elmsford
21/9/12 .

L32a

THE GREATEST GOOD FORTUNE

ANDREW CARNEGIE

THE GREATEST GOOD FORTUNE

Andrew Carnegie's Gift for Today

SIMON GOODENOUGH

EDINBURGH:
MACDONALD PUBLISHERS
1985

© Carnegie UK Trust 1985

ISBN 0 86334 055 5

Published by
Macdonald Publishers
Edgefield Road, Loanhead, Midlothian EH20 9SY

Printed in Great Britain by
Macdonald Printers (Edinburgh) Limited
Edgefield Road, Loanhead, Midlothian EH20 9SY

DEDICATED TO
DREAMERS AND DOERS
WHO COMPREHEND THAT LIFE IS A
WONDER AND WORKSHOP
AND TO MY FRIENDS

Acknowledgements

My thanks must go to a great many people for their help in compiling the information in this book but foremost I owe thanks to the trustees and staff of the Carnegie United Kingdom Trust for their support and assistance and particularly to Geoffrey Lord, Secretary of the Trust, for his personal encouragement and confidence over the three years in which the book has been planned and written. His initiatives and the work of the CUKT first attracted me to look further into the activities of all the Carnegie trusts. Jane Paterson and Moira Scott of CUKT have also contributed more than their share of work in the preparation of this book.

I am also greatly indebted for their personal interest and ready help to Alan Pifer and Sara Engelhardt of the Carnegie Corporation of New York; to Fred Mann of the Carnegie Dunfermline Trust and the Carnegie Hero Fund Trust; to Thomas Hughes, Larry Fabian and Susan Fisher of the Carnegie Endowment for International Peace; to Ernest Boyer and Verne Stadtman of the Carnegie Foundation for the Advancement of Teaching; to Jennifer Wada of Carnegie Hall, New York; to Robert Off and Walter Toerge of the Carnegie Hero Fund Commission; to James Mellon Walton and John Lane of the Carnegie Institute; to James Ebert, George Wetherill, Hatten Yoder and Ray Bowers of the Carnegie Institution of Washington; to Richard Barnhart and Angel Jordan of the Carnegie-Mellon University; to C. E. Bond of the Carnegie School of Physical Education, Leeds Polytechnic; to Anthony Ritchie of the Carnegie Trust for the Universities of Scotland; to Betty Smith of the Children's Television Workshop; to Lisa Taylor and Elaine Dee of the Cooper-Hewitt Museum; to Ulrike Klopfer of the Council on Religion and International Affairs; to the Registrar of the International Court of Justice at The Hague; to Ian McNee and staff of Macdonald Publishers; to William Greenough and Francis King of TIAA-CREF; and to Foster Murphy of the Volunteer Centre. I have not forgotten the many others within those and other organizations who have offered help or contributed to the work of putting this book together; I hope they will regard the few names I have had space to mention as representatives of their efforts and cooperation.

My special thanks also go to Carnegie's biographer, Professor Joseph Wall of Grinnell College, Iowa, who corresponded with me and permitted me freely to plunder his own reflections on Andrew Carnegie. I owe thanks as well to Caroline Bidwell for her invaluable research assistance and to Simon Butler for his help in drafting the typescript.

Contents

List of Illustrations

with acknowledgements

Author's Note

The 150th anniversary of the birth of Andrew Carnegie, steel magnate extraordinary and philanthropist, is being celebrated in 1985 by the Trusts that he founded, for education, peace and the welfare of the community, on both sides of the Atlantic, and by those who are still Carnegie's beneficiaries. The Carnegie United Kingdom Trust asked me to write this book about the work of all the Trusts and each has given me a great deal of help and support. I was offered a free hand to select whatever material and themes I thought might interest the general reader.

The formidable character of Carnegie himself, the multifarious activities of the Trusts and their immediate relevance to current issues quickly impressed me. Most of us, without knowing it, seemed in some way to be touched by Carnegie's influence. It was impossible to do justice to the man or to the full extent of the Trusts in one book but I have tried to display at least the range of their work and, out of curiosity, to explore some of the incidental as well as the major themes.

In the first chapter, I have tried to pick out these themes; the second is a brief account of Carnegie's life and the origins of the Trusts. The sections on each of the Trusts are in chronological order, though the peace foundations have been kept together. Each section is preceded by a short summary of that Trust, with some basic facts and figures, for easy reference. The conclusion attempts to sum up what I learned about Carnegie and the rôle of the Trusts. For all the omissions that readers will find who know the Trusts far better than I, my apologies cannot suffice but I hope they will be accepted.

The Greatest Good Fortune

Andrew Carnegie—boy to man

Introduction

ANDREW CARNEGIE, the son of an impoverished Scottish weaver, arrived in America along with two million other immigrants from the British Isles in the 'hungry' 1840s. He made his fortune in the manufacture of iron and steel during the years of opportunity between the American Civil War and the death of Queen Victoria, forty years of extraordinary personal and national vigour. When he retired from business in 1901, at the age of sixty-five, Carnegie possessed the largest private negotiable fortune in the world; it was locked safely in the vault of his own bank in Hoboken, New Jersey. During the next thirteen years, before the onslaught of the First World War, he gave almost all of it away—nearly three hundred and fifty million dollars—between two and three *billion* dollars in the values of today.

If that part of the story is not remarkable enough, there is a sequel that in many ways is even more remarkable. Carnegie did not give his money away simply to benefit his contemporaries but for the benefit of future generations, for ourselves and those to come. He distributed the bulk of his fortune with such forethought that even now, more than sixty years after his death, it is still contributing to the 'improvement of mankind.' The trusts he set up, for education, research, peace and the welfare of society, have already spent more than two billion dollars and, from current capital of much more than one billion dollars, they are spending each year throughout parts of the world well over one hundred million dollars, or nearly four dollars every second. Those figures are very conservative. They do not include the capital assets of buildings, museum and art collections and scientific equipment, nor the multitude of independent offshoots given birth with trust financial help: one pension fund alone is worth more than thirty billion dollars.

There is an obvious danger that the sums of money involved in the story of Carnegie's philanthropic gifts might overwhelm the much more interesting story of how that money has been used. In fact, it would be almost impossible to calculate the real total of 'Carnegie money' now at work among us, touching all of us, usually in ways of which we are not aware. It is equally difficult to add up the total benefits created by that money—not just the number and variety of activities but the sum of their worth: the buildings created and supported, the organizations encouraged, the individuals helped, the books and reports, the ideas discussed and developed, the seen and the unseen projects and programmes. They range from Carnegie Hall, in New

York, to the children's television favourite, *Sesame Street*; from the Mount Wilson Observatory to the 'Home of the Dinosaurs'; from 2,500 free public libraries to 7,600 church organs around the world; from J. K. Galbraith's *The Affluent Society* to a study of the effects of the First World War in 155 volumes; from pre-school playgroups to Nobel laureates; from village halls to the Peace Palace in The Hague; from 90,000 Scottish university students to several thousand awards in eleven countries for civilian bravery; from a taxidermy apprenticeship to help for the disabled and unemployed; from minority rights to world peace; from the welfare of children to concern for old age; from high school curricula to poverty and pensions; from concerts to conservation; from modern art to the study of plants and animals; from Egyptian mummies to genetic surgery. All these have benefited from Carnegie's fortune.

What were the characteristics and circumstances that enabled Carnegie to acquire his fortune and what persuaded him to give it away? His upbringing was radical and infused with the politics of social reform, entirely opposed to the accumulation of wealth. 'I was a violent young Republican whose motto was "death to privilege",' he wrote, but in America he found boundless opportunity. He had all the qualities for material success: he was ambitious, competitive and single-minded; he was quick-witted, adaptable and ready to recognize any chance; his discovery of the world of capital delighted him; his grasp of the potential for growth in an expanding economy was matched by an insatiable appetite. 'Whatever I engage in, I must push inordinately,' he said. The novelist J. M. Barrie once wrote, 'There are few more impressive sights than a Scotsman on the make.' He might have had Carnegie in mind, for this particular Scotsman was a most impressive sight indeed; it was as if he could not stop himself from getting rich, despite his upbringing and his social principles.

What marked Carnegie out was that he remained deeply conscious of his principles even while he let nothing stand in the way of his goals. When he was only thirty-three and already had an annual income of fifty thousand dollars, he began to think about retiring and spending his surplus wealth for benevolent purposes. 'The amassing of wealth is one of the worst species of idolatry,' he wrote. 'To continue much longer... must degrade me beyond hope of permanent recovery.' He did continue—for another thirty-three years—but he began the business of giving money while he was still in the business of making money. The giving became his excuse for the making. The dollars were transmuted into service for others. There never ceased to be a struggle in his mind between his great wealth and the principles of his upbringing but he found a way to justify his life by returning what he had taken. His *Gospel of Wealth* called upon the millionaire 'to sell all that he hath and give it in the highest and best form to the poor by administering his estate himself for the good of his fellows.'

Carnegie revealed the essence of this inner conflict when he quoted the words of the poet Burns, 'which fortunately burnt themselves into my conscience in youth and remain with me in old age: "Thine own reproach alone do fear".' It was a sincere belief that 'the man who dies rich dies disgraced' that persuaded him to argue that the millionaire should be a trustee for the poor and would thus earn their affection and gratitude. 'Rich men should be grateful for one inestimable boon,' he wrote. 'They have it in their power during their lives to busy themselves in organizing benefactions from which the masses of their fellows will derive lasting advantage, and thus dignify their own lives.' In his view, the rich man could administer his wealth for the benefit of the poor man better than the poor man could administer money for his own needs—the accumulation of great wealth was permissible, therefore, so long as the rich man returned his surplus wealth in a way that would not destroy society's own responsibility to preserve individual and community initiative: he should help people to help themselves.

This 'self-help' principle lay at the root of Carnegie's gifts; it was the reason why most of them concerned education in some way. He had no wish simply to give charity. 'The main consideration should be to help those who will help themselves,' he wrote; 'to provide part of the means by which those who desire to improve may do so; to give those who desire to rise the aids by which they may rise, but rarely or never to do all.' He would provide a library building for a town but only on the understanding that the community would stock and maintain it. 'When the library is supported by the community,' he said, 'all taint of charity is dispelled.' Or to put it another way, in his avowed intent to 'elevate the masses,' he wrote: 'You cannot push anyone up a ladder unless he is willing to climb a little himself.'

This emphasis on self-help derived from Carnegie's own experience of life; likewise, many of the qualities that had enabled him to make money were put to good use in the distribution of that money. His gifts reflected what had influenced him and was important to him. 'Two women, my mother and my wife, have made me all that I am,' he wrote but he also admitted the great debt that he owed to his roots in the town where he was born and the town which he adopted, to Dunfermline and to Pittsburgh. 'Nothing disappoints me so keenly as the omission of wealthy men and women to remember their own cities when they must dispose of the surplus wealth they cannot take with them,' he said, and so he provided a substantial endowment 'to bring more of sweetness and light' into the monotonous lives of the Dunfermline townsfolk, and he provided a collection of endowments in the town where he had made his millions.

Carnegie took great care in establishing his trusts. He was good at organizing, he was practical and he liked to see results. 'A great man *settles* things,' he wrote; 'a small one nibbles away at petty reforms. That this talent for organization and management is rare among men is proved by the fact that it invariably secures enormous rewards for its possessor.' He combined with this ability a suitable philosophy: 'Our duty of today is with today's problems. We have nothing to do with those of the distant future. We cannot legislate wisely for posterity.' This attitude enabled him to concentrate on, and solve, the immediate problems of his business; it also enabled him to foresee that his trustees needed to have flexible powers so that they, too, might be able to deal with the immediate, and possibly different, problems of the future. This outlook, more than anything, has ensured that the trusts can fit themselves to the needs of the time.

In business, he was single-minded. 'Put all your eggs in one basket and then watch that basket,' he wrote when concentrating into one business all the processes and resources for the manufacture of steel. It was a highly successful formula. When it came to his gifts, the eggs were just as various—colleges and schools, museums, music halls, men's and women's clubs, laboratories, libraries, temples of peace—but there was similarly one wide basket into which they all went—the 'improvement of mankind.' Carnegie was refreshingly optimistic, if at times a little naïve; he believed that the eggs were sure to hatch. He had no reason not to be optimistic, for everything in his own life had worked out well for him. 'All is well since all grows better,' he wrote.

The concept of the eggs and the basket applied, in Carnegie's opinion, to the importance of backing the individual also. 'The exceptional man in every department must be permitted and encouraged to develop his unusual powers, tastes and ambitions in accordance with the laws which prevail in everything that lives and grows,' he wrote. 'No great institution and no great thing, nor any great man, is truly great without differing from others....There must be individualism.' He was the living proof of his own philosophy, the spirit of America, individualism and independence, but Carnegie also saw independence as the necessary prelude to something more: 'A man's first duty is to make a competence and be independent. But his whole duty does not end here. It is his duty to do something for his needy neighbours who are less favoured than himself. It is his duty to contribute to the general good of the community in which he lives.' That was the corollary, and bound up with that was the self-help principle again. Carnegie believed that only some people would rise above the masses; he wished to encourage them as much as possible and to help them to advance themselves so that they in turn could help the masses from whom they had escaped. Carnegie's hope was to provide the means for more and more people to develop their individual talents so that eventually the whole of society was raised up and was helped to rise further still by the continued encouragement of the exceptional men and women in its midst. It was a glorious picture of an ever-rising society, with a cautionary note of commonsense added by Carnegie himself: 'It is only by degrees that a community is led upward to higher things.'

Education was the key to success, for the exceptional person and for the masses. 'The taste for reading is one of the most precious possessions in life,' wrote Carnegie. 'There is no human arrangement so powerful for good...as that which places within reach of all the treasures of the world which are stored up in books.' It was the once-poor radical youth who remembered in later life how much he had yearned for those treasures in order to educate himself, and libraries put learning within the reach of everyone. 'Upon no foundation but that of popular education can man erect the structure of an enduring civilization,' he believed.

In Carnegie's mind, education and peace went hand in hand; peace would follow hard upon the heels of universal education: 'Peace wins her way not by force; her appeal is to the reason and conscience of man.' Education elevated the moral consciousness of individuals and communities and thus of nations and would therefore, Carnegie was convinced, persuade others to agree with him that 'my first wish is to see this plague of

This cartoon from a 1905 edition of *Life* magazine
satirises Carnegie's plans to give away his fortune

OUR ANGEL OF PEACE

Carnegie's interest in international peace
was satirised in this famous cartoon

mankind—war—banished from the face of the earth.' He tried to approach the business of peace in the same way that he approached all other business and believed that by doing so he could 'settle' the problem once and for all time. 'It is by concentrating upon the one issue that great causes are won,' he said, and would not let go of his dream for 'the reign of peace and the brotherhood of man.' To all those who would listen, in his efforts to bring world leaders together to discuss peace, he promised that, 'So far from the idea being visionary that there can be a reign of peace thus secured, I place upon record the opinion that this century will not pass without seeing it accomplished.' The First World War shattered his hopes.

There is no doubt that Carnegie relished the fame that wealth brought him. He actively cultivated the companionship of the great and enjoyed discussions and friendship with leaders in the world of music, letters, the fine arts, drama, politics and the Church. He revelled in the private and public accolades that came his way as a result of his philanthropic interests—whatever was thought about his fortune-making, his fortune-giving fascinated everyone. 'How sweet it all was! Never so busy, never so happy!' he wrote in the midst of his philanthropic enthusiasm, before he began to tire. All the same, he was well aware of the pitfalls: 'The name philanthropist is a very dubious one to apply to anyone. It usually means a man who has more money than sense.' Not so in Carnegie's case.

Work was not everything to him; he believed that leisure was important, too, in his own life and in education. 'Life must not be taken too seriously,' he wrote. 'It is a great mistake to think that the man who works all the time wins the race.... I attribute most of my success in life to the fact that, as my partners often say, trouble runs off my back like water from a duck.' Recreation and the arts were, in his opinion, vital ingredients toward a better life for everyone: 'Let no one underrate the influence of entertainments of an elevating or even an amusing character, for these do much to make the lives of the people happier and their natures better.' The organ music that he loved appealed to his belief in improvement and also to the sentimental side of his nature; it was all in the character of the Scot, as Carnegie himself acknowledged: 'Touch his head, and he will bargain and argue with you to the last; touch his heart, and he falls upon your breast.' Speaking in New York, in 1935, on the centenary of Carnegie's birth, the President of one of the Trusts remarked that, 'He was an extraordinary combination of all the ruling, dominating and attractive characteristics of the Scot, transfused with the elasticity, the adaptability and the quick-moving progress of our American way of life and thought.' As the English writer, Dr Samuel Johnson, once said, 'You can make a great deal of a Scot if you catch him young enough.'

What Carnegie saw around him, not just in his native Scotland at the time of his childhood but in America also at the end of the nineteenth century, was great underlying social turmoil. The Industrial Revolution had created a homogeneous and interdependent new working class which began to see clear goals for personal achievement that had not existed previously, and in this newly-created competitive environment there grew opportunities for self-betterment—a great need for mass education arose. It was the birth of the age of the 'public.' At the same time, local and government agencies were both financially and administratively unable to provide the facilities for which the people craved. Responsibility was thrown on to the shoulders of wealthy and well-meaning individuals who, for many reasons, supported the need for civic growth; by 1900, the time was ripe for a man such as Carnegie, with money to spend on such enterprises.

But the twentieth century has seen great changes. Today in Britain, for example, the State provides many of the basic amenities and has taken over most of the duties formerly undertaken by voluntary finance. Now the public takes these amenities for granted, in education and welfare, where the State at local and central level has intervened. The result is that the extra work needed from the Carnegie and similar trusts is different. Luckily, and by Carnegie's good judgment, his trusts were endowed not only with money but with trust deeds that have allowed them to adapt to the needs of society in an ever-changing world. What the trusts can achieve today is determined by a subtle blend of what Carnegie originally intended and those current needs seen by the trustees, presidents, chairmen and secretaries. The worth of Carnegie's contribution to the world depends largely on the judgment and skill of the men and women who direct the trusts in interpreting how best to use the special qualities of their private foundations to match contemporary problems.

Most importantly, the trusts are *independent*. They are able to pursue policies as appropriate to the changing needs of society or science, normally without interference from government and without pressures from industry or public grant-making bodies. They are free to make mistakes, to experiment without fear of being closed down if the experiment does not produce immediate results or fails completely. They are free to criticize government—for example, government education policies—and by so doing they can bring influence to bear on government policy. In the words of the Carnegie Trust for the Universities of Scotland, 'there's no one to run to, nor do we have to beg for funds.' All the trusts feel the importance of this; at the same time, it gives them a tremendous responsibility. 'It is well to remember,' wrote Carnegie in the *Gospel of Wealth*, 'that it requires the exercise of not less ability than that which acquires it, to use wealth so as to be really beneficial to the community.'

Being independent, they are also able to act with *swift response* when necessary. 'He who gives quickly gives twice,' remembers the Secretary of the Trust for the Universities of Scotland. The Carnegie Foundation for the Advancement of Teaching regards this quick reaction as very important. The Carnegie United Kingdom Trust and the Carnegie Corporation of New York both value their ability to respond swiftly to new ideas.

Flexibility is another word that crops up frequently among the trusts: the flexibility which enables them to seize unexpected opportunities. Carnegie-Mellon University recognizes that 'flexibility has not only resulted in vigorous research efforts but has enriched the learning process itself.' Flexibility makes use of the freedom of independence. It enables the Carnegie Corporation, by far the largest of the trusts, to be free to act when it identifies critical issues and to avoid being tied down to long-term support. It enables the United Kingdom Trust to 'remember that new deeds are constantly arising as the masses advance' and to be sensitive to change. It enables the Dunfermline Trust to match its efforts to the developing needs of the community.

Adaptation is the result of making the best use of that flexibility. 'I can imagine that it may be your duty to abandon beneficent fields from time to time,' wrote Carnegie to the Dunfermline Trustees, 'when municipalities enlarge their spheres of action and embrace these.' Adaptation has ensured that the trusts have been able to establish new relationships with the State as the latter has become increasingly involved in community interests. That same adaptability has enabled the Carnegie Institution of Washington, for example, to cease its successful archaeological work in Mexico and Central America and move on to pioneer new fields elsewhere when it felt that others had taken up the original work satisfactorily.

The concept of *pioneering* is fundamental to the work of almost all the trusts. By avoiding long-term administrative commitments, the Carnegie Corporation and other trusts can use their money as 'venture capital.' This involves some risks and some mistakes but it does something that no public money could politically afford to do. The aim is to address problems the consequences of which can only dimly be perceived on the horizon. The Carnegie Endowment for International Peace, in one way, aims to anticipate what will be the problem areas of the world. The Carnegie Institution of Washington avoids the 'safe' projects of business-sponsored research and provides the resources and environment for those 'dreamers and achievers' who are attempting to 'break the ground and prepare the way for others' in scientific research. Carnegie-Mellon University likewise looks ahead in its graduate and undergraduate programmes, providing a lead particularly in its computer and robotics departments to all other universities. The United Kingdom Trust regards its main purpose as 'priming the pump' and supporting the experimental in matters of social welfare and recreation; it looks for potential matters of concern and for projects with flair; it seeks to break some of the old moulds and find new ground on which to develop new responses; it picks out those enterprises that may subsequently be publicly supported so that it is free to pioneer yet again. The natural history research projects of the Carnegie Institute at Pittsburgh are similarly concerned with gathering information with which to meet present and future problems. The *High School Report* recently published by the Carnegie Foundation for the Advancement of Teaching is pioneering a new concern for American secondary education. Carnegie himself stressed the point in his instruction for the Dunfermline Trustees: 'Your work is experimental. Remember you are pioneers and do not be afraid of making mistakes; those who never make mistakes never make anything. Try many things freely but discard just as freely.' In this context, a major concern of many of the trusts is to draw attention to issues on the horizon that lack immediate appeal and are therefore ignored.

A large measure of this pioneering 'venture capital' is invested in ideas and *individuals*. 'Find the good men and back them,' said Carnegie. The Carnegie

Institution of Washington exemplifies this attitude in its tradition of providing sustained support for the exceptional man or woman; Barbara McClintock, for example, a Nobel Prize winner in 1983, worked for forty years on the genetics of maize before her research was fully recognized outside the Institution. The Carnegie Corporation seeks out the gifted mind and talents to find new solutions to old problems in advancing social justice and improving educational opportunities. The staff who run the programmes of the Endowment for International Peace are selected individuals who have specialist experience in academic, government and operational fields. The United Kingdom Trust echoes its fellows in seeking out the talented and enterprising individual. One speech at the 1935 centenary summed it up as follows: 'We have learned or are learning: in the distribution of funds, money is never the main consideration, convenient though its presence may be. The essential factor is the human element.'

The trusts are not simply looking for people with ideas; they are looking for the *implementation* of projects and policies, for practical results. The Carnegie Foundation for the Advancement of Teaching refers to the importance of 'moving from thought to action,' so as to 'make a positive difference' to society. The Endowment for International Peace has 'an aversion to research for the shelf, to research without recommendations.' The Carnegie Hero Funds do not simply give awards for acts of civilian courage, they give financial help and, even more important, they give practical friendship to the bereaved. The Carnegie Institute at Pittsburgh does not simply provide a museum for people to gaze at; it backs that museum with its own practical research programmes; it takes the museum out to the community; it concentrates much of its energy on making the museum readily accessible to everyone, from the children to the handicapped; it attempts both to give pleasure and to educate.

This element of combined *wonder and workshop* appears in several of the trusts, reflecting Carnegie's personal view of the world. It is evident in the scientific research of the Carnegie Institution of Washington and the Institute at Pittsburgh; in the Dunfermline projects to improve the quality of life in that town through educational, welfare and leisure activities; in the arts and heritage projects and in the volunteer and community programmes of the United Kingdom Trust; in the technical, business, arts and computer programmes at Carnegie-Mellon University; in the 'wise extravagancies,' as Carnegie called them, of the Museum of Art, the Music Hall and the Three Rivers Arts Festival in Pittsburgh. Carnegie believed strongly in the 'wholeness' of life; the Institute at Pittsburgh was founded to 'develop the moral, intellectual and aesthetic life' of the community.

The concept of 'wholeness,' of cutting across disciplines, of bringing together disparate programmes is another important attribute of the trusts' independence and their ability to experiment; it enables the trusts to play the rôle of the *catalyst*. The Carnegie Institution of Washington has developed this by linking its geographically separated departments in a loosely knit 'family'; the desirability of bringing scientists of many disciplines into a common research environment underlies current consideration of combining the Institution's department of Terrestrial Magnetism and the

Geophysical Laboratory. Carnegie-Mellon University also encourages the cross-fertilization of ideas; its computer studies department, for example, is a common resource for all the departments. The United Kingdom Trust believes that one of its main duties is to provide neutral ground for people of different disciplines to come together and pool their ideas, as does the Endowment for International Peace. The Carnegie Corporation makes a point of sounding out all possible sources before entering on new programmes and has adopted as one of its major programmes the assembling of all the main viewpoints on nuclear disarmament in order to clarify objectives. The Institute at Pittsburgh actively brings together the public, the museum staff, community volunteers and its researchers—research proceeds in the same building as the museum itself. The Foundation for the Advancement of Teaching encourages discussion about the improvement of education, between government, administrators, teachers, students and parents.

This approach is enriched by the *international breadth* of many of the trusts, which are concerned with offering help and exchanging ideas on a range of matters of international relevance: scientific research, racial and minority intolerance, disability and the social rôle of government, the development of human resources, the quality of education, the value of the arts, the quest for peace and the protection of the environment, and the welfare of the family. The Carnegie Corporation is currently concerned with poverty and with legal rights in South Africa. Researchers from the Carnegie Institution of Washington and the Carnegie Institute of Pittsburgh have been all over the world on exchange visits and fellowships; investigators worldwide in turn come to the Carnegie centres for periods of collaboration, research and training. Students and staff from the Scottish universities are also provided with the means to travel widely. The Foundation for the Advancement of Teaching has invested in comparative studies on education in many countries besides America. The Endowment for International Peace is naturally involved in conferences and issues throughout the world. Carnegie-Mellon students come from fifty foreign countries, as well as most of the United States, and carry their skills back home. The International Exhibition at the Museum of Art in Pittsburgh brings together every two or three years the best of modern art from all over the world. Both the Dunfermline and the United Kingdom Trusts inquire at home and abroad for ideas that might be adapted for their own work.

In bringing ideas and people together, in cherishing the flexibility to pioneer, in drawing critical issues to the attention of the public, all the trusts have in common Carnegie's wish that they should provide an *initiative for self-help*—for communities and for individuals. The Dunfermline Trust pursues this policy in pioneering projects for which responsibility, it hopes, will eventually pass to the local authority and therefore the community. The United Kingdom Trust looks not simply for bright ideas but for those that have already shown some practical roots—seedlings strong enough to become self-supporting with a little encouragement. The trusts that are directly concerned with education intend their efforts to be ploughed back into the community by those who have been educated through their endeavours and support. The Institute's Museums of

Art and Natural History demand a response from the people of Pittsburgh. The free public libraries are maintained by local taxes. The Foundation for the Advancement of Teaching has fathered a vast contributory pension scheme. The Carnegie Institution of Washington provides the resources for its staff to develop their own capacities unencumbered by administrative or classroom responsibilities. Carnegie's entire concept of education, as a resource, was that it would break down class barriers and encourage equality of opportunity—it was the opportunity that he saw as important; the rest was up to the individual. (He had little to say about those who, for whatever psychological, social or physical reason, remained helpless in the face of opportunity).

These themes are all represented by the trusts that bear Carnegie's name. There are seven 'Carnegie' trusts in America, four in Britain and eight Carnegie Hero Funds in Europe. Carnegie also established some other trusts that did not bear his name and he made a great many other smaller gifts along similar lines; in addition, he provided for numerous private pensions. This was what he called the 'retail' side of his giving, as opposed to the 'wholesale' or public side, and in many ways his heart was more in these private gifts to old colleagues and subordinates, to personal friends and people he admired, than it was in his multi-million endowments. Inevitably, too, he received hundreds of requests for money each day; sometimes, if he thought a cause or project was particularly deserving, he would write out a personal cheque. These gifts must swell the sum of his beneficence well beyond the official figure.

All the major trusts and some of Carnegie's other gifts and endowments and a few of the buildings with which he is associated are included in the following pages, with brief descriptions of their history and a closer look at their present work. The 'Carnegie' trusts are in chronological order, because that shows the development of his own plans; only the peace foundations are kept together, so that they can be seen as an issue in themselves. It was first intended to construct this account, chapter by chapter, around certain basic themes related to the trusts: education and opportunity; understanding and research; concern for the needs of the community; appreciation for the quality of life; peace and humanity. All the trusts would be covered under one or other of these headings but it soon becomes clear that most of the trusts overlap into several of these themes—there is, indeed, a 'wholeness' about the trusts beneath the surface; they pursue related issues by different routes. It seemed therefore more sensible, and a great deal more clear, to look at each trust in turn, relating it to Carnegie's underlying interests.

Each trust has a different character, as will quickly be seen in the nature of the projects and programmes with which it is concerned: the personal style of the Hero Funds; the community interest of the Dunfermline, United Kingdom and Pittsburgh trusts; the scientific detail of the research trusts; the work of the education trusts in schools, colleges and universities; the international policies of the peace trusts. Side by side, these characteristics present several facets of a single picture; together, they represent, in the phrase of the philosopher Ralph Waldo Emerson, 'the lengthening shadow of one man.'

Andrew Carnegie's birthplace

Andrew Carnegie's Life

Fortunate in my ancestors, I was supremely so in my birthplace. I was born in Dunfermline, in the attic of a small one-storey house... of poor but honest parents, of good kith and kin.

The historic town of Dunfermline, where Carnegie was born on 25th November 1835, a few miles north of Edinburgh, had been the first capital of a united Scotland. The town became the seat and burial ground of Scottish kings. Robert the Bruce was buried there; Mary Stuart held court in the Palace; Charles I of England was born there. 'All is redolent of the mighty past,' wrote Carnegie. 'No bright child of Dunfermline can escape the influence of the Abbey, Palace and Glen.'

As a boy, he played among the ruins of the Abbey and the Palace but was denied the Park and Glen by the laird who disliked the radical views of the Carnegie family. Carnegie's father, William, was a skilled weaver from a line of weavers, and in 1835 Dunfermline's most important industry was linen weaving. There were 3,500 hand looms in a town with a population of 11,500; two-thirds of the looms were used for damask weaving, for such products as table linen. But this traditionally proud, independent and self-employed industry was threatened by the industrial slump after 1815, with the end of the Napoleonic conflict and increasing competition from cheap cotton imported from the European mainland. The development of mechanized looms in factories that exploited women and children and those out of work after the war, working long hours for low pay, often in unhealthy and unsafe conditions, aggravated the situation. The weekly earnings of the hand-loom linen weavers dropped from one pound to one-quarter of that sum. William Carnegie was affected like anyone else. 'I began to learn what poverty meant,' wrote his son, Andrew.

Economic distress provoked social unrest and demands for political reform. In Scotland, only one in ten male adults was qualified to vote. A 'People's Charter' set out six major demands: universal male suffrage, a secret ballot, annual Parliaments, equal electoral districts, the end of property qualifications for members of Parliament, and payment for members of Parliament. Several times, the Charter was unsuccessfully presented to Parliament. On its rejection in 1842, there were riots and strikes. The army was called in to many towns, including Dunfermline, 'long renowned as the most radical town in this kingdom,' wrote Carnegie, whose family, on his mother's side, played a leading rôle in this political action in Scotland.

Dunfermline became one of the centres of Chartism in Scotland thanks largely to the activities of Carnegie's grandfather, Thomas Morrison, by trade a shoemaker, by temperament a radical political and social reformer, a friend of William Cobbett and a contributor to Cobbett's famous *Register*; Morrison also published his own radical paper, *The Precursor*. This was the background to Carnegie's own commitment to social reform; his upbringing in a poor, proud, politically active environment, where education was highly prized but hard to come by, influenced him enormously. 'It is not to be wondered at that, nursed amid such surroundings, I developed into a violent young Republican whose motto was "death to privilege",' he wrote. It was not to be wondered at that the Laird of Pittencrieff Park and Glen shunned the family whose activities challenged the stability of the old ways.

William Carnegie tried to remain independent and failed. In 1848, together with his wife Margaret and their two boys, Andrew, then aged twelve, and Thomas, aged five, he sold up all he owned to raise the fare for the passage to America in the 800-ton sailing ship, *Wiscasset*. They had to borrow an extra £20 to pay their way. Then they became just one more family among the more than two million people who emigrated from Britain to the United States during the 'Hungry Forties,' most of them fleeing from the potato famine but many of them skilled craftsmen, ousted by the factories, seeking jobs and a better life. Many emigrants experienced appalling squalor on such voyages but the Carnegies were lucky; they were luckier still in having somewhere to go to. Margaret Carnegie's sisters lived in Pittsburgh. There was no rail link then from New York to Pittsburgh and so it took the family another three weeks after the voyage to reach their destination.

Once in Allegheny City, across the river from Pittsburgh, the family took up residence with a brother of an uncle Hogan, above a weaver's shop owned by an aunt Aitken. Carnegie's father began weaving table-cloths which he sold from door to door. Evidently, Carnegie had little faith in his father as head of the family; it is his mother to whom he devotes his sympathies. 'She towered among her neighbours wherever she went,' he wrote. His mother was equally devoted to her son. When uncle Hogan's brother suggested that the boy should peddle 'knick-knacks' about the unwholesome environs of the Allegheny wharves, she protested with vehemence, 'What! My son become a peddler and go among rough men upon the wharves! I would rather throw him in the Allegheny River.' Instead, the young Carnegie joined his father, who had been forced to give up his meagre independence and was working in a cotton factory owned by a fellow Scotsman. Andrew Carnegie was taken on as a bobbin boy at one dollar and twenty-five cents a week.

A short time later, at two dollars a week, he went to work for another Scotsman, John Hay, who manufactured bobbins. Here, he had to look after a steam-engine that

Andrew and his younger brother, Tom, pose for a photograph
soon after they arrived in the United States

fired a boiler in the factory, and such were the dangers of the job that he found himself waking at night with visions of the engine about to explode. Hay discovered that Carnegie was good at figures, and used him to make out bills and do other office work. His duties, however, still included immersing the bobbins in a vat of boiling oil, the smell from which caused Carnegie to vomit, 'but if I had to lose breakfast, or dinner,' he wrote, 'I had all the better appetite for supper.'

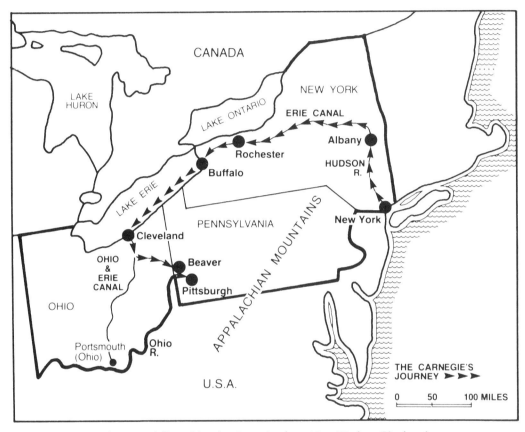

The route followed by the Carnegies from New York to Pittsburgh

When he heard that the Western Union telegraph office was looking for a good young man to act as a messenger boy, Carnegie went along for an interview, accompanied by his father, whom he asked to wait outside. 'I imagined that I could make a smarter showing alone with Mr Brooks than if my good old Scots father were present, perhaps to smile at my airs,' he wrote. He got the job, at $2.50 a week, and at once set about making himself into the best messenger in town. 'I felt that my foot was upon the ladder and that I was bound to climb,' he wrote. He spent his nights memorizing the name of each business along the streets of Pittsburgh, so that, 'before long I could shut my eyes and, beginning at the foot of a business street, call off the names of the firms in proper order along one side to the top of the street, then in regular order to the foot again.'

The Pittsburgh of 1850, in which Carnegie was making his way, was still very much in its infancy; most buildings were of timber and represented a considerable fire risk. Much of the business quarter had already been razed in a conflagration in 1845. The population at this time was around 40,000. In his first year as a messenger, Carnegie made use of the library of a Colonel Anderson, which had been opened for use by boys in Pittsburgh. 'Every day's toil and even the long hours of night service were lightened by the book which I carried about with me,' he remembered. It was the enlightenment gained from his reading that later led Carnegie to devote so much of his fortune to library buildings and educational institutions.

After twelve months, Carnegie's diligence was rewarded; he was selected to look after the office while the manager was out. This elevation did not endear him to his messenger colleagues, whose dislike Carnegie recalled with some humour: 'I was not popular with the other boys, who resented my exemption from part of my legitimate work. I was also taken with being penurious—mean, as the boys had it.' But meanness is not held altogether as a fault by Scotsmen and the Carnegie family thrived upon the careful budgeting of their resources. Promotion in the telegraph office brought an increase to $13.50 a month in Carnegie's pay, an extra $2.25 a month on his previous salary which he kept back from his family until breakfast on a Sunday morning: 'Then father's glance of loving pride and mother's blazing eye soon wet with tears, told their feeling.'

Carnegie quickly picked up the rudiments of receiving telegraphic messages and eventually could interpret incoming messages merely by listening to the sound of the key tapping. This skill led him to obtain the position of relief telegraphist at an out-of-town office in Greensburg. At the age of seventeen, he was promoted again to telegraph operator back in Pittsburgh at $25 a month.

Through this job, and through his obvious eagerness to learn and ability to work, Carnegie was lucky to meet Thomas Scott, the Superintendent of the Pittsburgh Division of the Pennsylvania Railroad. In 1853, Carnegie went to work for Scott and flourished under Scott's encouragement. With his keen mind, ambition, and his flair for mastering the necessary skills of his job—often regardless of the feelings of colleagues—he soon made himself indispensable to Scott. Preoccupied with his work, the death of his father in 1855 seems to have had little impact on him; his mother remained his close counsellor.

A year later, Carnegie had the opportunity to make his first investment. Scott advised him to buy ten shares of Adam Express stock, a blue chip investment not available on the open market. The shares were priced at $600. Carnegie did not have even $60 with which to buy them. According to him, his mother raised the money by mortgaging their home but according to his biographer, Professor Wall, it is more likely that Carnegie borrowed the money from Scott himself. It was only after some adroit juggling of further loans, partial repayments, notes of credit, further investments with

Pittsburgh in the 1840s was a bustling town situated where the Allegheny and Monongahela Rivers joined to form the Ohio. Despite the fact that it was not yet linked to the east coast by railroad, it was already a rising industrial centre, known by the nickname 'Smoky City'.

savings and interest payments that might have been used to pay off the loans, that Carnegie's mother stepped in to arrange through her brother to mortgage their home in Allegheny to secure the necessary funds to pay off the main loan—some two years after the purchase of those ten shares! By then, Carnegie knew all about the rewards that investment could bring. Within a month of buying the Adam Express shares in 1856, he received the first $10 dividend:

> I shall remember that check as long as I live....It gave me the first penny of revenue from capital—something that I had not worked for with the sweat of my brow. 'Eureka!' I cried. 'Here's the goose that lays the golden eggs.'

The next few years were crucial in developing Carnegie's professional as well as financial interest in the railroads; it was the beginning of the boom time in American railways. While he developed his talent for juggling with the few hundred dollars of his first investments and loans, he proved himself in his work as well. In December, 1859, Scott was promoted and Carnegie was chosen to replace him as Superintendent of the Pittsburgh Division.

It was only a year earlier that he had met the celebrated T. T. Woodruff, the inventor of the sleeping car, which filled a great need on the long-distance journeys across North America. According to Carnegie, he 'discovered' Woodruff; according to Woodruff, his invention had already been well-tried and recognized. In September, 1858, a contract was signed between Woodruff and the Pennsylvania Railroad Company. Whatever the origins of the contract, Carnegie had, by 1859, obtained an extremely valuable one-eighth interest in the new Woodruff Sleeping Car Company, for which he was allowed to pay in monthly instalments. He obtained a bank loan for the first instalment of $17.50 but thereafter was able to use the dividends to pay the further instalments. That sum was therefore the only money he had to raise and contribute from an outside source. Within two years, this investment was returning to him an annual income of nearly $5,000—more than three times his yearly salary from the Pennsylvania Railroad Company.

In April, 1861, the first shots were fired in the war between North and South, between the Union and the Confederacy. Carnegie had already cast his vote for Lincoln. When Scott was summoned to Washington to oversee the running of the railroads to supply the Union Army and to keep Washington open to the north, he asked Carnegie to join him and Carnegie responded eagerly. He played a colourful part in reopening the lines of communication between the north and a temporarily threatened capital by riding in the cab of the locomotive with the engineer and fireman and by receiving a cut above the face from some fallen telegraph wires when trying to clear the track for the troop train. He arrived in Washington boasting that he was the first man to be wounded in the defence of the nation's capital. After helping to organize further trains to carry supplies and ferry the wounded during the run-up to the first battle of Bull Run and following the Union defeat, he stayed for a while in Washington as Scott's assistant in charge of railroads and telegraphs but he was frustrated by the heat and inaction and got permission from Scott to return to Pittsburgh, in September, 1861, where he felt he could contribute more to the war effort by continuing his previous job.

Carnegie helped to run railroads and telegraphs during the early years of the civil war

He did not limit himself to the war effort, or to his job. Almost at once, he took an interest in the oil wells at Oil Creek, in one of the most isolated parts of western Pennsylvania, and seized the opportunity to become involved in a newly formed Columbia Oil Company. Using his dividends from the Woodruff Sleeping Car Company, Carnegie purchased more than 1,000 shares at $10 each, investing a little more than $11,000. In the first year alone, Columbia Oil gave a return of 160%, providing Carnegie with a return of $17,869.

Exhausted by several uncomfortable trips up to Oil Creek to supervise operations—and by his war effort—Carnegie took his first vacation since starting work in America fourteen years earlier. In June, 1862, Carnegie and his mother travelled first class on the steamship *Aetna* and reached Liverpool in two weeks; it had taken them seven weeks to cross the other way. Carnegie was disappointed by what he found in

Dunfermline. 'You are all here; everything is just as I left it,' he wrote, 'but you are now all playing with toys.' He found, too, antagonism in Scotland to the Union cause. He returned, feeling that he could no longer combine the two ends of his world; he was dedicated to the American way of life.

With increasing dividends from the Woodruff Sleeping Car Company (reorganized as the Central Transportation Company; his partnership survived legal battles against the famous Pullman Company, with which he eventually merged) and the Columbia Oil Company, he had funds to invest elsewhere—in such things as Pennsylvania Oil, the Western Union Telegraph, and the Iron City Forge. It was in the manufacture of iron, railways and bridges that he saw his real future. From the early 1860s date his interests in, for example, the Freedom Iron Company, for the manufacture of iron rails; the Superior Rail Mill and Blast Furnace set up in Pittsburgh in 1864; the Pittsburgh Locomotive Works (also Carnegie and Miller); and a one-fifth interest, for $1,250, in the newly formed Piper and Shiffler Company, for the manufacturing and erection of iron and wooden bridges. In the first year of operation, the Company returned $7,500. From this developed the creation of the Keystone Bridge Company, for the construction of iron bridges. Together with the Union Iron Mills, which developed from the Cyclops Mills, Keystone became Carnegie's major interest in the latter half of the 1860s.

At the end of 1863, Carnegie's total income for the year was $42,260, of which his Pennsylvania Railroad salary was a mere $2,400. In view of the relative time and effort that small sum took him to earn, Carnegie vowed to retire as soon as the war was over. He did so at the end of March, 1865, in order to give more time to his investments. Three years later, at the end of 1868, a year after moving to New York, he reassessed his investments and his annual income. His investments in sixteen companies and a few odds and ends amounted to $400,000; his annual income was $56,110. He sat down in the St Nicholas Hotel in New York and wrote himself a note:

Thirty three and an income of 50,000$ per annum.

By this time two years I can so arrange all my business as to secure at least 50,000 per annum. Beyond this never earn—make no effort to increase fortune, but spend the surplus each year for benevolent purposes. Cast aside business for ever except for others.

Settle in Oxford & get a thorough education making the acquaintance of literary men—this will take three years active work—pay especial attention to speaking in public.

Settle then in London & purchase a controlling interest in some newspaper or live review & give the general management of it attention, taking in public matters especially those connected with education & Improvement of the poorer classes.

Man must have an idol—The amassing of wealth is one of the worst species of idolitary (*sic*). No idol more debasing than the worship of money. Whatever I engage in I must push inordinately therefor should I be careful to choose that life which will be the most elevating in its character. To continue much longer overwhelmed by business cares and with most of my thoughts wholly upon the way to make more money in the shortest time, must degrade me beyond hope of permanent recovery.

I will resign business at Thirty five, but during the ensuing two years, I wish to spend the afternoons in securing instruction, and in reading systematically.

Carnegie had given himself two years; he stayed in business for another thirty-two years or more and increased his fortune several hundred times. There were too many opportunities for a man of his energy, ambition and ability; he could not turn away from them, whatever his good intentions. Before his allotted two years were up, the construction of the Lucy Furnace was under way, for the manufacture of pig iron; it was named after his sister-in-law. But already he had realized that steel was about to replace iron. In 1868 he was attempting to produce limited quantities of Bessemer Steel at the renamed Freedom Iron and Steel Company. In 1872, he visited the Bessemer steel-making plants in Sheffield and Birmingham. 'The day of iron is past,' he wrote, 'Steel is King.'

Henry Bessemer was an English inventor who, in 1856, had discovered that the impurities could be removed from pig iron (the name came from the 'pigs' or channels—like piglets sucking a sow—along which the molten iron flowed from the base of the furnace) by blowing cold air through the molten pig; as a result, steel could be produced, and steel was a great deal stronger than iron. The Bessemer process had

The high tower of the Lucy Furnace produced over a hundred tons of pig iron a day

26

Pig iron produced at the Lucy Furnace came to the Edgar Thomson works to be made into high-quality steel. Much of its production was rails for the growing American railroad network.

first been used in America as early as 1860, but Carnegie was able to buy the American rights to the process and thenceforth dominated the rise of the United States as the world's largest steel producer. Carnegie also understood that it was not enough simply to own one part of the manufacturing process:

> The one vital lesson in iron and steel that I learned in Britain was the necessity of owning raw materials and finishing the completed article ready for its purpose.

It was this total control of raw materials and the entire manufacturing process that was the key to Carnegie's success and wealth. At the same time, he believed in high production rates and low costs as the foundation of profits. His men worked long hours in high temperatures to keep the furnaces going.

In 1873, a financial crisis throughout America temporarily halted Carnegie's construction programme but he weathered the storm. In the same year he made two of his first major gifts: he gave the money for an organ to the Swedenborgian Church in Allegheny, to which his father had been used to go, and he gave $25,000 for public baths in his home town of Dunfermline; eventually, he gave about $6,250,000 for more than 7,600 organs, and, besides other gifts, he provided Dunfermline with its own endowment of $3,750,000. The following year, his steel mills at the Edgar Thomson Works were ready to begin work, using pig iron from the Lucy Furnace.

With command of the entire process of steel manufacture, from raw material to finished product, Carnegie extended his empire to include a range of related interests and so keep down the price of his final product and thus remain unbeatable. From the mining of high quality iron-ore in the Mesabai Mountains in Minnesota, to the ships that took the ore across the Great Lakes, to the railroad cars that transported it on the last leg of its journey to the Carnegie steel mills in Pittsburgh, Carnegie was in control; iron-ore, coal and coke, limestone, manganese ore, railroads, mills—all belonged to him. As this commanding position built up, so did the size of the company and the profit. In 1881, Carnegie Bros & Company Limited was formally organized, with Carnegie's younger brother, Tom, as Chairman of the Board. The new company included the Edgar Thomson Steel Works, the Union Iron Mills, the Lucy Furnaces, the coal mines and coke ovens at Unity and a four-fifths interest in the Lorimer Coke Works. It was capitalized at $5,000,000 and in that same year it made a profit of $2,000,000. Carnegie had no official position in the company but he did have fifty-five percent of the capital.

True at least to the spirit of his resolution in 1868, Carnegie left the managing of his companies to his brother and to others, though his orders and advice were never long absent, even when he himself was travelling in Europe. In 1877, he joyfully received the Freedom of Dunfermline. It was the first of many Freedoms granted to him, usually after the gift of a library building to a town. Proudly, he beat Gladstone's record of fourteen Freedoms and then he reached a peak of six Freedoms in six days. *The Times* became so confused that it once reported he was about to receive the Freedom of one town—much to the consternation of the unprepared town—when in fact he was on his way to another. In 1878, he went on a journey round the world and wrote a book about it. Three years later, in 1881, he went on a coaching trip through England and Scotland and subsequently wrote another book, *An American Four-in-Hand in Britain*. He wrote in that volume, 'They also work who plant the roses.' Carnegie was a great believer in relaxation from business through other pursuits. 'No doctor like Doctor Golf,' he wrote much later; 'his cures as miraculous as those sometimes credited to Christian Science, minus its unknown and mysterious agencies, which are calculated to alarm prudent people.'

In 1881, he also gave his first library building, for a free public library in Dunfermline, and in the same year he offered one to Pittsburgh and was at first refused, because Pittsburgh could not meet his condition that the city should stock the library and pay for its maintenance. In due course, Carnegie gave more than $56,000,000 for more than 2,500 library buildings around the world. All but three were given on the same terms, that the community supported them. Contrary to public belief, Carnegie did not insist his name be engraved over the entrances but he did supply on request a photograph of himself to be hung in a place of honour.

Painting of Mr Carnegie's arrival in Dumfermline to open the first Carnegie Library in Britain

Throughout the 1880s and into the 1890s, Carnegie divided his life between America and Britain, greatly enjoying the intellectual life and politics of the latter. He regarded Matthew Arnold as 'the most charming man I ever knew' and persuaded him to go on a thoroughly unsuccessful lecture tour of America. He became part of the distinguished company of Liberals that included Gladstone, and he attempted to enter the newspaper business in order to reawaken the old Chartist movement he had known as a child. In 1884, he acquired a two-thirds interest in the London *Echo* and by the end of that year he owned or held a controlling interest in seven daily newspapers and ten weeklies, with an emphasis in the Midlands and the North of England. His papers called for the abolition of the monarchy and the House of Lords, and the disestablishment of the Church of England. Naturally, he rejoiced at the final extension of male suffrage in the

Cartoon of Carnegie as a mason, building 'a very solid temple' of fame

Reform Bill of 1884. But his enthusiasm did not last long. He lost on his investments in most of his papers, though he did not surrender his final shares in the London *Echo* until 1902.

In 1886, he published *Triumphant Democracy*, which became immensely successful on both sides of the Atlantic. It was confident, energetic and portrayed the triumph of the American Republic's 'Gilded Age' in contrast to the fading force of the British monarchy. In the same year, both his mother and his brother, Tom, died of typhoid within a few weeks of each other. It was a doubly bitter blow; he had leaned on each of them heavily for support, one in his private life, the other in his business. Indeed, his mother had been the dominant character in his existence, for so long as she had been alive. It was her presence that had delayed his marriage. The year after her death he married at last Louise Whitfield. Their daughter, Margaret, was born ten years later, in 1897.

In 1889, there appeared in the June and December issues of the *North American Review* Carnegie's famous articles on 'Wealth,' which explained his principles of 'scientific philanthropy'; the articles were adopted by the *Pall Mall Gazette* under the better-known title, *Gospel of Wealth*. 'The problem of our age,' wrote Carnegie, 'is the proper distribution of wealth.' He dismissed inheritance in favour of distributing his wealth during his lifetime for public benefit. This, Carnegie said, was:

> The true antidote for the temporary unequal distribution of wealth, the reconciliation of the rich and the poor—a reign of harmony....Under its sway we shall have an ideal State, in which the surplus wealth of the few will become, in the best sense, the property of the many, because administered for the common good, and this wealth, passing through the hands of the few, can be made a much more potent force for the elevation of our race than if distributed in small sums to the people themselves....
> The man of wealth thus becomes the mere trustee and agent for his poorer brethren, bringing to their service his superior wisdom, experience, and ability to administer, doing for them better than they would or could do for themselves.

Specifically, Carnegie recommended that the wise trustee of surplus wealth should invest in seven fields of philanthropy; these were universities, free libraries, hospitals, parks, local halls suitable for meetings and concerts, swimming baths, and church buildings. He admitted that he did not expect there to be 'general concurrence' on this list. Not surprisingly, his whole philosophy came under attack. William Tucker, a liberal American theologian and subsequently President of Dartmouth College, replied in 1891 that Carnegie's assumption that wealth was the inevitable possession of the few was unacceptable, just as people no longer accepted that political power should remain in the hands of the few because it could be better administered; nor could Tucker accept that the millionaire could necessarily administer his wealth better for the community than it could do for itself. But Carnegie persisted in his view—perhaps to make sense of his own life—that the accumulation of great wealth was permissible so long as he accepted responsibility for returning that wealth wisely to the community and in a way which encouraged the community to help itself. His library buildings were the best example of this philosophy in practice. In 1890 he renewed his offer to Pittsburgh, increasing it to $1,000,000. Pittsburgh accepted. Five years later, the Library and Music Hall were opened and Carnegie declared his plans for a further gift to endow Pittsburgh with a Museum and Art Gallery as well. Thus was born the first of the major Carnegie endowments, the Carnegie Institute, to which, in 1900, he added plans for a Technical School, which in due course became the Institute of Technology and eventually became part of Carnegie-Mellon University.

Meanwhile, Carnegie Bros continued to grow through the 1880s. In 1882, Carnegie purchased half of the stock in the Frick Coke Company, and Frick himself subsequently became Chairman of Carnegie Bros before turning into an entrenched enemy of Carnegie. Ever-increasing demand for steel led Carnegie to purchase also the Homestead Steel Mills, a rival mill, a mile down the river from the Edgar Thomson Steel Works at Pittsburgh. Carnegie gained control of Homestead partly through the fierce competition he offered and partly through its own labour problems; it was ironical that Homestead's labour problems subsequently caused him some of the worst Press he received. That was in 1892. In that year, the capital of Carnegie Bros had risen to $25,000,000 and profits were averaging $4,500,000 a year. In July, 1892, the Carnegie Steel Company was formed, to embrace this enlarged business. It was already the largest steel company in the world.

Homestead Plant workers in a rare moment of relaxation

The notorious Homestead strike also took place in July, 1892; it tarnished Carnegie's reputation both in America and in Europe. On the face of it, through his published views, Carnegie was a conscientious employer and a supporter of organized labour, but his Company needed to put an end to the power of the unions in the mills, since they imposed costly restrictions. A proposal was put to the men for a reduction in the minimum wage scale and in tonnage rates. The men, believing that Carnegie would not wish to enter into conflict with his workmen, rejected the proposal, but Carnegie was safely out of the way in Scotland, and it was left to Frick to resolve the situation. Frick had no such scruples as Carnegie had expressed about the use of blackleg labour. Frick knew that wider issues were at stake—the future of labour-employer relations throughout the American steel industry. He also knew that he could easily lay his hands on plenty of willing immigrant labour. He was determined to break the strike. From Scotland, Carnegie urged caution but kept his distance. Frick brought in 300 special armed operatives from the Pinkerton Detective Agency to convoy the blackleg labour across the Monongahela River at night into the Homestead works. There was a bloody fight between the Union men, armed with staves, rifles and other weapons, trying to keep the blackleg labour out and the Pinkerton men, caught by a sudden alarm cowering in their barges, trying to get the labour in. The Pinkerton men were forced to surrender and suffered further onslaught from enraged women as they were marched to the town jail. Four men lost their lives and all the Pinkerton men were injured. That was on July 6/7th; on July 12th, the National Guard was called in and the Company regained control of the Homestead Mills.

The *London Financial Observer* commented:

> Here we have this Scotch-Yankee plutocrat meandering through Scotland in a four-in-hand, opening public libraries and receiving the freedom of cities, while the wretched workmen who sweat themselves in order to supply him with the ways and means for his self-glorification are starving in Pittsburgh.

Carnegie, on the other hand, gave several accounts in his autobiography of how the rich and famous wrote to him after the Homestead troubles offering their sympathies. He also quoted a telegram received from the workforce at Homestead: 'Kind master, tell us what you wish us to do and we shall do it for you.' He did not mention in his autobiography a telegram he sent to Frick on the day after the Homestead battle:

> All anxiety gone since you stand firm. Never employ one of these rioters. Let grass grow over the works. Must not fail now. You will win easily next trial.

Evidently Carnegie was staunchly behind Frick, despite his public affirmation prior to the strike: 'Thou shalt not take thy neighbour's job.' There was a postscript to the affair, when, on 23rd July, a twenty-five-year-old anarchist of Russian descent made an unsuccessful attempt to assassinate Frick.

The next year, 1893, Carnegie suffered another scandal; he was accused of supplying the U.S. Navy with sub-standard armour plate. Carnegie had at first refused to

A drawing of the scene at the Homestead works in 1892
following the surrender by the Pinkerton detectives

compromise his principles of peace by making armour plate for navy warships but the potential profits and prestige persuaded him to see it purely as a defensive measure. In 1890, he signed a contract for 6,000 tons of nickel steel, worth 300 percent profits to his company. Three years later, there was a public scandal over accusations that Carnegie had short-changed the government. The Company was ordered to pay damages but was not prosecuted; the steel passed some rigorous tests and the contracts continued. Once again, Carnegie had weathered the storm.

By 1899, Frick, as Chairman of the Carnegie Steel Company, had increased its profits from $4,000,000 to $21,000,000 a year. He had become restless under Carnegie's control; in turn, Carnegie was suspicious of the prominence that Frick was taking. A bitter battle ensued, in which Carnegie ousted Frick. Carnegie's loyal colleagues, Henry Phipps and Charles Schwab, finally persuaded him to make a reluctant peace. Agreement was reached, in March, 1900, to consolidate Carnegie Steel and Frick Coke into the Carnegie Company, with an issue of $320,000,000 half and half in bonds and stock. Carnegie's share was fixed at $174,000,000; Frick received $31,000,000; the remainder went to sixty junior partners and heirs of deceased members of the combined firms. Schwab became President of the new company.

Within four months, Frick, keeping well out of the management of the company, wrote a letter to Carnegie, highly critical of Schwab. That could not have been the only thing that made Carnegie think of selling out. Competition was increasing. The banker, J. Pierpont Morgan, had already formed his giant $200,000,000 Federal Steel Company. In response, Carnegie made a series of proposals for the expansion of his own company that so alarmed his rivals that they approached Morgan to buy out Carnegie, just as Carnegie hoped; he knew that Morgan was the only man who could handle a deal of that size. It was finally Schwab who introduced to Morgan the idea that Carnegie might be willing to sell. Schwab delivered the note to Morgan on which Carnegie had scribbled down his price:

Capitalization of Carnegie Company: $160m bonds to be exchanged at par for bonds in new company:	$160,000,000
$160m, stock to be exchanged at rate of $1000 share of stock in Carnegie Company exchanged for $1500 share of stock in new company:	$240,000,000
Profit of past year and estimated profit for coming year:	$80,000,000
Total price for Carnegie Company and all its holdings:	$480,000,000

Morgan's only comment was, 'I accept this price.' A few days later, he visited Carnegie for fifteen minutes and shook his hand. 'I want to congratulate you on being the richest man in the world,' he said. Quite probably, it was indeed the largest ever fortune in liquid assets; yet some thought it possible, had Carnegie asked for it, that Morgan would have paid another $100,000,000 for the company. Within such a vast sum, it didn't seem to matter that Carnegie had missed out on the extra!

For his bonds (par value $86m) and capital stock (par value $93m), Carnegie accepted in payment bonds for $225,639,000 par value of the newly formed United States Steel Corporation, 'to be secured by a mortgage upon all of its property now held or hereafter held.' U.S. Steel was capitalized at more than one billion dollars; it was the first such billion dollar company. A special vault was constructed in Hoboken, New Jersey, to house nearly $300,000,000 worth of bonds belonging to Carnegie and his sister-in-law, Lucy. Many of his erstwhile partners spent their own share of the sale with lavish exhilaration; Pittsburgh had hardly ever known such a spree.

After the sale was completed, and before Carnegie left for a holiday in Europe, he began his philanthropic giving in earnest by leaving a note with instructions for his agent to arrange the provision of more than $11,000,000 for pensions and libraries: $1m for maintaining libraries at the Braddock, Homestead and Duquesne works; $4m to provide certain pensions for employees of the Carnegie Company; $5.2m to New York City for sixty-five branch libraries; and $1m to St Louis for branch libraries. Of the pensions, he wrote:

> I make this first use of surplus wealth upon retiring from business, as an acknowledgement of the deep debt I owe to the workmen who have contributed so greatly to my success.

Of his interest in libraries, he had already written:

> Whatever agencies for good may rise or fall in the future, it seems certain that the Free Library is destined to stand and become a never-ceasing foundation of good to all.

Carnegie knew the general area in which he wanted to spend his money; it was mostly to go to education in one form or another; community welfare and peace were issues that went alongside this. It seemed straightforward enough; after all, Carnegie had been thinking about spending his surplus for benevolent purposes since the note he wrote to himself in 1868. But his friend, the English statesman John Morley, wrote to him a month after the sale, quoting a phrase: 'I don't envy, I do admire.' Morley added, 'You'll have some difficulty tho' in adapting the principles of accumulation to the business of distribution.' Carnegie's reply conceived of no problems:

> tenacity and steady sailing...supreme confidence in one's own ideas, or conclusions rather, after thought—and above all placing *use* above popularity.

As canny as he had been in business, Carnegie took equal care to see that the trusts he established were properly administered. He was generally careful to enter into any charitable venture only after carefully examining the effects of his involvement; sometimes he set up commissions to inquire into every aspect of a proposed trust. In many instances, he refused all charitable aid, firm in his belief that financial support could have a deleterious effect. Once his mind was made up that a project was worthy of his support, he was extremely generous; rather than risk a shortfall in the amount that a trust might need, he sometimes gave double the amount requested.

Having decided to establish a trust, Carnegie devoted a great deal of care to formulating the trust deed which set out how each fund should be administered. These documents, addressed to the trustees (their numbers varied with each trust; twenty or so was a common number), are masterpieces of concise and clear thinking; they combine a firm outline of what the trust is about together with a degree of flexibility that allows the trustees to meet changing circumstances. Thus, the Carnegie United Kingdom Trust, one of whose first duties was to provide funds for library buildings and church organs, now involves itself with arts and disabled people, with the unemployed and community projects and with conservation. Carnegie's perspicacity in this regard has done much to ensure that the trusts have remained an effective force in education and social welfare, despite the great changes that he could not have foreseen.

In the year of his retirement, besides the money he gave immediately for pensions and libraries, he also established the Carnegie Trust for the Universities of Scotland, which he endowed with $10,000,000, bringing his total giving in the year to more than $21,000,000. This fund was to help pay the fees for deserving students at the four Scottish universities and to improve the opportunities for scientific research at those universities; the gift made clear his interest particularly in higher education.

In 1902, he moved in, with his wife and daughter, to the Carnegie Mansion in New York; thereafter he divided his year between that house and Skibo Castle in Scotland, which he had bought in 1897, the year his daughter was born. Also in 1902, he established the Carnegie Institution of Washington with an initial endowment of $10,000,000 and subsequently another $15,000,000. This independent scientific research institution was intended to provide backing for all the universities in the nation through 'research and discovery and the application of knowledge to the improvement of mankind.' It offered a step beyond higher education in the sciences.

His interest returned to his home town the following year, when he established the Carnegie Dunfermline Trust, with an endowment of $2,500,000, 'to bring into the monotonous lives of the toiling masses of Dunfermline more of sweetness and light,' through welfare, social, educational and recreational activities. By this fund, the inhabitants of Dunfermline probably became the community with the largest private endowment in the world. In the same year, 1903, he made his first contribution to the least successful of his peace funds, The Simplified Spelling Board; there were more serious peace efforts to follow. One of these was the first of his Hero Funds, the Carnegie Hero Fund Commission, which he endowed with $5,000,000 in 1904. Its purpose was to honour civilians who risked their lives in saving or attempting to save the lives of others. Four years later, Carnegie established a similar Trust in Great Britain, with an endowment of $1,250,000 and, between 1909 and 1911, he founded nine more such Trusts in Europe. In sum, he endowed the Hero Funds with $10,540,000.

In 1905, Carnegie returned to higher education, with the Carnegie Endowment for the Advancement of Teaching, for which he provided $10,000,000 initially and a subsequent $6,250,000. His aim was to improve the standards of education in universities and colleges by improving the conditions of teachers through the provision

Andrew Carnegie with his wife and daughter

of retiring pensions; the Endowment later concentrated on studies and reports on various aspects of education. Carnegie provided buildings and endowed chairs at many individual colleges, beyond his major educational trusts; it was mostly the smaller colleges that he preferred. When Woodrow Wilson (later, President of the United States), as President of Princeton University, tried to persuade Carnegie to donate a graduate college, a school of law and a school of science, he simply got a lake, so that Princeton boys could take their minds off football, which Carnegie disliked, and switch their efforts to boating competitions with Harvard, Yale and Columbia. In sum, Carnegie gave more than $15,000,000 to individual colleges, universities and schools. Two recipients were the Hampton and Tuskagee Institutes, which both provided for black youths from the rural south.

The art gallery and museum of the Carnegie Institute, in Pittsburgh, opened in 1907, to join the Library and Music Hall, and to complete, with the Technical Schools, Carnegie's educational and cultural 'package' for Pittsburgh. The schools were reorganized into the Carnegie Institute of Technology, in 1912, to provide higher education and professional training in engineering, the fine arts and home economics. These endowments for Pittsburgh cost Carnegie, from his own funds, nearly $20,000,000. Through the Carnegie Corporation funds, they received a great deal more of Carnegie's money.

After seven years of giving, Carnegie was slowing down and looking for another cause than education. He was persuaded to take up the theme of peace, which already interested him to some degree. He was known to be vehemently against imperialism and had made valiant efforts before 1900 to prevent the acquisition by America of the Philippines, even suggesting at one point that he himself might purchase the islands from the United States. He was also firmly opposed to war. Indeed, he was keen on using his considerable financial resources to engineer a number of peace conferences and to attempt to bring together world political leaders in the quest for peace. Theodore Roosevelt, who became President on the assassination of McKinley in 1901, and the German Emperor, Kaiser Wilhelm II, were his prime targets.

In 1907, Carnegie wrote an article in which he was among the first to consider the idea of a League of Nations. In the same year he became President of the National Arbitration and Peace Congress and made a speech in which he said that the power to abolish war rested in the hands of the Kaiser. He seemed confident that the Kaiser would hold the chance securely, particularly when he met him for the first time that summer on an invitation to Kiel. 'I know I offer H.I.M. the plan that makes him the greatest agent known so far in human history: The Peace Maker,' wrote Carnegie. As for Roosevelt, Carnegie at first regarded him as 'an unknown quantity, capable of infinite mischief,' and the new President was equally suspicious of Carnegie: 'I have tried hard to like Carnegie,' he wrote, 'but it is pretty difficult.' He also referred to Carnegie's 'utterly stupid condemnation of war' and 'hopelessly twisted ideals' but this did not stop him, after his term of Presidency was ended, from accepting money from Carnegie to help finance an extended safari to Africa on condition that he, Roosevelt,

Andrew Carnegie and his guest, Lord Weardale, one of the twelve representatives of Great Britain, at the Peace Meeting in New York's City Hall

would agree to combine the trip with a visit to the Kaiser to help the cause of the League of Peace. As it happened, the death of King Edward VII, in 1910, put an end to all Carnegie's plans of a grand peace conference. Roosevelt met the Kaiser but the situation in Europe was too delicate to allow detailed discussion of peace. Roosevelt's plans to visit London for further peace talks were also cancelled due to the nation's mourning.

There were more constructive aspects to the year, however. On his seventy-fifth birthday, Carnegie announced the foundation of the Carnegie Endowment for International Peace and endowed it with $10,000,000 'to hasten the abolition of international war' by any means it could devise, including publications, conferences, discussions and through liaison with kindred organizations. In the same year, 1910, two of Carnegie's three 'temples of peace' opened: the Pan American Union Building in Washington, to which he contributed $850,000, and the Central American Court of Justice in Costa Rica, to which he eventually contributed $200,000. His third 'temple' was the International Court of Justice, in The Hague, the 'Peace Palace,' to which he contributed $1,500,000 and which was officially dedicated in 1913, after ten years of planning and building.

By 1910, Carnegie had given away $180,000,000 of his fortune but he had almost the same amount left in his possession, because of the interest that constantly accrued on his capital, at the rate of anything up to $15,000,000 a year. He feared that he would die in disgrace as a wealthy man after all, so he set up the Carnegie Corporation of New York, in 1911, with an endowment of $25,000,000, to which he added another $100,000,000 in 1912 and another $10,000,000 in his will, so that the trustees could worry about the distribution of the remaining bulk of his fortune; their responsibility was for 'the advancement and diffusion of knowledge and understanding'—Carnegie was back to education again. He had hoped to use funds from the Corporation to establish a final trust in Great Britain but this proved to be legally impossible, and so he had to produce from his own pocket another $10,000,000 to endow the Carnegie United Kingdom Trust, in 1913, 'for the improvement of the well-being of the masses.' In 1914, the Corporation itself provided $2,000,000, at Carnegie's behest, for the foundation of the Church Peace Union, addressed to the 'Gentlemen of Many Religious Bodies, All Irrevocably Opposed to War and Devoted Advocates of Peace.'

Even at the beginning of that year, Carnegie had thought that peace was assured. The Kaiser was his 'Hero of Peace...the foremost apostle of peace in our time.' On the day he received word that Great Britain, France and Russia were at war with Germany and Austria-Hungary, Carnegie had just finished his *Autobiography* on a high note of hope, concluding with his meeting with the Kaiser the year before and congratulating him upon his long and peaceful reign. Subsequently, he added: 'As I read this today, what a change! The world convulsed by war as never before! Men slaying each other like wild beasts.' His wife added in a preface, when the book was published:

> Henceforth he was never able to interest himself in private affairs.... Optimist as he always was and tried to be, even in the face of the failure of his hopes, the world disaster was too much. His heart was broken.

Despite his energy, he was, of course, an old man of nearly eighty by 1914. His views on world peace were idealistic and had not kept pace with events. His idealism held little appeal for the leaders of the European powers who saw in the turmoil an opportunity to assert themselves; nor could his dreams hope to find favour with the industrialists who stood to profit from the conflict and who, in turn, had the ear of those in power. It is possibly a further irony that Carnegie might have had a greater influence on the course of the war, and on his cause for peace, had he retained his steel-making interests.

One further curiosity is worth considering: why he himself never went into politics. His correspondence with presidents, kings, emperors, chancellors, prime ministers and ambassadors, his meetings with the Kaiser and his last-ditch efforts to avert war, these were all the actions of the would-be politician—perhaps frustrated at not in actuality being a politician, or resolved that he could wield greater power from outside—or perhaps there were more complex reasons of character, inclination and opportunity. There is no question that Carnegie counted among his friends men and women of high social and political rank on both sides of the Atlantic. He entertained lavishly at his properties in America and Scotland. He enjoyed meeting the famous, and was particularly proud of having had the opportunity of seeing something of President Lincoln during his telegraph work in Washington in the Civil War. 'I never met a great man who so thoroughly made himself one with all men,' he wrote of Lincoln. In Britain, Prime Minister Gladstone was one of his correspondents. In 1890, Gladstone turned to Carnegie for help when Lord Acton threatened to sell his magnificent private library. Carnegie gave £10,000 to enable Acton to keep the library during his lifetime but forbade mention of his name to Acton. A closer friend was Herbert Spencer, a complex and brittle character, whose socialist writings, advocating the rise of the fittest, were influential in guiding social attitudes; it might be said that Carnegie tried to put into practice what Spencer advocated in his published works. Rudyard Kipling and Booker T. Washington, one of the most famous American negroes of his generation,

Carnegie was one of the first people to interest himself in helping black people of America. He was a friend of Booker T. Washington and made many donations to black institutions

were both on Carnegie's private pension fund. Samuel Clemens (Mark Twain) was among his literary friends and enjoyed teasing Carnegie:

> Could you lend an admirer a dollar & a half to buy a hymn book with? God will bless you. I feel it. I know it. N.B. If there should be another application this one not to count. P.S. Don't send the hymn book, send the money. I want to make the selection myself.

Though the money was not sent, the humour of this spoof begging letter was thought not to have been lost on the sober Scot. It was estimated by his secretary that he received from 400 to 500 letters a day, rising to about 700 after the announcement of some major benefaction. Most men, with that kind of public and private correspondence, those contacts and that ambition might well have sought a public platform.

With war a reality, the Carnegies left Skibo for America in September, 1914. In March, the following year, he suffered from pneumonia, recovered but was greatly dispirited. He spent the winter of 1915-16 cruising on his yacht aimlessly in Florida; in the winter of 1916-17, as US-German relations worsened, he wrote to President Wilson urging war: Germany, he said, was 'completely insane.' He had bought Shadowbrook, a large mansion near Lennox, Massachusetts, in the fall of 1916, and he spent his time between there and New York. The Armistice, on 11th November, 1918, revived his spirits; the marriage of his daughter Margaret, in April, 1919, was his final pleasure. He died from another bout of pneumonia on 11th August, and was buried at the Sleepy Hollow Cemetery in North Tarrytown, New York. Three months later, the US Senate turned down the League of Nations.

Carnegie's immediate peace plans had undoubtedly been frustrated but his long-term, carefully laid philanthropic plans were only just beginning to bear fruit. He was not being over-optimistic in the hope he expressed at the end of his life:

> My chief happiness, as I write these lines, lies in the thought that, even after I pass away, the wealth that came to me to administer as a sacred trust for the good of my fellow men, is to continue to benefit humanity for generations untold.

Manet—*Still Life with Brioche*, Museum of Art

The Carnegie Trusts for Education, Research and Welfare

CARNEGIE INSTITUTE

By the time it was completed, Carnegie's first major philanthropic trust had set the pattern for many of the themes that most concerned him. The Institute is remarkable chiefly because it contains so much under one roof and is rooted so firmly in the community; it is the first pointer, in practical terms, to the underlying wholeness of Carnegie's somewhat *ad hoc* plans for the distribution of his fortune. He had written in the *Gospel of Wealth*:

> Not until the dollars are transmuted into service for others, in one of the many forms best calculated to appeal to and develop the higher things of the moral, intellectual, and esthetic life, has wealth completely justified its existence.

Whom better to serve with his wealth than the city which had shown hospitality to the poor young immigrant and from which his fortune derived? He was proud to announce that the Institute was 'built by a Pittsburgher with Pittsburgh money for Pittsburgh,' so that the city should become a leading cultural centre as well as the leader of industry that it was already.

His gift began with money for a library and Music Hall, completed and dedicated on 5th November 1895, to provide Pittsburghers with a resource for education and cultural appreciation. To these were added in 1907 a building to house the art gallery, the Foyer of the Music Hall, and the museum of natural history, to extend appreciation and develop understanding of the world around. An essential aspect of the museum was scientific study and research, to deepen understanding. To further the practical side of education, Carnegie also put under the care of the Institute a technical school.

The technical school developed into the Carnegie Institute of Technology in 1912 and eventually into Carnegie-Mellon University in 1967 (see p. 64), quite independent of the original Institute. The library, too, became legally independent of the Institute but has remained under the same roof. The building now houses the Museum of Art, Carnegie Museum of Natural History, the Carnegie Music Hall of Pittsburgh and the Library.

The Carnegie Institute comprises the first three: art, natural history and music. In 1974, the Sarah Scaife Gallery was added to the Museum of Art; it was built at a cost of $12,500,000 and endowed with $5,000,000. Fifty miles east of Pittsburgh, the 2100 acres of the Powdermill Nature Reserve (a field research facility) also belongs to the Institute as part of Carnegie Museum of Natural History.

In 1981, the Vice-President of the Board of Trustees declared with reasonable pride:

> Carnegie built thousands of libraries, here and all over the world, but this Carnegie Institute, with a museum of natural history, a museum of art, a music hall adjoining a library, this is unique. Carnegie built only one of these—here in Pittsburgh.

Carnegie Museum of Natural History now ranks among the six largest such museums in the United States. Besides its exhibitions and collections, it conducts education programmes in the community both in and out of schools and for those with disabilities; it has a loan collection and an extensive volunteer programme; it welcomes researchers from abroad and sends its own research staff on expeditions to the farthest corners of the world. The Museum of Art, world-famous for its Carnegie International exhibitions of contemporary art, and with extensive permanent collections of paintings, sculpture, prints, drawings, photographs and decorative arts, has added collections of film and video and has initiated a widely-praised community art festival. The Music Hall is used not only for concerts but for lectures and films as well. The Library completes this all-embracing cultural service to the whole community of Pittsburgh; it is a service which reflects on the whole country and, certainly in its scientific aspects, contributes to world-wide understanding.

Carnegie Institute

Foundation: Library and Music Hall: 1895
           Art Gallery and Museum of Natural History: 1907

Purpose: The celebration of art, science, music and literature, through the Museum of Art, Carnegie Museum of Natural History and the Music Hall; Carnegie Library of Pittsburgh is a separate entity in the same building.

Finance:

Original endowment (1901):	$1,000,000
Additional endowments by Carnegie (1901):	$1,000,000
(1907):	$4,000,000
Additional gift for other purposes by Carnegie:	$5,729,472
Additional endowment by Corporation:	$2,094,000
(Other funds also provided by Corporation)	
Current endowment fund (1983):	$60,485,700
Actual receipts (1983):	$13,789,000
Actual expenditure (1983):	$11,959,000

Monetary gifts, grants, contributions from individuals, foundations, corporations and government agencies (1983):	$4,750,000
Specified funds and gifts expended on new permanent exhibits, additions to the collections, building renovations, research activities, special programmes, including Three Rivers Arts Festival, education and temporary exhibitions (1983):	$4,030,000

Attendance and collections (1983):

Number of visitors and participators:	700,000
Volunteer Program—services to public, research assistance, outreach programs:	
Number of volunteers:	600
Total hours of service:	44,000
Special Events—attendances at Music Hall, Lecture Hall, Museum of Art Theatre, etc:	158,000
Individual members of the Institute (approx.):	20,000
Continuing Education Dept.—enrolment in craft, dance, painting programmes, etc:	1,353
Items on display at Natural History Museum:	10,000
Specimens held by Natural History Museum:	minimum 12-15,000,000
Works of art held by Museum of Art:	18,000

Administration:
President: Dr Robert C. Wilburn (also President of Carnegie Library of Pittsburgh)
Vice-President: James A. Fisher
Secretary: Henry P. Hoffstot, Jr.
Director, Museum of Art: Dr John R. Lane
Director, Carnegie Museum of Natural History: Dr Robert M. West
Staff: approx. 300 full-time; equivalents approx. 600 volunteers
Address: 4400 Forbes Avenue, Pittsburgh, Pennsylvania 15213

Carnegie Institute

Pittsburgh refused Carnegie's first offer of $250,000 for a library building. The offer was made shortly after his visit to Dunfermline in 1881 when his mother had laid in the city of his birth the cornerstone of the first Carnegie Public Library. Wishing to repay his adoptive city in a similar way, Carnegie's only condition was that Pittsburgh should provide a site and $15,000 annually for maintenance. The mayor declined because the City was prevented by law from spending tax monies to maintain a free library. Carnegie transferred the offer across the river to Allegheny, where it was accepted.

There was surely a fine sense of one-upmanship in Allegheny when in 1890 the dedication of their library was attended by Benjamin Harrison, President of the United States. The city of Pittsburgh changed its law and asked Carnegie to renew his offer. He was glad to: he quadrupled it to one million dollars on condition that the city would provide $40,000 annual support. This time, the mayor accepted the price.

At the dedication in 1895 Carnegie made clear his reason for requiring Pittsburgh, or any other beneficiary, to pay its way:

> The taste for reading is one of the most precious possessions of life. I would much rather be instrumental in bringing the working man or woman this taste than mere dollars. When this library is supported by the community, as Pittsburgh is wise to support her library, all taint of charity is dispelled.

In the same speech, Carnegie announced his decision to inaugurate a museum and art gallery in association with the library but he saw these additions as less important at first, even though subsequently they were to cost him a great deal more:

> We now come to another branch, the Art Gallery and Museum, which the city is not to maintain. These are to be regarded as wise extravagances, for which public revenues should not be given, not as necessities. These are such gifts as a citizen may bestow upon a community and endow, so that it will cost the city nothing.

For the construction and establishment of the additional buildings required for the Art Gallery and Museum, Carnegie provided another five million dollars endowment and nearly six million for other purposes. It has been estimated that the real cost of the enterprise to Carnegie was closer to twenty-five million, since he supplied much of the steel from his own mills without charge. The new buildings were dedicated to the public in 1907, with three days of celebrations attended by Heads of State from around the world.

The building was an imposing three storeys high, of light grey sandstone, in an architectural style known then as 'American Renaissance'; more recently it has been described as 'a monument in the beaux arts tradition.' The interior was expensively decorated, with lavish use of variegated marble. A guide to the museum refers to it as 'a palace of culture—perhaps the last such edifice to be built before twentieth century conditions ended forever the tradition of building palaces.' The walls and staircase were decorated with murals by John White Alexander, depicting the 'Triumph of Labour,' a fitting tribute to the force that had brought Pittsburgh to prominence as an industrial city. Unfortunately that same industrial air, that Pittsburgh smoke, increased the labour of early museum directors in attempting to preserve the building and its collections.

Within the entrance, the atmosphere was not so much of Pittsburgh but of the ancient and mediaeval world. The great Hall of Architecture still contains the original life-size plaster reproductions of civilization's heritage from across the Atlantic. Crowded together in one vast room, these architectural treasures produce an overwhelming impact and one that is slightly claustrophobic: here is a complete recreation of the tomb of King Mausolus of Halicarnassus in Asia, one of the seven wonders of the ancient world; here are the magnificent eastern doors of the Baptistry of St John in Florence, designed and built by the Renaissance sculptor Ghiberti; here is a

Gothic portal from Bordeaux; and here is the entire facade of the twelfth-century Romanesque Church of St Gilles du Gard, for which special permission to take impressions directly from the structure itself had to be obtained from the French Government. The casts were carefully packed in crates for shipment to Pittsburgh and reassembled only just in time for the opening of the Institute.

There was a time, at the turn of the century, when some twenty museums in capital cities relied on such plaster casts for their displays of great architecture but as world travel became more available to the general public and tastes became more sophisticated art critics disdained the casts and most museums dismantled their displays and many were broken up. Pittsburgh resisted the trend and public affection for the plaster pillars has remained faithful. Now other museums look to the Institute with interest and with an eye, perhaps, on an old ruse that still has great potential.

More casts appear in the Hall of Sculpture and Balcony, which is patterned on the Parthenon, the temple to Athena on the Acropolis in Athens. Pentelic marble from the same quarries that supplied the original marble for the Parthenon itself was used for the construction of this scaled-down replica in Pittsburgh. Around the walls inside the Hall there is a plaster reproduction of the sculptured frieze that once adorned the outside of the Parthenon. The original marble frieze, well-known as part of the Elgin Marbles removed to the British Museum in London by Lord Elgin in the early 1800s with the explanation that these important monuments of Greek antiquity were being preserved from 'acts of pillage,' is now being urgently demanded back by the Greek Government. Meanwhile the replica remains safely in Pittsburgh, providing great pleasure and no discontent, among other bronze reproductions from Pompeii that were uncovered in the eighteenth century.

The Museum of Art

The architectural works and casts properly belong to the Museum of Art, within the Carnegie Institute. In the Deed with which he established the original Art Gallery, Carnegie specified 'that there be purchased each year two or more pictures by American artists, exhibited in that year, preferably in the Carnegie Art Gallery.... My object in so providing is to secure a chronological display of American art, from this time forthwith as shown by these pictures.' Purchasing and exhibiting modern paintings was quite as important to Carnegie as collecting antique monuments.

The Pittsburgh Exhibition of Contemporary Paintings and Sculpture was inaugurated in 1896 and is probably the event for which the Museum of Art became most widely known. It enabled Carnegie to write proudly that paintings were sent to Pittsburgh 'by the first artists of Europe.' The style and format of the Exhibition, subsequently known as the Carnegie International, has changed, chameleon-like, to reflect changing tastes and financial restrictions but the selection and representation within the exhibited works are now more truly international than they were in the beginning.

Carnegie had hoped that the Exhibition would 'spread goodwill, understanding, and peace among nations.' He also intended that it should 'enrich the permanent collection of the museum' and 'educate Pittsburgh audiences and inspire American artists by providing the best examples of international contemporary art.' Leon Arkus, writing in 1959, believed that the Internationals had 'probably brought more fame to Pittsburgh than any other civic activity.' He also thought that at least one of Carnegie's hopes had been fulfilled: 'That the Internationals spread goodwill among nations through art understanding,' wrote Arkus, 'is to be affirmed by the popularity of the Prix Carnegie abroad.' Among the winners of the first prize at Internationals over more than eighty years have been Winslow Homer, Frank Benson, Lucien Simon, Gaston La Touche, Augustus John, Pablo Picasso, Georges Braque, Ben Nicholson, Francis Bacon, Joán Miró.

There were those critics who were not inspired. In 1909, the *Pittsburgh Gazette Times* wrote of George Sauter's *The Bridal Morning* that it was 'interesting mainly because it shows to what extremes men will go and still call it art.' The paper added that 'it should be borne in mind that those who dislike paintings of the nude are not compelled to look at them.' In 1922, the *New York Tribune* paid a visit to 'modernism' in Pittsburgh and found, 'It was a sickening revelation. Some of them were so absurd that you could not make head or tail of them; they looked just as well upside down as right side up.' The *Pittsburgh Press* said of Carl Hofer's *The Wind* in 1939 that 'the girls look like a couple of flat-foot floogies on the fly-fly.' And in 1939, the *Pittsburgh Sun Telegraph* said of Marc Chagall's *The Betrothal* that 'the composition is ludicrous...the expression of the swain is moronic.'

Such views have not deterred the Internationals. Since they began, more than 300 paintings and other works have entered the Museum's permanent collection from the exhibition. Among these are examples of the highest quality of art-works of their respective periods: Winslow Homer's *The Wreck* (1896), the first-ever painting to be purchased; Rodin's bronze *Eve After the Fall* (1920); and Oskar Kokoschka's *Portrait of Thomas G. Masaryk* (1936). More recently it was proudly announced that 'a salient lacuna in the Museum of Art's contemporary holdings was filled with the arrival of a heroic-sized portrait of Andrew Carnegie by Pittsburgh's best-known artist-son, Andy Warhol' (see cover picture), though this portrait was not from an International.

The 1982 International, the forty-eighth, took place after a lapse of some years during rebuilding of the Museum. It was again the highlight of the Museum's programme and contained 189 works by 63 artists from 27 countries. It subsequently toured in Seattle. Works by David Hockney (Britain), Rackstraw Downes (USA) and Claudio Bravo (Chile) were included.

The Director of the Museum of Art, Dr Lane, is confident that the 1985 edition of this Pittsburgh classic 'will make a significant contribution to the "reinternationalization" of the contemporary American art world, a process that has become increasingly critical as visual evidence from abroad continues to affirm the end of the hegemony of New York as virtually the exclusive center of advanced contemporary art.' Dr Lane also sees the exhibition as one of the chief celebratory events associated with the 150th anniversary of Carnegie's birth.

The permanent collection houses not only contemporary art from the Internationals but distinguished masterpieces from the French Impressionists, the Post Impressionists and nineteenth-century American art, as well as old masters. As in all good art museums, it is with great satisfaction and the pleasure of meeting an old acquaintance that you come across, quite unexpectedly, the original of a painting that you have seen often before but only in illustrations. In 1984 the Museum received as a gift Edouard Manet's *Still Life with Brioche* (1880), the first Manet to enter the Pittsburgh collection. In the previous year, the Museum put on a popular survey exhibition of American abstract art of the 1930s which subsequently travelled around the country.

The Museum now owns more than 1,400 paintings and sculptures. It has a collection of more than 7,000 prints, photographs, drawings, watercolours, pastels and so on, from the fifteenth century to the present day. In all, the Museum owns more than 18,000 works of art, including collections of furniture and the decorative arts. The reference libary contains more than 10,000 volumes on all aspects of art. There is a Film and Video section, which has become one of the first museum-based Media Arts Centers in the United States; it presents educational programmes and appearances by leading artists in this field. Major displays and exhibitions are also part of the Museum's work. In 1983, an extraordinary compendium of objects was brought together in the Museum for an exhibition of 'The Heritage of Islam,' sponsored in Pittsburgh by a major grant from the Gulf Oil Corporation.

To make space for all this, the Museum of Art underwent major structural changes during the 1970s, with the addition of the $12.5 million Sarah Scaife Gallery. The Heinz Galleries, which house changing exhibitions, and the Ailsa Mellon Bruce Galleries for furniture and decorative arts are further additions to the original building. The Museum now has four main departments: Fine Arts; Antiquities; Oriental and Decorative Arts; Film and Video; and Education.

This last section takes seriously Carnegie's injunction to 'educate Pittsburgh audiences.' Staff duties include giving lectures, gallery talks and special exhibitions for children, students and adults. A graduate-level course, accredited to the University of Pittsburgh, on 'Using the Museum as a Resource,' is taught co-operatively by staff of the Museum of Art, the Natural History Museum and the University of Pittsburgh faculty. Staff also provide 'outreach programs,' which consist of series of slide lectures available to groups, clubs and organizations in the community. A variety of other programmes have been specially devised to take art into hospitals and for the benefit of blind and deaf people. An educational journal, *Prism*, is published and the bi-monthly *Carnegie Magazine* contains articles about the collections of the two museums and describes recent developments in all fields covered by the Institute.

Carnegie Institute has a long history of children's programming with studio classes for children established in 1923. A recent list of 'Summer Programs for Children' gives some idea of the imaginative range of enterprises aimed at the young. 'ARTexpress' classes for the four-to-ten age group explored the world of art through gallery games, creative art projects, story-telling and films. The children collected clues and tracked down treasures in 'Museum Mysteries'; they searched for old and new 'Magical Machines' and invented their own 'colourful kinetic contraptions'; they discovered the meanings of 'Symbols and Ceremonies' in many cultures and created their own costumes for a ceremony of their own devising. 'ARTventure' classes for the eleven-to-sixteen range developed their abilities and encouraged the students to examine their own ideas and feelings while working in the galleries of the museum, using printmaking, egg-tempera painting, drawing in black and white and in colour, clay sculpture and other means of exploration and expression.

By far the most significant and certainly the most popular event for taking art into the community is the annual 'Three Rivers Festival,' described in the Pittsburgh *Post Gazette* as 'The largest, longest and most popular event in this part of Pennsylvania.' Some would say, it has already earned a reputation as one of the best city festivals in the United States. Originating in 1960, activities involving local artists and crafts people take place in various 'display' locations throughout the city. The festival includes visual art exhibits, the performing arts and a film festival. Director John Brice explains the attraction:

> The people who come to the festival are often drawn by one particular event. They may come to see Ella Fitzgerald, but on the way to the stage they pause at a pavilion and look at a painting, or stop to watch a weaver at her loom. Next year, or perhaps the next day, they may return just to see the paintings or the weaver or even become regulars at the city's major cultural institutions.

Another way of putting it is this:

> What greater opportunity to introduce people to a new experience or art form than to have them stumble upon it on the way to pick up a blintz.

In 1983, nearly half a million people 'stumbled' upon, or came by intent to, the 'Three Rivers Festival,' the largest attendance in any year to date. The festival had to be extended from its traditional ten days to seventeen days to accommodate the demand.

Carnegie Museum of Natural History

> In the Carnegie Institute the great rooms, with their freight and plunder of the past, seem to float, as it were, above a multitude of workshops and laboratories; they are upraised, supported and maintained by a marvelously active little city that is essential to the structure's very existence.

This description in *An American Palace of Culture* by James Van Trump reproduces Carnegie's own image of the Museum: a combination of wonder and workshop, of education and research, side by side, which quickly became one of the most respected institutions of its kind in the world. Carnegie's own hand guided the policies of the museum in the early years and he contributed through enthusiasm and cash to the build-up of the collection.

The nucleus of the collection came from the Pittsburgh Academy of Science and Art, through Carnegie's 'good offices.' Among his many other gifts were 'two mummies, with cases, from Egypt'; a collection of 12,000 specimens of 3,000 species of moths from British India; several Atlantic walrus, purchased from Lt Robert Peary, the famous Arctic explorer, who, as Admiral Peary, reached the North Pole in 1909; a large number of anatomical models of mammals, including 'a complete man'; and reproductions of classical statues. There followed specimens of birds, reptiles, fish, fossils, plants and minerals but it was the 'Carnegie Dinosaurs' that set the seal on the ultimate success of the museum and won for it the affectionate title, 'Home of the Dinosaurs.'

Reading through the *New York Journal* of November 1898, Carnegie's eye was caught by the headline, 'Most Colossal Animal Ever on Earth Discovered Out West.' He sent a note to the director of the museum, Dr Holland: 'Dear Chancellor, Buy this for Pittsburgh.' Enclosed was a cheque for $10,000. Dr Holland travelled to Wyoming and persuaded the 'discoverer,' Mr Reed, to sign a contract in which all the fossilized bones he dug up would become the property of the museum. Reed did not explain that the massive thigh bone he presented to Dr Holland was so far the only remains he had unearthed but two months later he began to uncover the fossilized skeleton of an almost complete giant dinosaur, more than eighty-four feet from nose to tail, so huge that it was not until the museum itself was enlarged in 1907 that it could be mounted for display. There was no argument about the name: it became *Diplodocus carnegii*. Critics quickly relished the opportunity to draw comparisons between the dinosaur and the man's vast empire.

Carnegie was delighted with the prize. Acting on a broad hint from the British royal family, he sent a full-size reproduction to London and then one each to Berlin, Bologna, Buenos Aires, Leningrad, Madrid, Mexico City, Munich, Paris and Vienna. More bones were discovered by Reed and his team throughout Wyoming and Colorado, and over succeeding years hundreds of tons were delivered to the museum. Preparators working on Dinosaur Monument materials are still chipping away at the great lumps of rock encasing dinosaur remains shipped to Pittsburgh in the early 1900s. There they are, in the basement of the museum, waiting to be opened out. Of those revealed, one demonstrated Carnegie's respect for equality between the sexes: Mrs Carnegie also had a namesake—*Apatosaurus louisae*.

It was the influence of the Institute that contributed to the preservation of the famous dinosaur quarries in northeastern Utah. The public can view the fossils exactly at the site where the creatures perished millions of years ago, at what is now the Dinosaur National Monument. Today, new discoveries are keeping alive the Carnegie tradition. In 1981, an expedition to Ghost Ranch, near Santa Fe, New Mexico, produced the biggest single block of dinosaur-containing material in the museum's history.

Carnegie's Dinosaurs

by Helen J. McGinnis
Carnegie Museum of Natural History, Carnegie Institute

A Book of the Collection from the Carnegie Museum of Natural History

The public remains as fascinated with these giants of the past as visitors were when the museum began, reflecting an intriguing aspect of the Institute: the enduring quality of the exhibits and the number of things that have *not* changed over the decades. The dinosaurs and the great plaster reproductions still draw the crowds; so do the Egyptian mummies, the diorama of the camel driver being attacked by Barbary lions now extinct, the Indian rain dancers, the reptiles, the vultures and the other habitat groups. Pittsburghers who came as children to gaze in wonder at these things now bring their grandchildren to do the same.

At the same time, the museum has not stood still; it has been determined that the massive collection should not stagnate, as Craig Black, the director, reported in 1981:

> I find, in looking over the year's activities, as well as those of the past five years, that Carnegie Museum of Natural History is a place of constant change. . . . What does not change is our commitment to excellence.

Today the museum ranks among the six largest natural history museums in the United States. It is among the ten most-visited places in Pennsylvania. Apart from the famous dinosaur collection, it houses one of the foremost collections of butterflies in the world. It contains the fifth or sixth largest grouping of birds in the country, the fourth or fifth largest grouping of amphibians and reptiles, and one of the ten most extensive collections of mammals. There are sections on verbetrate fossils, invertebrate fossils, botany, amphibians and reptiles, birds, entomology, mammals, minerals, man and education. There is a section for exhibit design and production, and a 'visitor center,' which uses audio-visual aids to explain how the museum works and what it contains. Information is also provided through a number of publications, including the *Annals of Carnegie Museum*, published continuously since 1901; the *Bulletin of Carnegie Museum of Natural History*; Special Publications and the *Carnegie Magazine*, containing articles about all the Institute's activities; and a considerable flow of pamphlets and guides both popular and technical.

It is the work of the exhibitions to bring to the surface, for public delight and education, the tip of what lies beneath the museum—the research and the collections. The workshop that creates the eye-catching displays does so with great skill and imagination, building display cases, constructing bodies and modelling faces, designing dioramas, creating icebergs and illuminations. The workshop itself, and all that goes on in it, is one of the best exhibits in the whole museum, certainly one of the most intriguing.

Recent work has included the display in The Hillman Hall of Minerals and Gems, opened in 1980, and the Polar World: Wyckoff Hall of Arctic Life exhibition, opened in 1983. Hillman Hall presents a dazzling display of rocks and minerals made exciting by mirrored walls, rear-projection audio-visuals, track-lighting and hands-on features. One of the star pieces was a 14-carat diamond from India, which disappeared from its supposedly secure case within a year. The vacuum was filled in 1982 by a light yellow, round, brilliant cut diamond weighing 15.5 carats, but in the meantime the space left vacant received as much or even more interest than the original stone. The new Polar World exhibit represents the first major anthropological installation since 1913. Within the dramatic display of Arctic life, there are six life-size dioramas, including Inuit, an igloo, a walrus and a kayak. Construction took several years, including drawings, preparation of plants, animals and people, photography and assemblage. The exhibition itself contains many of the results of thirty-eight expeditions mounted by the museum to the Arctic and sub-Arctic since 1902, together with collections of modern Inuit art.

The visiting public see only a small percentage of the work that goes on in the natural history museum. It functions also as a major centre for scientific research. More than fifty scientists and staff members care for and study the fourteen million specimens and artefacts stored behind the scenes. International exchanges and fieldwork expeditions throughout the world play an important part in this work. A brief glance through the collections and the activities can give only a small impression of what exists and what goes on but it demonstrates the range. The truth is that you would need very many visits to comprehend even one part of it all.

There are 140,000 computer-catalogued specimens in the Section of Amphibians and Reptiles, most of which are not on the exhibit floor. In 1983, more than 1,380 specimens were handled in seventy-seven loan transactions to scientists using the museum's research facilities. A further 3,434 specimens were added to the reference collection that year, and a reorganization of the turtle collection was achieved to house a backlog of 15,000 unprocessed specimens. The museum has been particularly successful in researching into the reproductive biology of sea-turtles, once abundant in tropical oceans, now decimated by over-utilization but still an important potential human food source. It has been discovered that the temperature at a critical phase of incubation determines the sex of the hatching turtle and since one male can fertilize the eggs of many females the deliberate production of a majority of females could speed replenishment of depleted breeding populations. Research of this kind into endangered species often begins at the museum's collections, to establish from earlier specimens the original spread of the species and so help to identify how much the species has been reduced.

The study collection in the Section of Invertebrate Fossils is measured not by individual specimens but by lots—75,000 in all, ranging from one shell to several hundred, housed in sixty-six cases. During 1983, there were 422 specimens of land, freshwater, marine and fossil molluscs donated by collectors. In the Section of Entomology, in 1980, some 257 cabinets with 7,552 drawers and innumerable insect specimens received a thorough grooming. In any single year, from 1,000 to 2,000 insect identification requests are made to the section; in 1983, about 235 of these enquiries were made by the general public. In the same year, individual labelling of 100,000 specimens in the type-rich Ulke beetle collection greatly improved accessibility.

The Botanical collection contains more than 500,000 plant specimens from all the world's major plant groups. More than 2,000 of these are 'types'; that is, specimens that were new to science when they were first collected. There is a botanical library of

Bird banding—Powdermill Nature Reserve

10,000 volumes and periodicals, with many eighteenth-century volumes among them. There is also a laboratory for plant classification. In 1983, there were 12,180 specimens added to the collection from staff field work (10%), various gifts (30%) and the exchange programme (60% of which 30% came from Asia). In the same year, there were 11,721 specimens sent out from the museum on exchange to thirty-eight institutions, of which half were in Asia.

There are about 1,000 birds on display to museum visitors. Behind the scenes, there are 6,000 skeletons, about 10,000 sets of eggs, and 4,000 alcohol specimens for dissecting tissues for research; there are also 160,000 bird skins, stuffed with cotton, stored in wooden drawers in huge metal filing cases. These are spectacular. It is unlikely that you would be allowed to hold the giant albatross, as old as this century, with a wingspan far greater than the height of a man, but the bird is there, in perfect condition, and it is an unforgettable experience to take it from its drawer. In 1983, computer cataloguing began on these study skins. In that year, seventy-four bird skins from the Ukraine were acquired, an area not previously covered by the collection. The public and other institutions donated 1,300 specimens. The public also co-operated in salvaging birds which died when hitting picture windows, television towers and automobiles. Of 798 specimens added in 1980, more than ninety percent were donated by friends of the museum in this way. The section contributes to art and education by lending specimens to recognized professional artists and carvers as models.

Bird-banding is a major programme in the Powdermill Nature Reserve, the 2,100-acre field research facility that is 60 miles east of the museum but plays a major part in its research. The nature reserve contains the third largest bird-banding facility in the United States. In twenty years, about 240,000 birds have been banded. In 1983, there were 14,630 new birds banded, representing 123 species. Powdermill is also a research station for plant and animal population studies and a field station for educational nature programmes for young people and adults in the area.

The Mammal Section in the museum contains 80,000 specimens in all, but the most marvellous room, without question, is the huge cold store where skins of the largest specimens are hung up for preservation. With its massive safe door, this giant freezer is like a bizarre clothes cupboard. There are skins of bear and moose and hippo and giraffe, hung up in heavy rows, brushing against you as you walk between them. These skins provide an invaluable gauge against which to measure changes in subsequent skins, to warn scientists of likely dangers to particular species, just as with the sea turtles.

In the Section of Man, there are more than five million anthropological and archaeological items, including pot shards and tiny arrow heads. Several thousand items may be added in any one year. Specialist collections include, for example, 1,000 native American baskets and 5,000 dolls. One of the rarest items is an Egyptian funeral boat from about 2000 BC. In 1983, museum scientists were investigating the impact of earthquakes on prehistoric cultures in southern Peru; on the islands of Barbuda and Montserrat in the West Indies, they were identifying prehistoric sites for excavation; on Martha's Vineyard, they were hastily surveying archaeological remains before housing development and land erosion obliterates all evidence of earlier settlements. In 200 years more than 2,600 feet of land have been lost to the sea—an average of thirteen feet each year.

Field expeditions are an essential part of the scientific research of museum staff, though they may range in duration from months in the High Arctic to a day within driving distance of the museum. Their work is often translated into new exhibits for the museum. In 1983, a special exhibition was mounted featuring eight field trips undertaken within recent years. It was called 'Carnegie Around the World.' The trips included the reopening of a dinosaur quarry in New Mexico, the discovery of a rich record of early Eocene land plants and vertebrates in the Canadian High Arctic, the study in Mexico of the endangered Bolson Tortoise, the study of a unique bird fauna on the Mexican island of Socorro, a joint effort to study the ecology and evolution of certain woodland herbs common to Japan and eastern North America, the discovery of four species of mammals previously unknown to science in Suriname in South America, the excavation in Market Street in downtown Pittsburgh of more than 15,000 artefacts from thirty wells and cisterns and a number of building foundations, and the collection and identification in a number of African countries of small mammals serving as hosts for organisms causing human diseases such as plague, typhus and spotted fevers, in a team effort to understand and treat public health problems in Africa.

Research and education combine in the museum's 'International Program,' through which resident museum specialists come from abroad to work for several years. There have recently been scientists from China, Japan, Kenya and Mexico, and shorter term 'Visiting Museum Experts' from Mexico, South Africa, New Zealand, Australia, Japan and England; there are now scientists from India, Singapore and Thailand. In return, a number of museum staff have recently visited India, Thailand, the Philippines, Peru and Belize.

Like the Museum of Art, the Museum of Natural History goes beyond the specialist and the enthusiast to educate by giving pleasure to the people of Pittsburgh, as Carnegie had intended. Museum tours, a loan collection, 'in-school programs,' a 'museum on the move' project, the Powdermill reserve, formal education classes taught by museum and university staff all make this properly a 'learning museum' for the general public.

In 1983, the Museum on the Move served 2,000 children by making 120 presentations at five hospitals. The In-School Program, conducted by thirty-three volunteers, met 13,600 children throughout Allegheny County. The Loan Collection benefited 60,000 individuals. The new Florence Lockhart Nimick Nature Center at Powdermill Nature Reserve hosted numerous education programmes in 1983 and the Leonard S. Mudge Environmental Education Program helped children interpret the natural world through direct experience of the outdoors. Encounters with Powdermill's creepers and crawlers; a visit of discovery about the management of a forest; a journey to the birthplace of the world's first petroleum industry and a trip through Pithole, a bustling city at the peak of the oil boom, now Pennsylvania's most famous ghost town; a fossil trail ending in a coal mine: these are some of the outdoor activities of the education programme.

There were 115,363 individuals in 1983 directly served by education programmes, an increase of nearly forty percent on 1982. Formal classes for children attracted 2,664 pupils, from three-year-olds to fourteen-year-olds. Classes ranged through an introduction to the museum, animal homes, backyard surprises, birds and their feathers, beetles, fruit and vegetable tastes, curious plant and animal companions, building a nature box, exploring a cave, and animal ancestry. For adults, the museum has special programmes, including a series of lectures called 'Man and Ideas.' In the last fifteen years, lecturers have included R. Buckminster Fuller, Margaret Mead, Mary McCarthy, Richard Leakey, George Segal, Gerald Durrell, Henry Kissinger, Isaac Asimov and Alvin Toffler. That list alone makes it easy to see why this is considered a museum for all.

Carnegie Music Hall

Carnegie's wish that Pittsburghers should be served by the Music Hall with the opportunity to listen to the best music has been amply fulfilled. In terms of acoustics alone, the Hall is considered to be one of the best in the world. In architectural terms, the foyer has been seen as one of the most splendid examples of Edwardian display in

America, with a mosaic patterned floor measuring 135 by 60 feet, a bronze sculpture of Carnegie himself presiding at one end, and marble from Greece, France, Italy, Galway, England and Africa used in its decoration and that of the adjoining smoking room. Today the foyer serves as a spectacular gallery for the works of a number of artists with Pittsburgh connections and for receptions.

Within a year of its opening, the Hall had its own orchestra, the Pittsburgh Symphony Orchestra, which was housed there from 1896 to 1910. In 1985, the Pittsburgh Symphony performs at the Edinburgh Festival in celebration of Carnegie's 150th anniversary. Another matter of particular pride to the Music Hall is its organ, which has 8,600 pipes; the largest is thirty-two feet long and weighs 1,000 pounds; the smallest is a fraction of an inch long.

Free organ recitals were given weekly from 1895, and monthly from 1966 onward; more than 4,500 such recitals have now been given. In any one year today, there are nearly 100 programmes of music in the hall, with aggregate attendances of almost 90,000; there is seating for 2,000 people. Lectures, poetry readings and film shows are

Music Hall Foyer

also held there, and the hall is available for hire. The Institute's Travel Film series attracts more then 1,000,000 people annually.

A roll call of famous musicians who have appeared at the hall would be an almost indigestible feast of names. Edward MacDowell, Richard Strauss and Sir Edward Elgar all appeared with the Pittsburgh Symphony in the early days. Elgar's *Enigma Variations* were played in the programme at the dedication of the foyer in 1907. Other visitors have included Percy Grainger, Dame Myra Hess, Fritz Kreisler, Paul Robeson and John McCormack. Sergei Rachmaninov came there in 1938 and refused to perform when he discovered that the enthusiastic crowd had overflowed onto the stage for additional seating space; it took great diplomatic skill to persuade him to change his mind. Similar overcrowding did not at all disturb tenor singer Luciano Pavarotti; and another cool head was that of Enzio Pinza, who sang at the hall in 1940. The audience watched in horror as a piece of plaster fell from the ceiling on to the stage in the middle of the performance, but Pinza smiled and kept on singing. Style and standards are both equally important.

Music Hall Stage and Organ

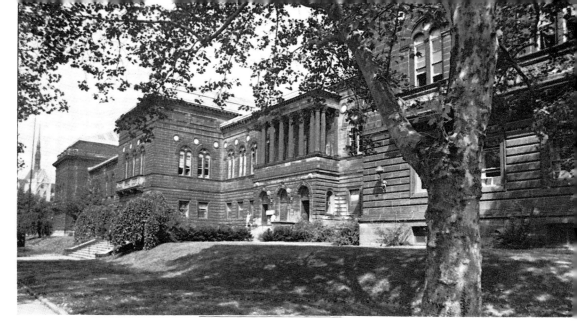

Carnegie Library

CARNEGIE LIBRARY OF PITTSBURGH

The Library, from which grew Carnegie's concept of an integrated arts, education and research centre, is now legally and financially separate from the Institute, though still housed in the original building. The Main Library has twenty-one branches and sub-branches, including a regional reference library, a library for the blind and physically handicapped, a reading centre and a district film centre. Eight of the branches were founded before Carnegie's death. Three bookmobiles serve areas without independent libraries, and there are eighty deposit collections and stations in schools.

The Library holds book stock of nearly 2,500,000 and non-book stock of nearly 2,000,000; the latter includes extensive collections of slides, records, cassettes and films. One of the best resource centres in the United States is contained in the Pittsburgh photographic library. The Library is also renowned for its collections in specialized fields such as technology, art, music, business and finance. Total circulation in 1983 of book and non-book stock was nearly 3,000,000, or approximately two items per head of population. The Library for the Blind and Physically Handicapped, with much the lowest stock, had markedly the highest circulation figures of any of the other branches and sub-branches, including the main library.

Finance comes almost entirely from tax funds. The people of Pittsburgh therefore support their own library service, which is what Carnegie intended. The library also makes its own efforts to raise money and to save money. In Andrew's Alcove is the used book store, where worn or donated books are for sale, to purchase new materials. In 1983, the book store raised nearly $10,000. In the same year, an amnesty was announced to overdue borrowers. During 'Forgiveness Week' there flooded into the main library, the branch libraries and the bookmobiles a total of 14,500 books.

Carnegie Library of Pittsburgh

Founded: 1895

Terms of use: Free borrowing privileges to all citizens of Allegheny County; free
reference services to all.

Income and expenditure, 1983:

Income:	City of Pittsburgh:	$3,710,000
	County of Allegheny:	$3,287,000
	Commonwealth of Pennsylvania:	$2,264,000
	Total:	$9,261,000
Expenditure:	County Bookmobiles:	$401,000
	Library for the Blind and Physically Handicapped:	$525,000
	Central and branch services:	$8,118,000
	Total:	$9,044,000

Additional expenditure from other funds for programmes,
administration, materials and facility improvements: $1,367,000

Additional monetary gifts and grants: $79,816

Stocks and loans, 1983:

Population served (1980 census):		
City of Pittsburgh:		424,000
County of Allegheny, outside city limits:		1,026,000
Number of agencies:		
Main library:	1	
Branch and sub-branches:	21	
Bookmobiles:	3	
Deposit collections:	77	
Stations in schools:	3	
Staff average:		
Monthly average number on payroll:	448	
Full-time equivalent of above figure:	346	
Buildings Department staff:	55	
Printing and Duplicating Centre:	4	
Total Book Stock:		2,424,427
Total Non-Book Stock:		1,812,445

(films, cassettes, slides, sheet music, recordings,
photographs, pictures, maps, microfilm, etc.)

Total circulation:
  City residents: 2,078,286
  County residents: 903,487
Total reference questions answered: 1,180,000
Total telephone reference questions answered: 435,000

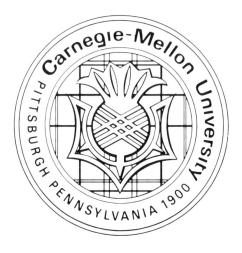

CARNEGIE-MELLON UNIVERSITY

The Technical Schools that in 1900 Carnegie decided to establish in Pittsburgh were an essential part of his total gift to the city. They represented the most practical side of his ideals for education. The library and music hall that had already been opened, and the museum and art gallery that were then being planned, were for the general educational improvement of the community; the Technical Schools were for the development of practical skills that would educate succeeding generations for work within that community. Leisure and work, side by side: Carnegie saw the need for education in both, for the advancement of mankind.

The Schools were officially opened in 1905, under the administrative care of the Trustees of the Carnegie Institute. Within a few years, they had grown so greatly that, in 1912, they were transformed into the Carnegie Institute of Technology, with full degree-granting status; they were separate from, but still under the care of, the Carnegie Institute, which administered further funds for the Institute of Technology provided by Carnegie and the Carnegie Corporation which had been created in 1911. The emphasis was placed on the development of professional skills in science, engineering, social sciences and the arts.

The Charter was revised in 1959, to provide for a separate Board of Trustees independent of the Carnegie Institute. In 1967, the Institute of Technology merged with the Mellon Institute to become Carnegie-Mellon University. The university now contains six major colleges—in engineering, fine arts, science, industrial administration, humanities and social science, urban and public affairs—each with its own departments.

Being a comparatively small university, with about 6,100 graduate and undergraduate students, Carnegie-Mellon has been able to concentrate on excellence and innovation and to select its research programmes carefully. For example, the original Carnegie Institute of Technology established the first school of drama in the United States in 1914; and the College of Fine Arts is now recognized as one of the leaders in its field in America. The Carnegie Plan for Professional Education included work in the humanities and social sciences and training in analytical thinking. It was a forerunner of the requirement that all engineering schools in the United States provide twenty percent of course work in the liberal arts. The management game by which students in the Graduate School of Industrial Administration learn the actual operation of a corporation was another Carnegie-Mellon innovation.

The university nurtures close links with industry in all its research and development programmes. Cooperation between its own departments has also been an important aspect of the university's success, with the Department of Computer Science acting as a major resource unit for all students. Carnegie-Mellon was the first university to establish a doctoral programme in computer science, and this department is numbered among the leading research centres in the United States. In 1978, the Nobel Prize in Economics was awarded to Herbert Simon, Professor of Computer Science and Psychology at Carnegie-Mellon.

With these and many other assets, Carnegie-Mellon has grown into a unique combination of major research university and small liberal arts college, breaking down many barriers between disciplines and providing what Carnegie himself would have welcomed as a full and practical education to enable graduates to make a major contribution to business and the community.

Carnegie-Mellon University

Founded: Technical Schools, 1900
Carnegie Institute of Technology, 1912
Carnegie-Mellon University, 1967

Original purpose: 'Schools of secondary education grade, providing technical training in the crafts and scientific vocations, so as to produce skilled workmen, such as machinists, mechanics, decorators, and so on.'

Current purpose: 'The establishment and maintenance in the city of Pittsburgh of a co-educational university of higher education, including an institute of technology, emphasizing liberal, professional education and specializing in teaching and research programs in selected areas of importance to the community and to the nation.'

Finance:

For original construction of Technical School (direct from Carnegie, 1905/06):	$1,500,000
For original endowment, from Carnegie, 1905/06:	$2,000,000
For construction enlargement, from Carnegie, 1910-13:	$1,500,000
For increased endowment, from Carnegie, 1910-13:	(approx) $2,300,000
	(approx) $7,300,000

From the Carnegie Corporation:

For salaries and equipment, 1914-21:	(approx) $1,200,000
For endowment, 1921:	$7,640,000
For gymnasium, 1921:	$400,000

In 1921, the Corporation agreed to increase the permanent endowment of the Carnegie Institute of Technology by $8,000,000 in July 1946 provided the Institute itself raised $4,000,000 by that date.

Further grants, 1965-84:	between $2-3,000,000
Grant from Hero Fund Commission, 1910-12:	$200,000

Additional endowment/grants above $5 million each:
  1949, Mellon Foundation, for School of Industrial Administration
  1958, Mellon Education and Charity Trust, for Fine Arts
  1967, Mellon Research Trust
        Mellon Institute General Endowment, for merger
  1968, R. K. Mellon, for School of Urban and Public Affairs

Current assets, June 30, 1983:

General Funds:	$25,575,086
Loan Funds:	$6,991,067
Endowment Funds:	$145,820,197
Life Income and Annuity Funds:	$6,896,821
Plant Funds:	$203,689,980
Agency Funds:	$279,287
	$389,252,438

Annual expenditures in early years:

1907-1908:	$208,125
1908-1909 (first graduating class):	$262,736
1909-1910:	$313,032

Annual expenditures at ten year intervals:

1919-1920:	$1,608,956
1929-1930:	$4,102,113
1939-1940:	$2,233,632

1949-1950:	$4,968,757
1959-1960:	$10,168,261
1965-1966 (before merger into C-M University):	$21,460,000
1966-1967 (after merger into C-M University):	$31,515,000
1969-1970:	$39,241,000
1979-1980:	$81,193,000
1982-1983:	$123,051,000
1983-1984 (projected):	$133,992,000
1984-1985 (projected):	$147,929,000
Total expenditures, 1908-1983:	$1,242,293,622

Students and faculty, Fall 1984:

	Undergraduate	Graduate	Faculty*
Carnegie Institute of Technology:	1,351	570	105
Mellon College of Science:	877	337	113
College of Humanities and Social Sciences:	880	184	94
College of Fine Arts:	877	147	78
Industrial Management:	227	—	—
Graduate School of Industrial Administration:	—	307	50
School of Urban and Public Affairs:	8	306	16
Other Faculty (Phys. Ed., Research, Admin.):	—	—	15
	4,220	1,851	471
Total enrolment at C-M University:		6,071	

* Faculty figures include full-time permanent faculty only (Department Heads are also counted here).

Administration:

President: Richard M. Cyert (former Dean of Graduate School of Industrial Administration, C-M University).

Secretary: Richard B. Barnhart

Staff:		
	Administrative staff:	267
	Instructional staff:	518
	Research staff:	315
	Other Professional/clerical:	589
	Support staff:	154
	Total:	1,843

Address: 5000 Forbes Avenue, Pittsburgh, Pennsylvania 15213

Aerial view of major academic buildings and mall of Carnegie-Mellon University

68

Carnegie-Mellon University

Carnegie liked to do things on a grand scale. His range of vision was responsible for his success in many ventures and enabled him to deal with vast amounts of money, time, materials and men; even in the disposal of wealth, Carnegie usually thought big. But one of his offspring foundations has made a virtue of its comparative smallness—in American terms. There are 'only' about 6,100 students at Carnegie-Mellon and the express aim of the university is the pursuit of excellence through careful selection of programmes within areas in which the university has a comparative advantage over other institutions. Like Carnegie himself, Carnegie-Mellon has not allowed smallness of stature to limit breadth of vision.

'How best to serve Pittsburgh is the question which recurs to me almost every day of my life,' wrote Carnegie in 1901, evidently not satisfied with the library and music hall he had provided in 1895, nor with the museum and art gallery he was planning to add. Another opportunity was already in his sights. He learned in late 1900 that the Pittsburgh Board of Education had modest plans for a technical school and so he made a proposal of his own that he 'might be the fortunate giver of a Technical Institute to our city fashioned upon the best models.' In his letter to the Mayor of Pittsburgh, Carnegie recalled the famous essay written by his grandfather to Cobbett's *Register*, which Cobbett was said to have pronounced the most valuable communication ever published in that paper. It was entitled 'Handication versus Headication' and in it Carnegie's grandfather had thanked God that in his youth he had learned to make and mend shoes. 'It is really astonishing how many of the world's foremost men have begun as manual labourers,' added Carnegie in his letter proposing a technical institute; he cited Shakespeare, Burns, Columbus, Hannibal, Lincoln and Grant.

The city welcomed the idea and agreed to provide a site; the Trustees of the Carnegie Institute agreed to accept stewardship of the new schools; but there was some disagreement about the nature of the schools. Carnegie sought the advice of a committee of educators, including 'professors from outstanding universities,' on how best such an institution should function. He disliked their suggestion for a university-level institute, so he sought the advice of a second committee, composed of representatives of industrial training institutions not of college rank and approved their suggestion that the schools should provide, at secondary level, technical training in the crafts and scientific vocations, so as to produce skilled workmen.

Carnegie had struck the right note; when the schools opened, they received substantial entries immediately. In 1905, the student roll was 765. In 1906, the Margaret Morrison Carnegie School for Women was opened. Carnegie was pleased at the Trustees' proposal to name the school after his mother: 'The tribute to my mother is exquisitely fine,' he wrote, 'and one she would have rejoiced in receiving. The interest she took in women wherever we lived was extraordinary.'

By 1912, it had become clear that the schools were getting closer to the aspirations of Carnegie's first committee and so Carnegie gave way to pressure to reorganize them into a fully-fledged, degree-granting Institute of Technology, still under the

Visit of Andrew Carnegie to Carnegie Technical Schools. At his left is Arthur A. Hamerschlag,
first President of the Institution (1903-1922)

management of the Carnegie Institute, and including the Margaret Morrison Carnegie
College. Funding for further endowment and for new buildings came through the
Carnegie Corporation of New York. There was rapid expansion and within three years
the student roll rose to 3,000; by 1917-18, there were 2,459 men and 690 women
students. The first master's degree was awarded in 1914 and the first earned doctorate in
1920; the first school of drama in the United States was established there in 1914.

In its early years, Carnegie Institute of Technology contained Divisions of Science
and Engineering, of Fine Arts, and of Industries; there was a Bureau of Salesmanship
Research and the Margaret Morrison Carnegie College, which offered a number of
courses including 'costume economics,' 'household economics' and 'secretarial studies.'
By containing a range of studies, Carnegie 'Tech' was among the first institutions to
develop an educational programme that integrated the humanities and social sciences
with the technical subjects required of engineers; it was also a pioneer in building its
technical education around an analytical approach to identifying and solving problems.
The 'Carnegie Plan' incorporating these ideas was adopted by many other leading
engineering institutions in the United States.

The Graduate School of Industrial Administration was added in 1949, with a
$6,000,000 gift from the Mellon family. It developed the widely-used 'Management
Game' to simulate, for student managers, 'real life' situations involving decisions in
marketing, accounting, manufacturing processes and personnel. Ten years later, in

Ceiling and main hall of College of Fine Arts building, constructed in 1912

Rotunda of Margaret Morrison Carnegie Hall, constructed in 1907 and named for Andrew Carnegie's mother

1959, the Carnegie Institute of Technology Charter was revised and the school became completely independent of the Carnegie Institute; at about the same time, a ten-year development programme was initiated to raise $28,000,000. New academic buildings were constructed for the Graduate School of Industrial Administration, the Hunt Library, Scaife Hall of Engineering, and Skibo; new dormitories were built; laboratories and classrooms were renovated; a new athletic field was laid out. In 1965, the first Department of Computer Science in the United States was established through a $5,000,000 gift from Richard King Mellon.

Carnegie-Mellon University came into existence in 1967, with the merger of the Carnegie Institute of Technology and the nearby Mellon Institute, which had been responsible for initiating several of the nation's major corporate research and development divisions. Since the Second World War, members of the Mellon family and the Mellon Foundation itself had made substantial grants to establish and endow new schools and programmes. Andrew Mellon (1855-1937), the patriarch of the family, had been a prominent financier, born and educated in Pittsburgh, with substantial interests in coal, coke and iron enterprises, aluminium manufacture and banking. He was President of the Mellon National Bank of Pittsburgh, U.S. Secretary to the Treasury 1931-32, and U.S. Ambassador to Great Britain 1932-33. Carnegie's was not the only philanthropic name to come out of Pittsburgh.

An important part of the Robotics Institute, established at Carnegie-Mellon University in 1979, is the Microbot, which is used in instructing students in the fundamentals of robotics

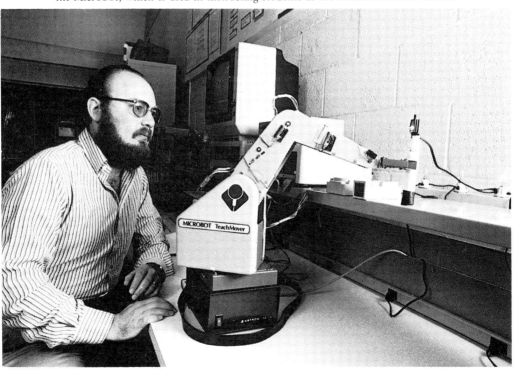

The creation of the new university naturally meant expansion. Expenditure increased by fifty percent, another $10,000,000, in the year of the merger. The following year, 1968, the College of Humanities and Social Sciences, incorporating some departments from the original Margaret Morrison Carnegie College, was established as the university's liberal arts college. The School of Urban and Public Affairs was established in 1969. Since the current president, Richard M. Cyert, came to office in 1972, the Robotics Institute has been added, so have Departments of Biological Sciences and Social Sciences; a personal computing project has been developed; there has been increased growth in the Department of Statistics; an 'Investments in Progress' campaign resulted in more than $100 million additional funds for the university; in November 1984, the Department of Defense awarded a $103 million contract to Carnegie-Mellon University to establish a Software Engineering Institute at the university.

These and other activities have gained for Carnegie-Mellon increased recognition nationally and internationally in its educational and research programmes. The main theme of the university has been its continued ability to carry on the traditions of both its Carnegie and its Mellon components in recognizing new problems and opportunities earlier than most other institutions. As the *Undergraduate Catalog* explains:

> Because of its modest size, it is able to tackle problems that cut across the boundaries of departments and disciplines, problems which larger and less flexible institutions find difficult to handle. This flexibility has not only resulted in vigorous research efforts but has also enriched the learning process itself.

In order better to understand the flexibility of the departments and the overall resources of the university, this might be the place to look briefly at the six degree-granting colleges at Carnegie-Mellon.

The Carnegie Institute of Technology (CIT) retains the original name and is the co-educational engineering college, with six engineering departments: chemical; civil; electrical and computer; mechanical; metallurgical engineering and materials science; and engineering and public policy. CIT has three main activities—undergraduate education, graduate education and research. Its continuing goal is to maintain excellence in all these activities. The degree to which this goal has been achieved is attested to by the demand for its students, the success of its alumni, the quality of its students and faculty, the adaptation elsewhere of its innovation, and the national and international recognition it receives in education and research activities.

Some of its research activities include biomedical engineering that maintains close ties with one of the largest and most active, well-equipped medical communities in the United States, with hospitals located within a three-mile radius of the university. The Department of Civil Engineering is widely recognized as a centre of excellence for computer applications in that field. The Department of Electrical and Computer Engineering has research activities in a number of areas, including computer-aided design, power engineering, solid-state electronics, and robotics. In 1983-84, a new

Computer training programme for teachers in Pittsburgh public school system, conducted by Carnegie-Mellon University, summer 1984

research centre, the Center for Iron and Steelmaking, was established within CIT—highly appropriate to the origins of Carnegie's wealth!

The Mellon College of Science (MCS) is a recognized leader in scientific research, with more than $12,000,000 in research grants and contracts; as with CIT, it promotes a combined emphasis on education and research, believing that this brings a special benefit to students. There are five departments: biological sciences, chemistry, mathematics, physics, and computer science. This last is particularly important. Undergraduates majoring in any field at the university will at some point come into contact with professors and students of the Department of Computer Science. Computing facilities are made available to all students and special courses are run for their benefit.

In 1982-83, the Center for Fluorescence Research in Biomedical Sciences and the Fermentation Institute were established; also, an interdisciplinary graduate programme in biochemistry and biophysics was initiated. The Pittsburgh Cancer Institute was established in conjunction with the University of Pittsburgh in 1983-84. Meanwhile, a new building is being constructed to house the Nuclear Magnetics Resonance Center, which comes into operation in 1984-85. This is a joint project for Carnegie-Mellon, the University of Pittsburgh, and a consortium of local hospitals. A Center for Applied Logic is also planned for the university.

The College of Fine Arts (CFA) contains five departments: art, architecture, design, drama, and music. The Department of Architecture was graduating students as early as 1908; by 1914, the College had become the first institution in the western world offering under the same roof a 'total' programme of these five elements. Today, within the departments, the aesthetics are centred on three areas: environment arts, performing arts, and visual arts.

In 1983-84, two new programmes were initiated, one in art history and the other a drama apprenticeship in cooperation with the Pittsburgh Public Theater. Also established was a programme to develop software for use in architectural design and education. In 1984-85, photography and theatre administration programmes are being added; so is an Electronic Imaging Center, to combine computer, video and photographic tools for use by students in art, design, drama and architecture. A Center for Art and Technology is also planned, to research the interaction between the two subjects.

The Graduate School of Industrial Administration (GSIA) has become one of the top business schools in the United States. Its Department of Industrial Management offers programmes for students who are interested in combining a broad educational base with a sound preparation for management. Its faculty pioneers research in economics and industrial administration. Three new executive education programmes were

Members of original cast of *Godspell*, a Carnegie-Mellon University Master's thesis project in 1971 of John-Michael Tebelak. A later world-wide success, the show at one time had 50 touring companies in the USA alone.

initiated in 1982-83, on economics, competitive strategy, and productivity. In 1984-85, two new research centres are planned, one for the Study of Private Policy, the other for the Management of Information and Technology in Organizations. A flexible, part-time 'Executive' master's degree is also under consideration.

The College of Humanities and Social Sciences (H&SS) has a dual emphasis on liberal arts and professional education. In 1977-78, the college replanned its curriculum 'to broaden perspectives, analytical skills and problem-solving strategies, while providing a base for the more specialized, professionally orientated courses.' In 1982-83, a new graduate programme in Psychology on Cognitive Processes in Human-Computer Interaction was initiated. In 1984-85, there will be a new curriculum for the Department of English; the Department of Statistics will offer an undergraduate degree in addition to its original graduate degree; and one former department will be split into two departments, that of History and Modern Languages, and that of Philosophy.

The School of Urban and Public Affairs (SUPA) deals with the management of urban organizations through its own professional and research programmes, and cooperates with many other of the university's divisions to handle a variety of problems. Some projects studied in SUPA have led to the drafting of new city, county and state laws; others have focused the attention of public officials on pressing problems in various fields of urban life. In 1982-83, the school offered jointly with the University of Pittsburgh's school of law a new mid-career master's degree in Public Management.

The inter-disciplinary *Robotics Institute*, established in 1979, undertakes advanced research and development in seeing, thinking and acting robots and intelligent machine systems; it also transfers this technology to U.S. industry. Its work focuses on robotics for hazardous environments and on automation and computer-integrated manufacturing. Recent developments include a collision-avoidance system for robots, an automated printed circuit board inspection system, and a position-sensing wrist for industrial robots; the institute has also researched into the reaction of workers to the installation of industrial robots in the workplace.

Besides these colleges, the *Mellon Institute* is worth a special mention. Two new research centres were established within the institute in 1983-84: these were for metals production and for battery testing. A fellowship was also established in Bio-engineering, sponsored by industry to undertake research in Biological Engineering. Two more research centres are planned for 1984-85: one for fossil fuels conversion, in which government, industry and academia will cooperate, the other for the development of solid-state gas sensors.

In November 1984, the Department of Defense of the United States Government announced its intention to establish a $103 million Software Engineering Institute at Carnegie-Mellon University. This institute is an effort by the Department of Defense to address one of the major problems with computers: creating and modifying software. In recent years, computer scientists have made steady improvements in tools and techniques for these purposes. However, these improvements have not satisfied the need for yet further improvements. Computer experts want to accelerate the rate at which these improvements are transferred from research laboratories to practical applications. The institute, which is expected to create 250 high-level jobs in Pittsburgh, will have an immeasurable effect on the regional economy. It should grow to its full complement of computer software, scientists, technicians, and support staff within five years.

On the broader front, in October 1982, Carnegie-Mellon and IBM jointly began to develop a prototype personal computing network that will give all CMU students, faculty and staff access to personal computers up to one hundred times more powerful than current home computers, linked together and to the mainframes in a campus-wide network that will also be accessible to off-campus users and will be tied into off-campus networks. The University Computing Center—the first new building in a decade—was completed in 1983-84. In the same year an agreement was signed between CMU and McGraw-Hill Publishing Company to develop university-level educational software. An inter-university consortium of seventeen universities and three auxiliary organizations was set up to stimulate the development of educational computing software. CMU also plans to introduce the latest computing technology into Middle and High Schools in Pittsburgh and Allegheny County. Meanwhile, the entire CMU campus is being rewired for a new telephone system and data-communicating network that will serve nearly 7,000 work-stations, making it the world's largest local-area network.

Carnegie-Mellon students come from almost every state in America and from about fifty foreign countries, with an approximate 2:1 men-to-women ratio. The professional achievements of the alumni are impressive: nearly 2,000 graduates are chairmen, presidents, or vice-presidents of corporations, and more than 1,400 alumni are now professors at other universities in management, engineering, the arts and sciences. The present distribution of students will continue; there may be a slight increase in the number of graduate students.

In 1972, the Andrew Carnegie Society was founded: 'to recognize and honor Andrew Carnegie...to encourage and inspire alumni and friends, in their support of Carnegie-Mellon University...and to encourage interest and participation of alumni and friends in the affairs of the University.' Members of the Society are recognized if they make annual gifts of $1,000 and more; Fellows support the University with gifts of $5,000 and more; the President's Circle contribute $10,000 and more per year; Life Membership is recognized by cumulative support of $25,000 and more. In 1983-84, Members and Fellows raised more than $3,600,000. Each year, a portion of the total support provided by the Society's members is directed toward general scholarship support. The special Andrew Carnegie Society Scholars Program recognizes four top students each year— one representing each undergraduate college. The first ACS Scholars were recognized in 1975.

Planning ahead, Carnegie-Mellon is determined to build on its greatest strength, the combined virtues of a major research university and a small, liberal arts college. Innovation in research, leadership in academic computing, interdisciplinary activities,

Warner Hall, administration building, named for Dr John C. Warner, fourth President of Carnegie-Mellon University (1950-1965)

78

the development of a core curriculum throughout the university, increases in the recruitment of undergraduates from overseas and of members of minority groups and of high-quality faculty, additional capital plant to improve the university's competitive position—these are some of the main goals of Carnegie-Mellon.

To support these goals, Carnegie-Mellon is also undertaking a major capital campaign. One important aspect of this support is to pay attention to issues related to the 'quality of life' for students, faculty and staff. This is central to the educational aims of the university; it also relates directly to Carnegie's own aspirations and to the aims of most of his other endowments.

CARNEGIE TRUST FOR THE UNIVERSITIES OF SCOTLAND

Carnegie's second major trust was also the first to bear his name after his retirement. With a library and music hall already provided for the people of Pittsburgh, and preparations in hand for an art gallery, museum and technical schools, his thoughts turned to the country of his birth, to Scotland, for which he retained a deep affection and where he had, for some years, been considering how best to serve the interests of higher education.

Education was at the heart of all Carnegie's plans; it remains the core that runs throughout his endowments. Education was in his eyes the means by which equality of opportunity might be realized and by which class barriers might be broken down; it was the logical prelude to a universal call for peace and the vital yeast for the elevation of mankind. Cultural appreciation, as provided at Pittsburgh, might be considered an important aspect of education; scientific research, as also provided there, might be necessary to underpin education; but practical, raw learning, as intended for the Pittsburgh technical schools and for the youth of Scotland, was the foundation stone of success from Carnegie's twin viewpoints: his upbringing as a lad and experience as a man.

The Trust Deed was signed in 1901. Its aims were threefold: to improve and expand the Scottish universities; to help pay tuitional fees for students of Scottish birth or extraction; to provide research and similar grants. There was much controversy about the Trust in Carnegie's lifetime and there have been certain shifts in emphasis since his death. The first change came in the 1950s, when State education released the Trust's funds for greater involvement in research aid and other areas. The second change came in the 1960s, when four new Scottish universities were added to the existing four. This doubled the spread of the Trust's responsibilities and made thinner the spread of its money.

Apart from the 90,000 students and others who have directly benefited from the Trust, its lasting mark can easily be found in a number of 'Carnegie' buildings for university purposes, ranging from laboratories to student residencies, but the cost of such major projects are now too great for the Trust's resources. Capital grants are still given to each university under a quinquennial distribution system; students are still occasionally helped with tuition fees; aid is still given to a library or university museum; grants are allocated for staff travel to conferences or for personal research; university expeditions are supported; Fellowships and Carnegie Scholarships are awarded. These last are regarded as the élite research awards for Scottish graduates. From Ecuador to the Orkneys, Paris to Papua, the Yemen to the USA, scholars and students backed by the Trust can be found researching into everything from robot systems to the treatment of wife abuse, from Islamic architecture to the behaviour of voles, from beach pollution to the forensic characteristics of human hair.

All in all, there can be little doubt that Carnegie's Trust and the trustees whose job it has been to interpret his Deed have contributed greatly to the fine reputation of education in Scotland.

Carnegie Trust for the Universities of Scotland

Founded: 1901

Purpose: 'Providing funds for improving and extending the opportunities for scientific study and research in the Universities of Scotland, my native land, and by rendering attendance at these Universities and the enjoyment of their advantages more available to the deserving and qualified youth of that country...' (*from the Trust Deed*).

Income and expenditure:

Original endowment ($10,000,000):	£2,000,000
Current assets:	£13,000,000
Annual distributions, 1901-1903:	(approx) £100,000
Annual distributions, 1983-1984:	(approx) £750,000
Total distributions, 1901-1984:	
(*a*) Grants to Universities/Research:	£9,610,696
(*b*) Assistance to students:	£3,549,302
	Total: £13,159,998

Capital grants to Universities, 1983-88 quinquennial:

Aberdeen	£102,000	Heriot-Watt	£66,650
Dundee	£67,550	St Andrews	£67,550
Edinburgh	£130,000	Stirling	£66,650
Glasgow	£130,000	Strathclyde	£108,400

Grants, Fellows, Scholars and Students:

Total named beneficiaries, 1901-1984:	(approx) 90,000

(As many again benefited indirectly.)

Annual beneficiaries, 1901-1903:	(approx) 2,000
Annual beneficiaries, 1982-1984:	(approx) 310

(The early figure is much greater because the Trust paid small sums of about £10 each to students as class fees. The system changed in 1948. Current figures include about 120 students; the rest are research awards.)

Publications received from beneficiaries, 1982-83:	81
Total scholarly volumes launched as a result of Trust publication support system, 1901-1983:	(approx) 900

Sample decade of support, 1973-1982:

Personal research support awards:	1,712
Publications resulting:	502
Research expeditions supported:	88
Learned society journals supported:	80
Full-time post-graduate researchers:	(approx) 100

Administration:

Chairman:	The Hon. Lord Cameron, KT, DSD, DL, LLD, DLitt, DUniv, HonRSA, PPRSE.
Secretary:	A. E. Ritchie, CBE, MA, DSc, MD, FCSP, FRSE; previously Professor of Physiology at the University of St Andrews and General Secretary of the Royal Society of Edinburgh.
Staff:	3 full time; 1 part time.
Address:	The Merchants' Hall, 22 Hanover Street, Edinburgh EH2 2EN.

Carnegie Trust for the Universities of Scotland

'We do a job which no other organization does,' wrote the Chief Executive of the Trust in 1984, 'and we do it quickly and equitably. The Scottish universities would not perish without us, and our contribution is financially small as compared to the early days...but I think we have done exactly what Andrew meant us to do.'

What educators in Britain feared that Andrew meant to do aroused such consternation that this proved to be one of the most controversial of all his endowments. Carnegie's views on education were already well-known. His preference for a practical education and his ambivalence toward the teaching of the classics caused uncomfortable stirrings in the depths of the Establishment. Since his own material success owed little to Shakespeare, Ovid or Homer, it was little wonder that he should extol the virtues of technical schools rather than classical classes. In 1891, in a speech at a

The MacMillion.

the Scottish-American millionaire

[Mr. Andrew Carnegie has provided £2,000,000 for the establishment of free education in the four Scottish universities.]

'The MacMillion' Cartoon of Andrew Carnegie on his endowment
of the Universities Trust

college of business studies in America, Carnegie told the students: 'I rejoice, therefore, to know that your time has not been wasted upon dead languages, but has been fully occupied in obtaining knowledge of shorthand and typewriting.'

If that was not alarming enough to the academics of Scotland's four ancient universities, then his scorn for the impractical and unwordly self-governance of the Scottish universities certainly gave them cause for thought:

> Americans do not trust their money to a lot of professors and principals who are bound in set ways, and have a class feeling about them which makes it impossible to make reforms [wrote Carnegie]. Americans put their money under the control of business men at the head of the universities. If I had my own way I should introduce that system into the Scottish universities.

Blackwood's Magazine turned to the attack, fearing that this was the thin end of a general assault on British principles:

> Maybe Mr Carnegie has never heard of the fable of Midas. If for a moment he can overcome his loathing of the past, we would urge him to read it....Push and screw; buy cheap and sell dear....To get money you must strangle joy and murder peace....Presently the American ideal of life will be our own....In old days, a rich man enjoyed his wealth—and if he did the community 'no good' at least he did not insult it with 'patronage.'

Their fears were exaggerated. Carnegie had a genuine affection for his homeland and a real concern for Scottish education, prompted by a newspaper article by Thomas Shaw (later Lord Shaw of Dunfermline) which pointed out that many poor people in Scotland were unable to pay fees for their children to attend university. It was also evident that Scotland's four ancient foundations, which had served the world well for five centuries, were finding themselves crippled by the shrinkage of their early endowments and unable to respond adequately to demands for expansion in the new age of research.

Whatever they thought of Carnegie's 'interference,' the outrage of his critics was definitely tempered by the size of the sum he offered: ten million dollars, equivalent to two million pounds at that time. It was almost overwhelming, for the combined endowment of the four universities was then less than £70,000, whereas the revenue alone from Carnegie's endowment came to £100,000 each year. It was, truly, 'an offer they couldn't refuse.'

The offer was accepted and the Deed drawn up. It contained thoughtful and straightforward terms as to the purpose of the Trust, and this certainly helped in the efficient running of the Trust in subsequent years, but it did not silence all objections. There were still those who found an unwelcome bias in the terms of the Trust that referred to 'improving and extending the opportunities for scientific studies and research...and such other subjects cognate to a technical or commercial education,' though medicine, history, English literature and modern languages were also mentioned. There were also those who insisted that financial aid for tuition fees would mean a lowering of standards: more pupils would mean worse pupils. It was not true. Carnegie grants became prizes worth working hard for, and the diligence of the trustees ensured that only the deserving benefited from the opportunity.

Carnegie's biographer, Professor Wall, noted that:

> There is no question that the Trust awakened Scottish higher education to an intellectual activity that it had not known since the golden days of the late eighteenth century. With funds available for equipment and research, Scotland was now prepared to advance into the twentieth century.

In the first thirty-five years, the Trust appointed more than 700 Fellows and Scholars, and awarded nearly 500 grants in aid of research. Nearly 200 beneficiaries later occupied University Chairs; a great number became Fellows of the Royal Society; and many had their lives' work recognized by knighthoods. Out of the first twenty Fellows and Scholars appointed in 1903, eight became Professors and three became Fellows of the Royal Society. One of these, Dr Kinneir Wilson, became in his day the most distinguished medical neurologist in Europe; another, Sir James Irvine, after an outstanding career as a chemist, became Principal and Vice-Chancellor of St Andrews University.

A US Steel Bond for one hundred thousand dollars
made out to the Universities Trust

There have, since the war, been so many other distinguished careers by erstwhile Carnegie beneficiaries that one example has to make do for all. The recent death of Professor William Fisher makes him an appropriate choice. Professor of Geography in the University of Durham from 1956 to 1981, he was once chastised for truancy by a headmaster who scorned the notion of going to university at all, but he subsequently gained a lectureship at Aberdeen in 1947 with a Carnegie Scholarship. At Durham he built up one of the largest and most progressive university departments of Geography; he also advised on geography teaching in schools, and achieved international recognition as one of the few major Middle Eastern geographers of the day.

Perhaps the most evident feature of Trust benefaction between the two World Wars was in the provision of buildings, which went on alongside support for student fees and research. In the Scottish universities there are Carnegie libraries, laboratories, student residencies, lecture theatres, student unions, all of which testify to the 'improvement and expansion' envisaged by Carnegie himself. In the 1950s, the development of State-supported education freed Trust funds to support 'qualified and deserving' students who wanted to take a second degree; as postgraduate research also came under the State wing, the trustees were able to provide more money for Carnegie Research Scholarships. State intervention in providing university facilities helped too. The Trust had been finding that the rising cost of buildings and equipment was proving too much for its limited exchequer; when it no longer had to fund complete projects, it was able to concentrate on giving aid for extra equipment and facilities not provided for in State aid.

The major change in the 1960s was the establishment of four 'new' universities in Scotland, to join the four ancient universities of Aberdeen (1495), Edinburgh (1583), Glasgow (1451) and St Andrews (1410). Three of the 'new' ones were developed from existing colleges; these were Strathclyde (1964), Heriot-Watt (1966) and Dundee (1967); only Stirling (1967) was an entirely new establishment. Such a development had not been foreseen by Carnegie, but the extensive powers granted by him to the trustees enabled them to prepare a new charter to incorporate the new universities within the terms of the Trust.

With eight universities to satisfy instead of four, and with the availability of massive State aid and major research awards from outside sources, the Trust has now decided on a policy which is, in effect, to fill in the gaps; to attempt to support any major projects would be to spread its resources too thin. The current areas of expenditure are in roughly equal parts: capital grants for equipment and facilities; block grants for staff travel; the pursuit of the original principle of providing aid in deserving cases, for despite State and Local Education Authority aid there are still cases where hardship might prevent a student from taking a degree. Other individual grants enable graduates and staff members to research abroad. Research scholarships and fellowships comprise the remaining part of the expenditure.

The Trust research grants are, for the most part, applied to travel. The range of interests and the variety of locations for research and travel grants approved in 1982-83 amply quash any criticism that a trust favouring the universities of Scotland might in

any way prove limited or parochial. Grants during this period enabled researchers to travel to Australia to study diseases in horses, commodity markets and environmental physics; to Brazil to study political systems; to Canada for manufacturing and comparative law; to China for river and rural development; to eastern Europe for adaptations of historic buildings for public housing; to Ecuador for glaciers; to Germany for wheelchair design; to Italy for sixteenth-century Florence; to Japan for robot systems; to St Kilda for beach pollution; to Mexico for agrarian reform; to Nigeria and Cameroon for the religious beliefs of the Chamba people; to the Orkney Islands for the behaviour of the Orkney voles; to Papua for the regrowth of logged forests; to Paris for two epic poems of the twelfth century; to Shetland for a Norse site on Papa Stour; to South Africa for the disposal of waste by long sea outfalls; to Sweden for the human response to vibrations of drilling and blasting; to Taiwan and South Korea for technological change and economic development; to the USSR for river sediment; to the Yemen for Islamic architecture; to Zurich for the Thomas Mann archives.

This constant flow of ideas and information between Scotland and the world presents an intriguing image in the research undertaken in the United States: Andrew Carnegie, a Scot, made his money in America, returned it to Scotland, to enable Scottish scholars to visit America to share their own ideas and return with new ideas to Scotland—a continuing exchange of resources between the two countries. Research grants for visits to the United States in 1982-83 included subjects ranging through the treatment of wife abuse, oesophageal disorders, computer-aided design, permafrost engineering, interpretations of Picasso's *Guernica*, the loading and strength of dentures, the forensic characteristics of human hair, business projects under Scottish influence in America 1820-1920 (which must include Carnegie himself), asphalt technology, libraries containing the works of T. S. Eliot, oriental Arabic manuscripts in Harvard and New York Universities, superconducting facilities, yeast genetics, British troops in the War of Independence, property taxation, electron microscopy of muscle, urban density, Free Electron Laser research, the operation of the lay midwife system, the origin of granites, and construction design and materials. In the same year, a fellowship was approved for a

OPPOSITE

TOP A moraine ridge deposited by the glacier Vestbreen (in the background) around AD 1920
BELOW A moraine ridge deposited by the glacier Blåisen (in the background) around AD 1920.

These are the most recent of a series of such moraines which mark the limits of advances or readvances of the glaciers of the Lyngen peninsula, northern Norway, over the past 12,500 years. Mapping and dating of such moraine systems, carried out as part of the objectives of research expeditions mounted by the Department of Geography, University of St Andrews, permits reconstruction of the former extent of the Lyngen glaciers at various times in the past. This in turn allows the nature of climatic changes associated with each glacier advance to be calculated. Understanding of the pattern of former climatic change is vital not only to the explanation of past environments, but also to prediction of future changes in climate.

professor from the Lunar and Planetary Laboratory in Arizona to work at the University of Edinburgh; a second fellowship was approved for a doctor from the Institute of Radiation Chemistry at Lodz in Poland to work at the University of Glasgow.

Scholarship awards and renewals for 1983-84 proved to be no less various. They ranged, for example, through study of how infants learn to think, rainwater harvesting in Mauritius and the behaviour of cracked structures under vibration, to the economics of crime and punishment, the identification of organic substances in certain Scottish burns and women as writers in twentieth-century France and England; they included the study of water supply and sanitation in developing countries and the religious and moral sensibilities of the eighteenth-century German novel; and, appropriately, there was research into prehistoric settlements in north-west Scotland.

Behind each research project lies an individual story—far too many to relate. Dr Schmitz, for example, went recently to Australia to research into the historical and economic background of the development of mining in that country between 1870 and 1920. His visit involved some hard travelling to the old abandoned mining sites but he also received help from the managements of major companies in such places as Broken Hill, and he was able to assess the technological changes. Many of these were due to the work of emigrant Scottish engineers; substantial Scottish investments had also assisted in the development of technology in the mines. Dr Schmitz's first-hand contacts with Australian academics and industrialists has proved to be of considerable help in his research.

Professor Sprigge did not find his own research in Prague quite so straightforward, in connection with meetings on political philosophies. In his report, he described the problems of reticence, security and evasion which bedevilled any discussions of political significance, though non-Marxist views were received with goodwill. 'It is certainly very difficult for a visitor from Britain,' he wrote, 'to know when he is being wise or absurdly cautious.'

Closer to home, members of the Heriot-Watt University Underwater Technology Group decided, in 1978, to investigate and photograph the remains of an aircraft believed to be a war-time Catalina flying boat, discovered by an earlier survey of Loch Ness. The team, led by Robin Holmes, a senior lecturer, identified the aircraft as a Mk 1A Wellington, the only surviving aircraft (to see active service) from the 11,462 produced during the Second World War; only one later training aircraft is extant and on display at the Hendon RAF Museum. Funds were granted to the Heriot-Watt team so that investigation could be made to see if the aircraft could be raised from more than 230 feet down in the murky depths of the loch. Early hopes were dashed when it was discovered that the aircraft was badly damaged and required a complex procedure for lifting. Further support, from an oil company, was sought before recovery might go ahead. Meanwhile, Dr Russell, also from the Underwater Technology Group, received a grant to visit the Massachusetts Institute of Technology to investigate comparable developments in unmanned, controllable undersea vehicles for surveillance, for repair of projects on the sea-bed, and for the invention of sensors to simulate human perception.

An immediate problem, close to home, has been the use of renewable energy in Scotland. A series of conferences on 'Energy for Rural and Island Communities' has been held at Strathclyde University. The Trust gave aid for experimental work to be carried out, providing the organizer, John Twidell, of the Department of Applied Physics, with a number of travel grants. One result of his work is a 300 kw aerogenerator in the Orkneys. John Twidell reported: 'I sincerely believe that the Trust's support over nearly fifteen years has enabled me to find a global view of energy programmes that would not have been possible otherwise.'

In line with its policy of providing grants for travel, the Trust also provides support for university expeditions of true exploration. In 1982-83, expeditions went to Iceland, Thailand, Sweden, Italy, Lemba, Eskmeals, Bavaria, Lyngen, Spain and Sabah. Each year, about seventy or eighty undergraduates are involved in explorations in arduous conditions of climate and living, and in significant field research, under experienced staff supervision. Their reports contain not only field observations but also experience and advice to those who may follow in their footsteps. As Dr Ritchie, the Chief Executive of the Trust, explains: 'The Scottish Universities still produce young men and women eager to spend their time and effort in pioneering unknown territory...in the wilderness ranging from tropical forests to the Arctic.'

A 300kW aerogenerator in Orkney, North of Scotland, manufactured by James Howden Ltd, Glasgow. Interest in the use of renewable energy in Scotland has been encouraged by the Strathclyde University's series of conferences 'Energy for Rural Island Communities.' The Carnegie Trust for the Universities of Scotland were able to support the practical aims of these conferences by awarding various travel grants to the organiser, Dr John Twidell, of the Department of Applied Physics.

Nicolas Poussin (1594-1665), *Baptism*, 1646. Duke of Sutherland Collection, on loan to the National Gallery of Scotland, Edinburgh. From the second series of Seven Sacraments, painted for Paul Fréart de Chantelou between 1644 and 1648. This picture was included in the exhibition at the National Gallery of Scotland, *Poussin: Sacraments and Bacchanals*, 16 October-13 December 1981. The Carnegie Trust contributed £500 towards the cost of the colour plates included in the accompanying catalogue.

A final area of support provided by the Trust is in publications. In 1982-83, nine publications were given aid, eight Scottish learned journals were helped, and small grants went to finance illustrations in a number of learned journal papers that would not otherwise have been able to afford them. Two publications from 1983 demonstrate the wide range of subject interest: Professor H. A. Bruck's *The Story of Astronomy in Edinburgh* and Dr W. H. Liu's *The post-Mao Economy in China*. The Trust also provided £500 in 1981 toward the cost of a catalogue to accompany an exhibition of Poussin at the National Gallery of Scotland.

Assessing the Trust in 1984, Dr Ritchie believes that it is respected and that its decisions are accepted without query because of its emphasis on independence and because the administration is not a hierarchy but a friendly arrangement between people with a common interest. The principals of all eight universities are *ex officio* trustees and themselves have a say in the operation of the Trust. Dr Ritchie stresses that this set-up makes it possible to give grants quickly; usually, without the several months' delay that is sometimes involved with other agencies. It is the few hundred pounds, more or less, often too little for a major research grant but too much for someone's personal resources, that are important in helping an individual to pursue an essential aspect of research. As the saying goes: 'He who gives quickly, gives twice.'

'This general encouragement of research,' writes Dr Ritchie, 'without producing any dramatic awards or major advances in Science, Medicine or the Arts, must nonetheless have a very valuable impact on the Scottish Universities.... It is worth bearing in mind the reply of Michael Faraday to a lady who asked him what was the use of one of his basic and novel experiments—"Madam, what is the use of a new-born baby?".' Carnegie must take the credit for encouraging all his endowments to experiment; successive trustees and executives should take the credit for carrying on that encouragement and for making their own experiments in order to adapt to the changing conditions of society.

CARNEGIE INSTITUTION OF WASHINGTON

Whereas in Scotland Carnegie decided to invest in higher education by supporting the four ancient universities, his ambition in America had long been to fulfil the dream of many American educators and statesmen to establish in Washington D.C. a *new* 'national' university. This proved to be impractical; instead, Carnegie decided to support existing universities by endowing an institution that would concentrate on pioneer research. The independent, non-profit research Institution in Washington, established in 1902, was the first of its kind in America.

The Institution now operates five research centres in various parts of the country: the Departments of Embryology, Plant Biology, and Terrestrial Magnetism; the Geophysical Laboratory; and the Mount Wilson and Las Campanas Observatories. It is an operating rather than a grant-making institution, and so all its work is done by its own departments. Each department has a director, a number of scientific staff members, a small support staff and a constantly changing roster of postdoctoral fellows. The Institution is funded out of income from the endowment, supplemented by grants from federal agencies, foundation grants and private gifts. About thirty percent of current income is other than endowment income.

In addition to the primary research rôle, the training of young scientists is an important goal. Students and Fellows from all over the world come to the Carnegie departments to work with the Institution's senior staff. Within the last three years, Fellows have been drawn from West Germany, Japan, Canada, Chile, Australia, Israel, Malaysia, India, Switzerland, Great Britain, China and several other countries. After about two years of close collaboration, these individuals leave to pursue careers elsewhere and in this way the Institution fertilizes growing fields of research in every country. A strong proportion of Japanese embryologists, for example, have been trained at the Institution.

In choosing its research directions, the Institution seeks areas of advanced study in which to prepare the ground before passing the work on to others for fuller development. This 'flexibility to pioneer' has been essential to the Institution's success; so, too, has been the tradition of the exceptional man or woman. There have been two Nobel laureates whose work has been done at the Institution: Alfred Hershey and Barbara McClintock. The work of George Ellery Hale and Edwin Hubble with the Institution's reflecting telescopes has also been world-renowned. The development of the proximity fuze by Merle Tuve was a major contribution to the Allies' effort in the Second World War. Archaeological excavations in Central America and the work of the non-magnetic ship *Carnegie* over 343,000 miles of ocean are also among the Institution's many past successes.

Today, the Institution is recognized as being at the forefront of scientific study in the physical and biological sciences. Its focus is primarily that of basic research—toward the understanding of nature—but such work often has eventual practical ends. Study of photosynthesis and the adaptation of plants to different environments is ultimately concerned with the world's precarious food supply; studies of minerals and rocks under high pressure deep inside the Earth are related to, among other things, our limited abundance of natural resources; studies of earth deformations before, during and after earthquakes are closely related to the search for earthquake prediction methods; studies of distant stars and galaxies are important for understanding our planet Earth and our star, the Sun; genetic studies lead to an understanding, and perhaps the treatment, of certain birth defects and genetic disorders.

Through these endeavours, the Institution plays a major role in the coordination of American scientific policy and contributes to the advancement of knowledge throughout the world—knowledge about ourselves and about the natural resources and environment on which we depend.

Carnegie Institution of Washington

Founded: 1902

Purpose: A research and educational institution in the physical and biological sciences which, in the words of the Trust Deed, should 'encourage, in the broadest and most liberal manner, investigation, research, and discovery, and the application of knowledge to the improvement of mankind.'

Finance:

Original endowment:	$10,000,000
Additional endowments by Carnegie (1909):	$2,000,000
(1911):	$10,000,000

Additional funding from Carnegie Corporation:

(*a*) Emergency aid because of economic conditions brought about by First World War:	$1,500,000
(*b*) Provided in 1925:	$5,000,000
(*c*) Provided in 1944:	$5,000,000
(*d*) Liberal funding for direct support of specific research ventures, including some supervised by the Institution at the request of the Corporation. In recent years the Corporation has supported fellowships in the Institution's departments.	

Assets, June 30, 1984:	$147,983,376

Annual monies in early years:	*Income*	*Expenditure*
1902, Jan-Oct:	$250,009	$30,187
1902, Nov-1903, Oct:	$508,254	$182,130
1903, Nov-1904, Oct:	$536,439	$315,790

Annual monies in recent years:	*Income*	*Expenditure*
Year ended 30 June 1983:	$13,700,933	$13,599,724
Year ended 30 June 1984:	$14,718,970	$14,425,169
1984-1985 (estimate):	$15,000,000	$15,000,000

Total income/expenditure, 1902-1984:	$250,000,000

(Total fund balances have increased from original endowment of $22 million to present $147 million due to unexpended capital gains and new endowment and special gifts; dividend and interest income was fully used for expenditures).

Restricted grants, balance 30 June 1984:

(*a*) Federal grants (from 10 agencies):	$3,034,831
(*b*) Private grants (from 24 sources):	$3,916,769

(Funds received from foundations, individuals and Federal agencies in support of scientific research and educational programmes).

Main areas of expenditure, 1902-1984:

Physical Sciences:		53.3%
Astronomy:	23.9%	
Geophysical Laboratory:	14.2%	
Department of Terrestrial Magnetism:	15.2%	
Biological Sciences:		22.9%
Department of Embryology:	10.7%	
Plant biology:	7.1%	
Genetics:	4.2%	
Other biological sciences:	0.9%	
History/Archaeology:		1.9%
Other research (minor grants):		4.2%
Publications:		2.6%
Administration:		15.1%

(The percentages above do not precisely depict the emphasis of work over the history of the Institution, as recent decades are weighted overmuch because of cost inflation and because of changing accounting procedures and inconsistencies over the decades in the distinction between Administration and Research expenses).

Scholars whose work has been supported:

Annual number, 1902-1904:	(approx) 200
(primarily small grants to outside investigators)	
Annual number, 1982-1984:	(approx) 180
(individuals serving as staff scientists and fellows)	
Total number of scholars, 1902-1984:	(approx) 2,700

Administration:

President: Dr James D. Ebert (also serves as Vice-President, National Academy of Sciences)

Staff:		
	Scientific-professional:	121
	Scientific-technical:	83
	Administrative:	50
	Maintenance:	21

Addresses: 1530 P Street, N.W., Washington, D.C. 20005

(*a*) Geophysical Laboratory, 2801 Upton Street N.W., Washington, D.C. 20008

(*b*) Mount Wilson and Las Campanas Observatories, 813 Santa Barbara Street, Pasadena, California 91101

(*c*) Department of Terrestrial Magnetism, 5241 Broad Branch Road N.W., Washington, D.C. 20015

(*d*) Department of Embryology, 115 West University Parkway, Baltimore, Maryland 21210

(*e*) Department of Plant Biology, 290 Panama Street, Stanford, California 94305

Carnegie Institution of Washington

It was George Washington who had first suggested a national university. The concept appealed to many interested parties, including Andrew Carnegie. A major obstacle to the idea, as Carnegie recognized, was that such a university, adequately financed, might serve not to strengthen but to weaken existing universities. Instead, encouraged by the progressive head of The Johns Hopkins University in Baltimore, he determined to support indirectly all universities by creating a central research agency which, according to one Secretary of the Carnegie Corporation, 'would seek to expand known forces and to discover and utilize unknown forces for the benefit of mankind.'

President Theodore Roosevelt, with whom Carnegie had already corresponded on the matter, himself agreed to become the first *ex officio* member of the new Institution's Board of Trustees. Roosevelt wrote:

> I will serve with the greatest pleasure. Let me congratulate you on the very high character—indeed may I say the extraordinary character—of the men whom you have secured as Trustees, and I congratulate the nation upon your purpose to found such an Institution. It seems to me precisely the institution most needed to help and crown our educational system by providing for and stimulating original research.

Support in the early years went to investigations in many fields, including astronomy, anthropology, literature, economics, history and mathematics; in the first year alone, departments were established in experimental evolution, marine biology, history, economics and sociology; within the next four years there were added the Departments of Terrestrial Magnetism and Meridian Astronomy, the Departments of Botanical Research and Marine Biology, the Geophysical Laboratory, the Department of Experimental Evolution (later named the Department of Genetics), the Department of Historical Research, and the Mount Wilson Observatory; the Nutrition Laboratory was added in 1908, and the Department of Embryology in 1914.

The ten million dollars with which Carnegie initially endowed the Institution, together with a further twelve million, was adequate for the variety of projects adopted at first. However, economic forces have brought about a number of changes in the administration of the Institution and income from the endowment is now supplemented by grants from federal agencies and foundations. As the current President, James D. Ebert, pointed out in a recent report: 'The Institution has modest financial resources and a total professional staff that is tiny in comparison to that of many universities.' For that reason and others, it concentrates on pioneering ventures and has sometimes even closed down highly successful endeavours, such as its acclaimed work in Middle American archaeology, in order to shift its limited resources to newer fields perhaps less able to attract funding from elsewhere. It is often said that Carnegie scholars are like explorers: the Institution seeks out new and promising areas for investigation, areas wherein to break down and prepare the way for others. Much new ground has been broken over the years.

The Caracol at Chichen Itza, Yucatan, was possibly used by the Mayans as an astronomical observatory. It was preserved by Carnegie archaeologists during the 1920s.

The archaeological excavations in Mexico and Central America were carried out by successor organizations to the Department of Historical Research from the 1920s into the 1950s and significant discoveries were made at the now famous sites of Chichen Itza, Utatlan, Ixcun and other cities of the Mayan empire. The Department's work was welcomed by the governments of those countries in which the 'digs' were carried out, particularly because all artefacts were returned to the host country when the studies were completed; the work also involved some valuable restoration on sites that were in danger of disappearing. The Department has now been disbanded, along with several other of the original departments.

Especially in its early years, the Institution was very active in the editing and printing of works arising out of research done within the Institution; in special cases, the Institution published results of research done elsewhere if considered to be of particular value to the scientific community. Early examples include *Judicial Cases Concerning American Slavery and the Negro, The California Earthquake of April 18, 1906*, and *The List of Prime Numbers from 1 to 10,006,721*, each of which was a valuable contribution to American scientific and social literature. The publication of such works remains a less active function of the Institution today, along with the Institution *Year Book*, which serves as an annual review, report and interpretation of the current programme.

The nonmagnetic sailing vessel *Carnegie* was operated by the Carnegie Institution's Department of Terrestrial Magnetism in long voyages exploring the earth's magnetism. After two decades of service, the ship was destroyed by fire and explosion in the South Pacific in 1929.

The work carried out in the voyages of the non-magnetic vessel *Carnegie* was one of the most renowned early projects. The *Carnegie* was a sailing ship with an auxiliary engine designed under the auspices of the Institution as a fully-equipped, ocean-going, non-magnetic laboratory for the collection of geophysical data from all over the world. Launched in 1909, she was on her seventh cruise when, in November 1929, she was destroyed by an explosion in Western Samoa and her captain was killed. She had in all covered 343,000 miles of ocean. As well as collecting much valuable scientific information, the precise data on the Earth's magnetism obtained, due to the vessel's non-magnetic quality, allowed mariners throughout the world to navigate more safely.

During the First World War, Institution staff directed the nation's production of optical glass for war purposes and developed sensitive instruments for detecting the magnetism of enemy submarines. Work on weaponry reoccurred during the Second World War, when the Institution was responsible for developing what has been described as 'probably the most important technical improvement in weaponry to come out of World War II.' This was the proximity fuze: in essence, a radio set inside an artillery projectile which triggered the fuze upon receiving an echo when close to a target. In conventional shells the timing of the fuze was a hit-and-miss affair, reliant upon determination of range and therefore subject to great error. The proximity fuze was particularly effective in anti-aircraft use and was crucial in helping to combat the V1 flying bombs sent against Britain in the last months of the war.

Work on the fuze was directed by Merle Tuve of the Institution's Department of Terrestrial Magnetism. Tuve's earlier work on the Earth's ionosphere by means of radio signals was a forerunner to the development of radar. Tuve's list of 'rules' for those working on the fuze included the following:

(1) I don't want any d--n fool in the laboratory to save money, I only want him to save *time*.
(2) We don't want the best unit, we want the *first* one.
(3) There are no private wires from God Almighty in the lab that I know about—certainly none in my office.

Though he was a hard task-master, there was another side to Tuve, which he expressed in 1954 when explaining the magic of scientific discovery:

When a new discovery is made [he wrote], a man is in some special way the vehicle for an expression of something outside of himself, not limited as he is in space and time, but immanent and pervasive throughout the universe. This is the basis for the silent wonder and satisfaction which come to a research man when his personal effort, often directed toward some visualized goal, results in finding a newly perceived aspect of the astonishing and beautiful creation in which we find ourselves.

Undoubtedly the Institution's war work was important. Under the prompting of Vannevar Bush, then President, the first discussions on the Manhattan Project (the atomic bomb) took place in the Institution's building. But it has been in more peaceful activities that the Institution has become famous in many fields today.

Originally known as the Department of Experimental Evolution, the Department closed in 1963 to be succeeded in 1971 by the Genetics Research Unit, and the facilities and equipment were handed over to Cold Spring Harbor Laboratory, New York. Some of the Institution's most exciting work was undertaken in this department. George Shull, famous for the development of hybrid corn, described as 'this country's most important scientific contribution to agriculture,' was one of the first staff members at the Department. Shull recognized that farmers used simple methods of selective breeding, choosing corn seed each year from the best specimens of the previous crop; in the long run, however, this technique produced a relatively fragile strain. Shull's work produced hybrid strains with yields up to three times greater. Almost all corn grown today in the United States and much of the world's corn comes from such hybrid strains. In addition, Shull's work has pioneered similar success in a wide variety of other plants and some animals.

Two Nobel laureates have emerged from the Department. In 1969, Alfred Hershey, director of the Genetics Research Unit from 1963 to 1971, shared the Nobel prize in medicine/physiology for work with viruses that provided critical evidence showing DNA to be the genetic material. Like many scientists, Hershey was also a philosopher, as he revealed in his report for the Institution's *Year Book* in 1965:

> The enduring goal of scientific endeavour, as of all human enterprise, I imagine, is to achieve an intelligible view of the universe. One of the great discoveries of modern science is that its goal cannot be achieved piecemeal, certainly not by the accumulation of facts. To understand a phenomenon is to understand a category of phenomenon or it is nothing. Understanding is reached through creative acts....The scientist tends to consider the path toward his goal as endless. Not too discontentedly, either, because human history is replete with glorious paths, not goals achieved.

The second Carnegie Institution laureate from Cold Spring Harbor is Barbara McClintock, who joined the Department in 1941 and spent the next forty years investigating the cause of the changing colour patterns on kernels of maize, or Indian corn. McClintock's years of painstaking work on corn mutations arose from her observation that patterns of pigmentation appeared to be under some sort of genetic control, and her growing awareness that segments of genetic material, which she called controlling elements, could turn on and off the activity of a gene by moving from place to place within the genome. This alteration of genes by the shifting of 'transposable elements,' she decided, could explain how the characteristics of cells from the same genetic lineage could become so different. It has only recently been realized that transposition may explain the erratic behaviour of tumour viruses. Transposition may also help to explain how cells rearrange their cells to produce antibodies which combat a host of different viral and bacterial threats, how bacteria can acquire immunities to antibiotics, and how certain cancer cells develop. For her discovery of transposition,

The Carnegie Institution of Washington's Nobelists: Alfred Hershey and Barbara McClintock, both of the Institution's former Department of Genetics

McClintock received the 1983 Nobel Prize in medicine/physiology. She continues her work at Cold Spring Harbor as a Distinguished Service Member of the Carnegie Institution.

It has been said in praise of McClintock that genetics would not occupy its present high estate were it not for her magnificent pioneering work, yet Cornell University once barred her, apparently because of her sex, from majoring in plant breeding. In October 1983, the *Washington Post* summed up her own achievement and the contribution made to that achievement by the Carnegie Institution:

> Until very recently Dr McClintock's work was so far out of the mainstream as to border on the heretical. While molecular biologists were marveling at the mathematical orderliness of the genetic world they were discovering, the genes in Dr McClintock's maize were jumping about and changing the characteristics of the cells they inhabited in disconcerting fashion. Only the timely intervention and continuing support of the Carnegie Institution of Washington made it possible for her to pursue—for more than four decades—her intricate and solitary research.

To get the government grants needed to support the expensive tools of modern science, researchers typically must work in groups and on projects in the mainstream of current theory. This is generally a very fruitful process. But there are exceptions to that rule, and it's worth remembering that Dr McClintock—working patiently and painstakingly in her laboratory, alone and unrecognized over the decades—is one of them.

Andrew Carnegie had set down as one of the guiding principles of the Institution that it should 'discover the exceptional man...and enable him to make the work for which he seems specially designed his life work.' That rôle undoubtedly fits Barbara McClintock and many other Institution scientists, who prove the Institution's claim that it invests its money in people and ideas without interference and without applying undue pressures to fulfil targets. It is one of the main advantages of an independent research trust that it can support long-term research in this way.

Department of Embryology

The focus of research in this department has changed markedly since its foundation. The original goal was a better understanding of the human embryo; with its own breeding monkey colony, it was able to investigate the nature and problems of primate reproductive physiology. The level of work became more refined as new discoveries and techniques opened up the world of the cell, and by the mid-1970s the monkey colony was tranferred elsewhere.

The Department's current concern was recently summed up in a publication of the Institution:

> Of all the problems of biology, few are more challenging than those of development—the processes whereby, under the guidance of the genes, there emerges from a single cell a complex adult organism....The great challenge at the Department lies in the question 'How?' How do genes direct the growth and differentiation of cells? How do signals from one cell, in turn, influence the gene activity in another?

The Department's director, Donald Brown, was one of the first to isolate a single gene—the first step in exploring how a gene works. His current work in defining gene control signals in Xenopus, a frog-like organism, has attracted wide Press interest in recent years. His discovery of fundamental differences in gene regulation between Xenopus and bacteria, for example, contradicted the previous assumption that animal genetics, though more complicated than bacterial genetics, followed the same basic scheme. In the future, such work promises to contribute to the solution of grave medical problems, among them cancer and birth defects. As Brown has written:

> Why do we study the nervous system of the leech, the eggs of a frog, the sperm of a worm, the genes of fruit flies and corn? We have selected these animals and plants because each provides some special advantage for studying a particular biological problem....Inherent in these studies is the assumption that what we learn will apply to analogous processes in humans.

This same principle applies to the recent work of the Department's staff member Allan Spradling and former staff member Gerald Rubin, whose highly successful experiments on the transfer of genes in fruit flies exploit the 'transposable elements' first described by McClintock. Though not a direct and immediate objective of their work, the understanding and treatment of genetic disorders may some day be enhanced as a result. As one newspaper reported:

> Laboratory-bred fruit flies have developed brown eyes instead of the red eyes of their cousins in the wild. This announcement brings forward the day when higher animals, even humans, could have such defects as the propensity to catch hereditary diseases removed by genetic surgery.

Another group of scientists at the Department of Embryology is exploring in intricate detail the fine structures and behaviour of biological membranes. Membranes—ultra-thin layers of organized proteins and lipids—surround the internal components of cells as well as the cells themselves. Richard Pagano, a staff member at the department, is currently investigating membrane lipids. He and his colleagues have devised a way to manipulate, in living cells, artificially derived lipid molecules that mimic their natural counterparts. Largely as a result of their pioneering work, lipids—once thought to be mere structural matrices—are now viewed as dynamic elements of membrane function.

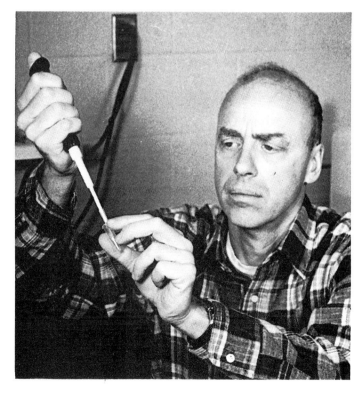

Donald Brown, Director of the Institution's Department of Embryology, was one of the first to isolate a single gene

Pagano's work, like other research at the department, is not directed toward practical goals. But in its promise of elucidating such important biological problems as membrane-cell interactions, it offers fundamental knowledge for understanding the mechanisms of disease. It is yet another example of the positive and relevant ends that can result from imaginative, pioneering research.

Mount Wilson and Las Campanas Observatories

The Institution's rôle in discovering and studying the galaxies is inseparable from the great instruments developed and built by Carnegie astronomers. When George Ellery Hale, prophet and leader of the 'new astronomy' in America, heard in 1902 that steelmaker Carnegie had founded an institution solely for research, he secured from the Trustees funds to begin solar observations and to mount, in 1909, a 60-inch reflecting mirror near the summit of Mount Wilson, in California, and became the observatory's first director. His successor, Walter Adams, in an article on 'Early Days at Mount Wilson,' explained Hale's enthusiasm:

> In the establishment of the Observatory, Hale found the complete fulfilment of his ideal of an institution devoted purely to research, free from many of the restrictions imposed by university affiliations, and able to build its equipment to fit the problems he had in mind instead of seeking the problems to fit existing or preconceived instruments.

Carnegie was equally enthusiastic and visited Mount Wilson with Hale in 1910. He was, apparently, in excellent form during the visit, as Walter Adams recorded:

> He was photographed repeatedly with Hale, always taking the higher position on a slope since he was somewhat sensitive about his height. On his return to New York he announced that 60,000 new stars had been discovered with the telescope at Mount Wilson, evidently a reference to Ritchey's photos of the Hercules cluster. Moulton, at the University of Chicago, cynically remarked, one might equally well speak of having 'discovered' 60,000 new gallons of water in Lake Michigan.

Subsequently, Hale persuaded Los Angeles businessman John Hooker, and Carnegie, to provide funds for the construction of the 100-inch Mount Wilson telescope (completed in 1917), which remained the world's largest for thirty years. It was understood that Carnegie's second ten million dollars was intended primarily to enable completion of this project. Both the 60-inch and the 100-inch reflector telescopes are still in productive operation.

Hale played a part in helping to provide the National Academy of Sciences and the National Research Council with a permanent building. The Academy had resided at the Smithsonian Institution for more than fifty years. After the First World War, the need for enlarged quarters to house the Academy and the newly created NRC became

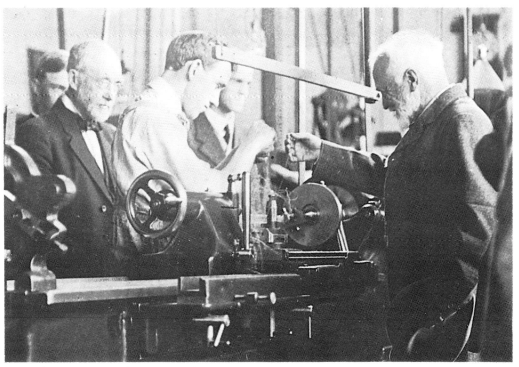

Andrew Carnegie at the Mount Wilson shops, 1910. The young machinist is Elmer D. Prall, who served the Observatory until his retirement in 1950.

urgent. The NRC, formed in 1916 as an entity of the Academy, broadened the Academy's rôle as adviser to the government and in the war-preparedness effort. It provided a framework within which governmental, educational, industrial, and other research organizations could cooperate to attack scientific problems. It was partly through Hale's efforts that in 1918 President Woodrow Wilson signed an Executive Order, requesting the Academy to perpetuate the NRC. Hale became chairman of an Academy building committee and in 1919 the Carnegie Corporation of New York agreed to contribute funds for construction of a building plus an endowment, if the Academy could secure a building site, which it did, near the new Lincoln Memorial in Potomac Park, Washington. The Corporation set aside $5,000,000 for the Academy and NRC endowment, with $1,350,000 thereof available for construction of a building, which was completed in 1924. It is most fitting that James Ebert, the current President of the Carnegie Institution of Washington, is also the Vice-President of the National Academy of Sciences.

Hale also initiated the giant 200-inch reflector at Palomar, in California, which was completed in 1948, with funds from the Rockefeller Foundation supplemented by substantial monies and technical support from the Carnegie Institution and the California Institute of Technology (Caltech). The reflector was designed and seen to completion with the participation of Institution staff, though it was owned by Caltech.

When it was completed in 1917, the 100-inch Hooker telescope at Mount Wilson, California, became the world's largest reflector telescope. Its superior qualities made possible Edwin Hubble and Milton Humanson's discovery in the 1920s that the universe was expanding.

It is said to have the power to detect the flame of a candle at 40,000 miles, though it is used for rather more serious purposes. Leadership in astronomical instrumentation is one of the Institution's most cherished traditions.

There are now in the world about a dozen optical telescopes of 100 inches or more; one of these is the third in the Institution's 'chain.' As early as 1903, the Institution's trustees had studied the idea of an observatory in the southern hemisphere; the idea moved toward reality in 1969, when the Institution acquired the ridge known as Las Campanas, or 'the bells,' in northern Chile. The 40-inch Swope telescope was completed in 1971 and the 100-inch Irénée du Pont telescope in 1977. The remote site is particularly good because there is very little atmospheric turbulence and the nights are very dark. The du Pont telescope is equipped for a wide range of photometric and spectrographic observations, and its optics produce images as fine as those of any telescope in the world.

Until recently, the Institution and Caltech jointly operated their facilities at Mount Wilson, Las Campanas and Palomar under the name 'Hale Observatories.' The joint

The Carnegie Institution's Las Campanas Observatory, Chile. The 100-inch Irénée du Pont telescope is at the far right.

operation has now ended but scientific ties among Carnegie and Caltech astronomers will remain strong and collaboration in research will continue, as will arrangements for the shared use of facilities.

Another great name in astronomy, Edwin Hubble, joined the staff of the Mount Wilson Observatory in 1919 and continued there until his death in 1953. His discoveries profoundly changed our understanding of the universe and remain at the heart of modern cosmology. Observing primarily with the 100-inch Hooker telescope, Hubble's fame was established with his confirmation that the faint spiral nebulae, long known to astronomers, were in reality distant systems, or galaxies, far beyond the Milky Way. Subsequently, it was Hubble who explained that these galaxies were receding from us at speeds proportional to their distances from us—in short, that the universe was expanding. His name lives on through the Edwin P. Hubble Space Telescope, scheduled for launch aboard the Space Shuttle in 1986. This 94.5-inch (2.4m) primary mirror and associated instrumentation will be housed in the orbiting observatory; Shuttle astronauts will visit the telescope periodically, returning with it to Earth for maintenance when necessary. The telescope will occupy the entire cargo bay of the Shuttle.

Hubble's vision of an expanding universe has been enlarged by many later scientists, among them another Institution astronomer, Vera Rubin, a remarkable scientist whose studies with her colleagues of how galaxies rotate have changed our understanding of the masses of spiral galaxies and, consequently, the mass of the observable universe. Rubin decided to become an astronomer when she was twelve; she first worked at the Department of Terrestrial Magnetism part-time so that she could be at home with her children. Soon afterwards she was told by the director that her 'part time' was more like 'time and a half.' Her discovery that 90-95 percent of the mass of a galaxy lies beyond the visible edge of the galaxy, perhaps in a dark heavy halo extending far into intergalactic space, means there is extra gravitational field that might retard expansion of the universe. If so, then the universe will contract and, according to Rubin, 'what started out as a Big Bang will ultimately finish as a Big Crunch.'

Astronomer Vera C. Rubin. She and her colleagues at the Department of Terrestrial Magnetism are best known for their investigations of the dynamics of spiral galaxies and the implications of the results for determining the overall mass of the universe.

Institution astronomers have also been involved in the development of the Carnegie Image Tube to enhance the sensitivity of optical telescopes; in the discovery and study of quasars; and in the discovery of a vast 'empty' region of space spanning a diameter one hundred times the distance to our nearest major galaxy, Andromeda, with a density approximately ten times less than average. At the Mount Wilson solar telescopes, Robert Howard made discoveries that suggest that the Sun has a deep-seated dynamo responsible for its sunspot activity; at the 100-inch Mount Wilson telescope, Allan Sandage has conducted a long-range programme for mapping the halo of our Milky Way galaxy; and at the du Pont instrument at Las Campanas, Carnegie's Paul Schechter, Alan Dressler and others are exploring faint, very distant galaxies, viewing the universe as it was half way back, and more, to creation. These are only some examples of the Institution's work in this field. George W. Preston, director of the Mount Wilson and Las Campanas Observatories, sums up that work as 'programs of astronomical research on the structure and dimensions of the Universe and the physical nature and chemical composition of celestial bodies.' He also provides some idea of the attraction of the work his department undertakes:

> Just as biologists would be entranced by the opportunity to study the forms and evolution of living organisms on another planet, so are astronomers captivated by the opportunity to make analogous studies of stars and regions of space very different from the solar neighbourhood.

A great strength of the Institution is in its expert technical people. One man for whom his work held particular appeal was Elmer D. Prall, who worked as a machinist and instrument-maker at Mount Wilson for forty-one years until his reluctant retirement in 1950. Prall's most prized possession was a photograph of Carnegie and himself at the Observatory, taken in 1910. He remembered Carnegie's remark to him at the time, that 'happiness cannot be purchased by money alone.' In late 1978, Prall celebrated his 77th wedding anniversary and his 93rd birthday. He died in December of that year, one of the last direct links to Andrew Carnegie.

For the future, the Institution is extending its strong tradition in the design and development of major instrumentation for optical astronomy. Various designs have been raised for constructing a major optical telescope of very large aperture (about five metres, or 195 inches) at Las Campanas. One proposal envisions the use of a primary fixed mirror, a design that sacrifices many qualities to hold down cost but which would provide a powerful instrument for spectroscopic work. Other concepts include the use of several smaller mirrors, controlled and their light integrated by computers. As ever, progress and practicality must go hand in hand. The vast promise of such instruments, and the magnificent Las Campanas viewing site, have led the Institution to seek ways of shifting resources away from Mount Wilson, without sacrificing the vital work that still proceeds there. At the time of writing, a committee is preparing a report on how this difficult change may be effected.

Department of Terrestrial Magnetism

The title of the Department derives from its early work to map the Earth's magnetic field and to obtain magnetic and electric data over extended time. Much of this work was carried out through the non-magnetic vessel *Carnegie*; its practical importance was emphasized by Carnegie himself, who was fond of telling about the costly shipwrecks that could have been prevented if the magnetic data obtained by the Department had been available earlier. Following the burning of the *Carnegie* in 1929, the Department moved on to a broader range of research.

During the 1930s, DTM, as it is known, became a centre in nuclear physics; this work led to later use of radioactive tracers in biological and geochemical studies. DTM scientists and engineers have also developed such new instrumentation as image intensifiers for telescopes, antennae and receivers for radio astronomy, and strainmeters for detecting earth deformations. Research now ranges from studies of seismic events in the Earth's crust to analysis of meteorites and investigations of far-distant galaxies. The aim that unites astronomy and isotope geochemistry in the same department is the search for the fundamental principles that underlie the order of the Earth and the Universe. As the director of DTM, George W. Wetherill, puts it:

> Until recently it was fashionable for practical geologists to regard discussions of the formation of the earth and the solar system as of little relevance to their work.... These times are over. The unity and interdependence of earth and planetary science as well as of stellar and even galactic astronomy are now apparent.

One group of DTM scientists has been investigating the regions of the Earth forming boundary zones between the Earth's plates, where much of the Earth's volcanic and earthquake activity occurs; their aim is to understand how the continents have evolved and might continue to do so. Evidence for the mobility of the Earth's crust can be seen in continental drift as well as in sea-floor formation and subduction, the processes by which the oceanic crust and mantle are being thrust beneath the continents; particular attention is being paid, for example, to the Andes and the adjacent portions of the South Pacific Ocean, where this activity is most evident, and to the mid-ocean ridges where the generation of new ocean floor replaces material lost by deep burial in subduction zones.

DTM's work has included studies of the Earth's interior by means of a worldwide net of broadband seismometers. DTM scientists are now concentrating on the development, installation and use of sensitive borehole strainmeters, cemented into subsurface rock as a means of obtaining data on Earth strain, with the aim of being able to predict earthquakes. Strainmeters have been positioned in Japan, Iceland, Peru and California; and DTM scientists have visited China twice to work with Chinese scientists in developing their own strainmeter instruments and installations—a good example of the international pooling of resources and ideas.

For the future, the Institution is providing seed-money for the development of an array of portable seismometers, with extensive software; if completed, the system will constitute an 'inverted telescope' capable of observing and mapping subsurface structure in unprecedented detail. The system would be moved from one locale to another and at each site would be laid out in patterns depending on the depth and area to be studied and the extent of detail desired. Staff members of DTM are taking leadership in developing the concept as a national enterprise.

Geophysical Laboratory

The Laboratory is one of the world's foremost centres for research and training in the earth sciences. In the early years, research was concerned mainly with determining the composition and properties of minerals and rocks that make up the crust of the Earth; that work still forms the core of much that is taught in university courses on petrology, geochemistry and geophysics. Today, in its own words, the Laboratory 'conducts physiochemical studies of geological problems with particular emphasis on the processes involved in the formation and evolution of the Earth's crust and mantle.' The aim, in simple terms, is the better to understand the evolution of our world.

Studies of minerals and rocks in conditions that simulate those deep within the Earth are among the most fascinating aspects of the Laboratory's work. Peter Bell, Ho-Kwang Mao and their colleagues have developed an instrument that enables them to conduct experiments with samples of material at extreme temperature and pressure. The material is squeezed between two diamonds to reproduce static pressures equivalent to that of the core-mantle boundary within the Earth and deeper. While under compression inside the diamond-anvil apparatus, samples can be studied under laser, x-ray and other kinds of radiation. Such flexibility makes possible a vast variety of experiments. In creating the instrument, Bell and Mao have shown once again that the pathfinder scientist must not only conceive new ideas but must often design and engineer his own equipment.

The headlines that greeted one of their experiments several years ago focused on an incidental result: 'Diamonds Pressed Together Until One Flows Like Butter'; 'Butter Soft Gems Clear Way to Core'; 'They Soften Jewels.' But there are far more fundamental results to the experiments, which are producing definitive experimental data—data with which future concepts of our planet and its evolution must conform. According to a recent Laboratory report:

> Deep Earth studies stand now in much the same position as did the space program in the late 1950s. The fundamental barriers to research are just being overcome and science is on the brink of having access to a vast new body of information. For the scientists involved this is a rare adventure. The inner earth is the last unexplored frontier of the earth. It is a large frontier: fully 99% of the earth is unknown.

Bell and Mao's diamond anvil is probing that frontier, far beyond the reach of drills, but their work means more than mere adventure. The director of the Laboratory, Hatten

110

Yoder, points to the growing awareness of the limited abundance of our natural resources; this intensifies the need to understand the accessible parts of the Earth's crust. The work of the Laboratory is extending the range of that understanding, and helping to determine why certain elements occur where they do; in the long term, such knowledge will be important in addressing our growing shortage of energy and minerals. In pursuit of such aims, Yoder declares that 'we grow rocks at the Laboratory' and it is literally true; by speeding up the growth of crystals to simulate the evolution of billion-year-old rocks, the Laboratory in its search to understand the Earth achieves what alchemists of old vainly boasted they might do.

The Institution is now exploring the exciting idea of bringing together the pursuits of the Geophysical Laboratory and the Department of Terrestrial Magnetism, perhaps at a single location in facilities not yet constructed. The Laboratory's experimentally orientated earth scientists and DTM's astronomers, planetologists, seismologists, geochemists and theoreticians would be brought together in pursuit of common questions.

Department of Plant Biology

The earliest Institution plant research programme was at the Desert Botanical Laboratory near Tucson, Arizona; the Institution's several botanical laboratories and field stations were centralized in 1929 at Stanford, California, a location which still offers two important resources—some extremely diverse plant habitats, and the faculty and students of several major universities in the San Francisco Bay area. The facilities of the Department are today used by Institution Fellows and by graduate students of Stanford and other universities. Department Director Winslow Briggs explains the Department's work:

> Many wild plants have an extraordinary capacity to tolerate the inconveniences of their environment. They survive water stress, extremes of temperature, onslaughts of disease, and insect attacks far better than the plants we attempt to cultivate for food and fiber. When we understand the genetics, physiology, and biochemistry of the mechanism by which wild plants are adapted to survive, we shall be in a far better position to design crop plants that can cope effectively with such hazards.

One aspect that staff are exploring is the molecular mechanisms by which plants convert light energy to chemical energy by photosynthesis, the primary source of all food. In capturing the light from the sun and converting it to energy, photosynthesis far surpasses any means yet devised by man, both in magnitude and efficiency, to capture solar energy. The Department has developed improved methods of studying photosynthesis and one current emphasis is on how chlorophyll functions in this process. Lessons learned both in the field and in the laboratory will greatly help us all in the future.

A second aspect of plants under investigation is their ability to adapt to environmental extremes. Work in this area of physiological ecology can be traced back to that of the original Desert Laboratory. The question at issue is how do wild plants growing in extreme environments manage to flourish where most other plants could not survive? High and low temperatures, dryness, and low carbon dioxide are among the environmental stresses being studied. The Department operates a mobile laboratory in a van, in which scientists travel to places like Death Valley for experimental work; one plant under investigation in this desolate spot grows and reproduces even during the hottest part of the summer. The hope is to help man make effective use of land that is now considered marginal or useless for agriculture.

The oleander plant provides an example of rare adaptability; it can thrive in climates ranging from the heat of Death Valley to cool, coastal regions, and can acclimatize itself with dramatic swiftness. 'Within two weeks,' reports the laboratory, 'a plant transplanted from high to low temperatures can barely be distinguished from ones grown continuously at low temperatures. Transfer in the opposite direction leads to an even faster adjustment. The acclimatization may be already half complete after only twenty-four hours.'

A third aspect of study is how plants develop in relation to light, and how the translation of genetic information changes during the plant's growth and differentiation. Plants are extraordinarily sensitive to light. The growth pattern of oat seedlings, for example, changes significantly when the seedlings are exposed to as little as one second of full moonlight. The redwood sorrel, *Oxalis oregana*, a resident of the Californian redwood forests, which prefers densely shaded sites, folds its leaves within six minutes if exposed to direct sunlight. Investigations of these phenomena, by increasing our understanding of the plants with which we share the planet, will contribute to our own survival.

A National Spirit in Science

Alongside their specific research programmes, all departments contribute to the Institution's aims in postdoctoral education, in which it is a world leader. The depth and intensity of modern scientific research demand an integration and synthesis of concepts and a command of advanced techniques well beyond those usually achieved by the young Ph.D., and even senior scholars need continued training in depth for their intellectual growth. The Institution's rôle in this has never been more important than it is today and, as a result, Carnegie-trained scientists have filled many key posts in research and teaching colleges, in medical schools, universities and in industry throughout the world.

Frontier research often requires costly instrumentation. Financial pressures in the 1970s forced the Institution to fall behind in this most important area but strong measures have been taken to resolve this problem. With one-third of the Institution's expenditure now provided by sources beyond the income from the endowment, this 'new money' has enabled the Institution to stretch its funds, upgrade its instrumentation on all fronts, and look to significant improvements in the coming years. Though the Institution may be less independent *financially* than it used to be, the directors and staff are confident that they are no less independent *intellectually*.

The Institution's President, James Ebert, points to a national spirit in science, in which the Institution plays a substantial part. This national spirit, he explains:

> means that our scientists and departments are part of a larger scientific enterprise, whose vigor rests fundamentally on the strength and the confidence of the whole national society. The data from our great telescopes and pace-setting laboratory instruments are at the disposal of others, just as our own scientists obtain help from workers elsewhere.

Ebert places great emphasis on one aspect of prime value to the Institution and of major concern to himself; that is, the preservation of the Institution's treasured flexibility to pioneer in new fields, to seize unexpected opportunities, and to support staff who are 'at once dreamers and achievers.' 'We buy a scientist's time,' says Ebert, 'and then, we give it back to him.' He admits that sometimes it is almost by accident of the individuals involved that particular areas of research might be stressed but he re-emphasizes the Institution's responsibility to pursue research that might otherwise be overlooked. The problem that heightens this responsibility is that so many young scientists are encouraged to expend themselves on safe projects that promise quick and certain results in order to fulfil the implicit agreement in their supportive grant papers and in order to assure themselves of achieving appropriate levels of conventional academic success; industry, too, is largely interested in providing grants in return for immediate results but, as Hatten Yoder puts it, 'If industry is asking about the applications of your work, you are not far enough ahead.'

The Institution is committed to avoiding these dangers and is determined also to avoid inhibitive procedures for assessing the work of its people; instead, it provides opportunities for staff members and fellows who are willing to run risks for high stakes. For those like Barbara McClintock, prepared to devote their lives to the pursuit of original research if only they are given the chance, the stakes and the rewards are very high indeed.

CARNEGIE DUNFERMLINE TRUST

The main thrust of Carnegie's endowments in the first two years of his retirement had been towards higher education and research, in Scotland and in Washington, but in his third year he turned again to the theme of community education. Through the Pittsburgh Institute and his gifts of library buildings and organs elsewhere in the United States, in Britain and in other countries, he had already begun placing within the reach of communities 'the ladders upon which the aspiring can rise.' His ambitious experiment for his native Dunfermline, in 1903, was to provide the townsfolk with social, educational and recreational opportunities beyond their previous expectations and so to increase their awareness of and appreciation for the quality of life. The plan was complementary to his previous schemes: he had recognized what money could do for higher education—he wanted to prove what it could also do for the elevation of the masses.

Carnegie's affection for his birthplace had persuaded him to provide it with public baths and a free library while he was still in the relatively early stages of making his fortune. Now came a massive and unique benefaction—the establishment of a Trust which would give the townsfolk '—especially the young—some charm, some happiness, some elevating conditions of life which residence elsewhere would have denied.' 'It is more than twenty years,' Carnegie wrote to the Trustees, 'since I provided in my will for this experiment—for experiment it is. My retirement from business enables me to act in my own lifetime....' The Trustees were immediately given the additional responsibility of looking after Pittencrieff Park, which Carnegie had triumphantly bought at the very end of 1902. Between 1903 and 1983, the Park absorbed thirty-four percent of the Trust's expenditure.

The main concern of the Trust is to provide for the people of Dunfermline something more than the local authority can provide and, indeed, something more than any other town of similar size might expect. In this endeavour the Trust has had to wrestle with a number of problems: the danger of experimental projects turning into long-term commitments; the need to keep ahead of the increased range of responsibilities adopted by the State and by local authorities; and the flexibility required to adapt to social changes which have removed many of the deprivations that Carnegie saw the need to combat. To these considerations, perhaps common to all the Carnegie Trusts, is added another more particularly of concern to the Dunfermline Trustees—the ability to observe the very narrow dividing-line which exists between helping a community and sapping its initiative.

Child health was a major concern in the early days; child education remains a concern of the Trust today. Physical training; community centres for men and women; public baths; libraries; museums; the provision and tuition of music; art collections and exhibitions; playing fields and youth clubs—all are among the variety of activities that have been fostered over the years. The arts, community activities, and recreation are still the major concerns of the Trust in the 1980s in pursuit of its essential quest, as valid today as it was eighty years ago, to improve the quality of life for the average Dunfermline citizen.

Carnegie Dunfermline Trust

Founded: 1903

Original Purpose: 'To bring into the monotonous lives of the toiling masses of Dunfermline more of sweetness and light.... The problem you have to solve is—"What can be done in towns for the benefit of the masses by money in the hand of the most public-spirited citizens?"' (*from the letter to the Trustees*).

Current Purpose: To improve the quality of life in Dunfermline by providing or supporting social, educational and recreational facilities over and above those which the central and local authorities may reasonably be expected to provide in a town of Dunfermline's size.

Finance:

Original endowment ($2½m):		£500,000
plus Pittencrieff Park, cost price 1902:		£45,000
Additional endowment, 1911 ($1¼m):		£250,000
Current assets:		£4,517,334
Balance sheet assets:	£1,735,370	
Surplus market value:	£581,964	
Properties, insured for:	£2,000,000	
Art collection, insured:	£100,000	
Equipment:	(approx) £100,000	
	£4,517,334	

Note: These figures do not take account of the value of assets such as properties and equipment which the Trust has handed over to local authorities and other organizations.

Expenditure:		Total	(Pittencrieff)
	1903-09:	£166,418	£36,138
	1910-19:	£340,339	£50,526
	1920-29:	£423,796	£78,613
	1930-39:	£398,136	£76,380
	1940-49:	£361,794	£89,779
	1950-59:	£601,362	£217,828
	1960-69:	£653,936	£320,275
	1970-79:	£1,072,918	£659,983
	1980-83:	£560,750	£42,467
Total—	1903-83:	£4,579,449	£1,571,989

Annual monies, 1983-85:		Income	Expenditure
	1983:	£192,925	£168,376
	1984 (estimate):	£185,000	£170,000
	1985 (estimate):	£200,000	£180,000

Administration:

Chairman:	James I. Scott
Secretary:	Fred Mann, MA, LL.B
Staff:	5 full-time (shared with Hero Fund Trust)
	1 special appointment for 1985 celebrations
	3 part-time
Address:	Abbey Park House, Dunfermline, Fife KY12 7PB

Carnegie Dunfermline Trust

There can be no doubt of Carnegie's affection for his birthplace; his autobiography and his many public speeches are liberally endowed with praise for Dunfermline. 'Fortunate in my ancestors, I was supremely so in my birthplace,' he wrote. Rather more extravagantly, he added, 'What Benares is to the Hindoo, Mecca to the Mohammedan, Jerusalem to the Christian—all that Dunfermline is to me.'

Though he left the town at the age of twelve—or perhaps *because* he left the town then—he retained a great fondness for it and a conviction that his subsequent success in America was attributable in no small measure to his roots and his ancestors. This affection was also nurtured by his closeness to his mother. In 1862, at the age of twenty-seven, and already on the way to making himself a wealthy man, Carnegie returned to Scotland for the first time, with his mother. 'No change ever affected me so much as this return to my native land,' he wrote. 'I seemed to be in a dream. Every mile that brought us nearer Scotland increased the intensity of my feelings.'

116

In 1877, he gave £5,000 to Dunfermline for a swimming pond and public baths (including a small gymnasium). These were so well used that in 1899 Carnegie announced the gift of a second set, completed in 1905 at a cost of £45,000. The New Baths included a full-size Swimming Pool, Slipper Baths, Russian and Turkish Baths, and a large gymnasium with ample apparatus and dressing-rooms. In 1881, he gave £8,000 to the town for a public library—the very first in his great chain of libraries. There were also many smaller gifts to societies and individuals in Dunfermline in the years before the foundation of the Trust.

On Christmas Eve, 1902, Carnegie achieved a very personal triumph. He became Laird of Pittencrieff. These sixty acres of park and glen lay close to the cottage where he had been born and contained a number of relics that figure large in the history of Dunfermline town and Scotland itself—sites such as Malcolm Canmore's Tower, St Margaret's Shrine, and the remains of the palace of the Stuart Kings. The property, long in private ownership, had been mostly closed to the people of Dunfermline, who, among other grievances against the Lairds of Pittencrieff, thought that the historic sites should be public. Carnegie's family had become involved in resisting attempts by the Laird to encroach upon the common lands of the town:

> Among my earliest recollections are the struggles of Dunfermline to obtain the rights of the town to part of the Abbey grounds and the Palace ruins. My grandfather Morrison began the campaign or, at least, was one of those who did. The struggle was continued by my uncles Lauder and Morrison, the latter being honored by being charged with having incited and led a band of men to tear down a certain wall. The citizens won a victory in the highest court and the then Laird ordered that thereafter 'no Morrison be admitted to the Glen.' I, being a Morrison,...was debarred.

Naturally, the growth of the family feud and the closure of the Glen gave Pittencrieff a symbolic significance in Carnegie's mind. 'When I heard of paradise, I translated the word into Pittencrieff Glen,' he wrote, but when much later he heard that the owners wished to sell, his business acumen did not desert him. He refused the original asking price of £70,000 and bided his time for two years until he had only to pay £45,000. The news of his success came to him on Christmas Eve and he could not contain his delight. 'My new title beats all. I am Laird of Pittencrieff...the most sacred spot to me on Earth.'

'No gift I have made or can ever make can possibly approach that of Pittencrieff Glen,' he wrote. It was '...the most soul-satisfying gift I ever made, or ever can make.' He decided to endow Dunfermline itself with an idiosyncratic trust fund. In 1903, he transferred to twenty-five citizens, to whom he also entrusted the management of Pittencrieff, bonds worth $2,500,000, which in 1910 he increased by another $1,250,000. Since the population of Dunfermline in 1903 was approximately 26,000 (in 1983 it was 126,000), this amounted to £19 endowment per person and £1 revenue per person per year at first, or nearly £29 endowment per person and £1.44 (£1.9s.0d) per person per year revenue after 1910. In current values, the latter represents nearly £900 endowment per person. Carnegie's letter of gift explained how he wished the money to be spent:

> In attempts to bring into the monotonous lives of the toiling masses of Dunfermline more of sweetness and light; to give them—especially the young—some charm, some happiness, some elevating conditions of life which residence elsewhere would have denied; that the child of my native town, looking back in after years, however far from home it may have roamed, will feel that simply by virtue of being such, life has been made happier and better. If this be the fruit of your labours you will have succeeded; if not, you will have failed.

Carnegie emphasized that the work was experimental:

> Remember you are pioneers, and do not be afraid of making mistakes; those who never make mistakes never make anything. Try many things freely, but discard just as freely....Not what other cities have is your standard; it is the something beyond this which they lack, and your funds should be strictly devoted to this....I can imagine it may be your duty in the future to abandon beneficent fields from time to time when municipalities enlarge their spheres of action and embrace these....As conditions of life change rapidly, you will not be restricted as to your plans or the scope of your activities.

Carnegie concluded his letter by commending what he believed to be a great truth: 'The gods send thread for a web begun.'

The Trustees, with their expanded responsibilities—far beyond the expectations of any comparable town—went quickly to work on a great variety of schemes. They took over from the Town Council the running of the New Baths and Gymnasium, keeping the Old Baths open free of charge. In 1905 a College of Hygiene and Physical Education was opened. Venturefair Playing Fields were created in 1909, with eight acres catering for football, hockey and cricket. A child welfare system was instituted: regular medical inspections of school children began in 1905, leading to the establishment in 1910 of a school clinic; in 1913-14, a dental clinic, and a massage and medical gymnastic clinic were opened. A craft school was developed in 1908. A series of institutes (reading rooms, libraries and baths) in outlying districts was begun in 1906, and a women's centre appeared in 1912. A museum, a speech therapy clinic, concerts and musical tuition, new baths, art collections and exhibitions, horticulture competitions, support for clubs, a range of youth schemes including bursaries and excursions, improvements to Pittencrieff Park and Glen in the form of refreshment facilities and conservatories—all these demonstrated the Trustees' determination to pursue their central aims: to promote efficiency for life's work and to provide for recreational interests. It was an awesome endeavour for the Trustees to tackle. Turning the pages of their Reports over eighty years, major activities and incidental ones equally catch the eye, alongside the continual wrestling with the inherent problems experienced by the

Early Gymnastic Class, Dunfermline 1909

Remedial Clinic 1913

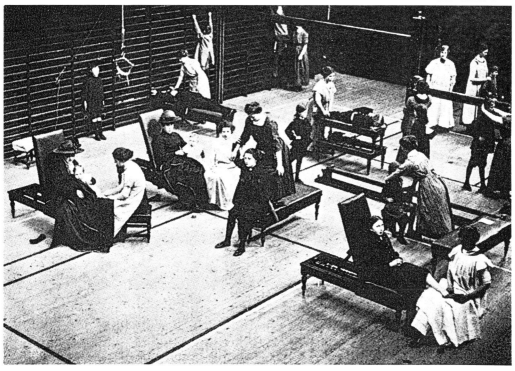

119

Trustees in implementing Carnegie's experiment to the full extent he would have wished. A passing review is probably the best way to catch the flavour of the Trust.

In 1903-04, the Park itself, the cornerstone of the endowment, formerly 'practically unknown to the people,' was already thronged by factory and shop workers. The Trustees had initially commissioned Patrick Geddes, sociologist and geographer, and Thomas Mawson, landscape architect, to advise them on the laying-out of the Park, but their plans were too ambitious and costly, and the Trustees settled for a more conventional scheme prepared by James Whitton of the Glasgow Parks Department. Paths and swings were provided, a tea house was made ready and there were horticultural exhibitions; in 1905 there was open-air music and a Trust band was formed. Music received special attention, as Mr Carnegie had 'expressed himself as desirous that the love of music which is common to every class should be gratified by a payment so small as to be within the reach of the humblest income.' A singing teacher was provided for schools; professional teachers were appointed for a School of Music; there were evening classes in vocal music and a teacher of elocution was appointed. By 1907, the Saturday evening concerts were attended by 1,600 people at one penny admission, and there were free concerts for 120 people in a small recreation room of the Model Lodging House. In 1906, there were 81,000 visitors to the New Baths.

Scotland's first College of Hygiene and Physical Education was opened in 1905. There were fifteen students in the first year, all women; the first course for men was in 1908 but demand was disappointing: it was found that the men who qualified had difficulty in finding jobs, and the only three entrants in 1914 all withdrew. Courses for men were reintroduced after the First World War and ran with the women's until 1931 when the men's course moved to Glasgow and the women stayed in Dunfermline. The college was ousted by the military during the Second World War and the Trust severed its connection with the College when it moved to Aberdeen in 1950; it is now situated at Cramond, Edinburgh, and is the only autonomous specialist college of education for training women teachers in physical education in Scotland.

The Trustees were very sensible of the problems and the potential in the first few years. In 1905, they recorded that they must 'help the people to help themselves'; in 1906, they 'must strive to permeate a glow of life and thought and to render the inhabitants of Dunfermline sensible to beauty and marked by their capacity for rational and refined enjoyment. In so endeavouring they will help to abolish class distinction.' In 1907, they were aware that 'It is only by degrees that a community can be led upward to higher things'; and in 1911, they were continuing 'to try to reach every part of the community by many roads of approach'—although some backs may have been put up by their pronouncement that 'There can be no doubt that throughout the community there is a certain amount of intellectual lethargy which it is the duty of the Trustees to try to dispel.' Already they were committed to a number of schemes regarded as indispensable, which threatened to absorb too much income at the expense of experimentation. This was a continual comment in their reports.

Meanwhile the activity continued. The new craft school, opened in 1908, provided qualified teachers and facilities for woodcarving, metalwork, metal enamelling, jewellery, illuminated manuscripts, gesso and gilding; there were 64 students in the first year. The inauguration of a school clinic in 1910 opened the Trustees' eyes to the extraordinary amount of 'preventable suffering of which we know nothing'; there were sometimes more than 100 cases in one day referred to the school clinic by doctors. In 1911, no damage was done to the Park by 12,000 miners who visited it on their annual holiday. In 1912, a Women's Institute was opened by Mrs Carnegie herself and 15,000 women enrolled for embroidery, cookery and similar classes. Carnegie gave an extra £5,000 toward an extension for the Library, and the Trustees provided another £6,000—finally (1920) increased to £15,000.

When war came in 1914, school gardens were soon providing cabbages, turnips and lettuces for sailors in the Fleet. Two years later, the Trust was supplying large amounts of writing paper to the armed forces: there were 48,000 letters posted in one Soldiers' Club in one year; but next year, 100,000 letters were despatched and 727,000 teas were supplied to Soldiers' Clubs in the same year. With the armistice in 1918, a remedial and curative clinic was installed at the baths for the treatment of disabled soldiers and sailors. Even in 1922, there were still 13,000 attendances of disabled men at the clinic.

The following year, the Chairman announced that:

Our principal duty is to the community as a whole and not to individuals—the time has come to deal seriously with such questions as the provision of a permanent recuperative home for children, art gallery, worthy entrances to Pittencrieff Park, a larger and smaller hall including an organ, play centres for young children and sports and playing fields for mature people, and finally a comprehensive scheme of child and infant welfare.

A sixth bowling green and pavilion were opened in 1924 and two years later, what is still the town's main outdoor recreation area was inaugurated with the leasing of 16 acres at Pitreavie Playing Fields: finally comprising 44 acres, with a 21-dressingroom pavilion, and Olympic standard running track (1952) and grandstand, it provided excellent facilities for football, hockey, rugby, cricket and athletics. In 1926 the industrial crisis persuaded many unemployed people to make increased use of institutes and libraries, and the coal strike made it necessary to close the baths, but there were proposals for artificial sunray baths. By 1928, plans were being introduced for psychological tests in local schools and a scheme for vocational guidance was in operation; the Birthplace Museum was opened and the Craft School was deemed to be one of the Trust's most successful experiments—'in many respects unique.' However, in the same year, it was noted that 'the Trustees are not attempting to hazard an opinion as to the wisdom or ultimate soundness of their actions: the reader must judge for himself....The Trust must build for posterity and posterity alone can be the judge.' Three years later, a report on the vocational guidance experiment found practically all children in recommended work were satisfied while only half in other work were satisfied.

Aeratone Therapeutic Bath, Dunfermline, 1938

There were two unsuccessful attempts to floodlight Carnegie's statue in the Park in 1932 and 1933, but new stables, stores and an aviary were built; the first Boys' Club in the town was formed; after an experimental year's operation, the centre for the study and control of juvenile rheumatism was abandoned because of lack of demand; and smoking was permitted in certain rooms of the Women's Institute—although in Baldridgeburn Institute there were so many unemployed people that the atmosphere was reported to be almost unbearable due to smoking. A clinic for children with defective speech was also opened and, after a flirtation with German gymnastics, the Carnegie Physical Training and Athletic Club reverted to Swedish gymnastics and keep-fit exercises. However, the appointment of a games organizer in 1935, particularly to interest unemployed young men in indoor and outdoor physical exercises, did not meet with much enthusiasm. On the other hand, a lecture by an Indian chief, 'although unique in its style, was sparsely attended by adults, but highly appreciated by the boys and girls who enjoyed the privilege of free admission.'

The Trustees noted in 1933-34 that the population of the town was 35,300 and the income of the Trust was £40,500; if all the Trust enterprises were undertaken by the local authority, the local rates—4s.3d for owners plus 5s.8d for occupiers, a total of 9s.11d (50p)—would have been increased by 3s.10d (almost 20p) in the pound. The community of Dunfermline had, during the last 33 years, 'to an ever-increasing extent looked to the Trust to keep abreast, if not ahead of, the times and to stimulate public interest by inaugurating some new scheme,' noted the Report in 1936, commenting that government and local authorities were providing many of the social amenities that had previously been run by voluntary organizations. The Report suggested that voluntary activity should be encouraged among energetic members of the community to give help and social guidance to their less fortunate or younger fellows. The next year, the Trustees were finding that pioneering was difficult when social conditions and demands change rapidly; it was 'far from easy to abandon a beneficent field once that field has become part and parcel of the life of the community'; not easy either (they admitted in 1938) to persuade the Council that it should take over and maintain some of the Trust schemes. The year 1938 saw a unique experiment, the introduction of an Aeratone Therapeutic Bath: the first of its kind in Britain, it was 'beneficial to people suffering from stiffness, rheumatism, faulty circulation and many other ailments,' as well as being a general tonic; there was already a long waiting list.

The Second World War virtually brought the Trust to a stand-still, as most of the buildings were taken over by the Services or other authorities. Although the Trust saved money during this period, it was recognised that increased costs of maintenance, salaries and wages would mean the Trust could not maintain all the pre-war activities on pre-war scale without exceeding income: 'The time has obviously come for the Trustees to discard.' Despite the off-loading on to the local authority in 1946 of the Baths and Gymnasium and the District Institutes, the Trust faced high expenses in making good the wartime damage in the Park. Once again, the Trustees were complaining about the problems of being landed with the permanent maintenance of what had started out as pioneering concepts. They decided that before entering any new field, the Trustees must feel it probable 'that in time the new project will be found to be such an integral part of the community life that it will become either self-supporting or the responsibility of the Local Authority.' In 1946 the Trustees were concerned about comments on the Carnegie Hall, opened in 1937 with a capacity of 640. Many touring companies were apparently 'amazed to find such a well-appointed dual-purpose building in a town the size of Dunfermline,' but the Hall was not adequately supported by locals because it was 'too far from the centre of town' or had 'no theatre atmosphere' and 'those who favour the more popular type of entertainment do not feel at home in such luxurious surroundings.' In general, the public of Dunfermline did not support high quality concerts; sometimes concerts which were not sponsored by the Trust attracted bigger audiences at double the ticket price. In 1948, it was noted that open-air attendances at concerts in the Park ranged from 1,260 to eight only; sometimes only a few people attended the concerts while thousands were elsewhere in the Park.

That year, £3,000 was spent in the Park on a Model Traffic Area, a miniature layout of roads and pedestrian crossings equipped with cars and tricycles so that children could practise road safety under expert tuition. The Trust also gave wider local circulation to the Town Council's Advisory Town Plan for Dunfermline by paying the extra cost of a larger edition. Even after the establishment of the National Health Service, the Trust continued to provide (as agents for the local authority) many of their existing medical welfare services for children, and in 1948 they commented that Trust expenditure in this area was still far in excess of anything a local authority could reasonably be expected to incur; there were 5,500 new cases and 19,700 attendances at general clinics during the year. In 1950, there was an average attendance of 1,000 at the educational and entertainment films for children in the Regal cinema; Youth Centre members paid a visit to Luxembourg and France. In 1951, Billy the cockatoo at the aviary collected £54 for charity (he died in 1971 at the reputed age of 47). In late 1952, the running track was completed at Pitreavie (opened 1954), and there was a production of *Carmen*. Interest-free loans were tried out for the first time in 1953, 'to encourage those who are prepared to help themselves.' On the musical front, the violins and cellos purchased some years earlier for the tuition of pupils in primary schools had proved so successful that in 1954 woodwind and brass instruments were also provided. Young musicians were subsidized to attend vacation courses and to visit the Edinburgh Festival. Attendance at drama societies and repertory companies was down, probably as a result of television, though light opera was still popular.

In the first fifty years of the Trust, approximately 30% of its expenditure had been on new building schemes and the improvement of Pittencrieff Park; 14% had been on projects within Pittencrieff Park; 10% had been on music and drama; 9% on baths and indoor and outdoor games; another 9% on institutes and bowling greens; 7½% on medical inspection and treatment of school children, and 3½% on arts and crafts. The total income from 1903 to 1952 was nearly £2,200,000.

Four major schemes were in prospect in 1959: the restoration as society meeting-

Carnegie Hall and Music
Institute, Dunfermline

International Sculpture
Exhibition in Pittencrieff Park,
1967

rooms of the sixteenth-century Abbot House; a covered stand at Pitreavie Playing Fields; a new car park in Pittencrieff Park; and the establishment of the Dunfermline Museum, in Viewfield, through which the Trustees hoped to demonstrate, 'especially to the young,' that a museum could be an attractive and fascinating storehouse. A Saturday night club for 13 to 15 year-olds was started in 1960 (membership of the Youth Centre was getting younger and younger). In 1961, the Report summed up some of the Trust's work and noted that there were 'few members of the community whose lives have not been touched by the Trust's operations—but the man in the street often does not realise just how much has been done'; the report added that much of what had been provided was 'the envy and the pattern for cities the world over.' Even so, the Trust's sphere of action had become more circumscribed; 'the central or local authority now administers as each man's right what the Trust originated as the Dunfermline man's privilege.' Finance was also a problem. In 1962, the Trust asked the local education authority to take over Pitreavie Playing Fields, the Craft School and Youth Centre, and asked the Town Council to acquire the Carnegie Hall, the Music Institute and Dunfermline Museum; these changes did not all take place immediately but the request was an acknowledgement that the Trust could not indefinitely carry on the administration of all their public services and also act as pioneers.

The next ten years saw the release of new energy. Between 1965 and 1974 the Trust sponsored an annual Festival of Music and the Arts, the centrepiece of which was a 70-strong Symphony Orchestra composed mainly of young Music College students. Billeted out on willing hosts and hostesses, they undertook ten to fourteen days of intensive rehearsal and concert-giving to schools and public under professional conductors. Round the Festival Orchestra was built a series of varied programmes of dramatic productions, concerts, brass band contests, recitals, talks, and a wide range of exhibitions. Among them was a memorable exhibition of sculpture, staged outdoors in Pittencrieff Park, which included works by world famous artists and encouraged the Scottish Arts Council to stage a sculpture conference in association with it. The Festival produced a photographic study of 'Dunfermline and its People' and a commissioned orchestral work (1967), and Festival spin-offs included the organization of weekend courses for amateur orchestral players, seminars on music for the handicapped, and the purchase of a Steinway grand piano. An artificial ski slope was opened, sub-aqua swimming equipment was provided, and a manikin was bought for artificial respiration practice by Girl Guides (1969). In 1970 the closed-circuit television experiment was developed further in secondary schools with a grant of £17,000—one of the largest single allocations by the Trust to that date, though the cost of replacing the old conservatories in Pittencrieff Park with a Floral Hall in 1973 required £40,000. A sailing dinghy was provided for secondary schools and a pool of musical instruments built up for loans to beginners or schools (1973). A scented garden for the blind was provided in the Park by voluntary effort in 1974. These are only samples of a decade's activities.

The year 1976 saw the beginning of even greater changes. An agreement was reached with the District Council that it should take over Pittencrieff Park, though the Trustees were to retain formal ownership and were to provide a grant of £250,000 over six years. The costs of the Park had become prohibitive for the Trust. In the first twenty-five years, the Park had represented about 10% of expenditure; in 1956 it had been 30%; in 1973 it had been 45%; in 1975 it had been 66% of total expenditure. By abdicating further responsibility for administration and maintenance, the Trust secured its own future and its freedom of action. In the same year, full-time employees were reduced to five in the office—in 1920, there had been 152 employees.

With freedom to innovate in prospect once more, plans were prepared in 1979 for several major projects: two mini-buses for use by the local primary schools at a cost of £10,000; a microfilm printer for Carnegie Central Library; a history of Dunfermline; loans of expensive sports equipment and musical instruments; seminars on aids for the elderly and handicapped; grants for mini-computers in local schools. Spending on community clubs was increased sevenfold between 1977 and 1979. In 1980, portable stage units were provided for Queen Anne High School, video equipment was supplied for the Dunfermline Sports Council, and there was a grant for visitor information in the Park.

In early 1981, a tapestry fifty feet square went on public show; it depicted 'Malcolm and Margaret,' the Scottish king and his queen who had originally made Dunfermline

Progress on the current Dunfermline Tapestry—a townscape super-imposed on a map of Fife

their capital. This was the culmination of two years' hard work by a group of citizens whose aims were to produce a celebration of Dunfermline's traditional weaving craft displayed in a historical setting. The Trust provided more than £9,000 towards the project and has since funded a second tapestry depicting Dunfermline and many of the themes with which the town is associated. In the same year, Ebenezer Henderson's astronomical clock was purchased for the Museum and £2,250 was paid for a portrait of King James VI of Scotland (James I of England).

Also in 1981, the Trust allocated £22,500, with an inaugural grant of £8,000, to establish a pioneer project to help people who themselves are caring for disabled people at home. Crossroads Dunfermline is a registered charity which provides Care Attendants who can take over the duties of those looking after the mentally and physically handicapped at home and thereby allow these 'carers' a much-needed rest, enabling them to get out shopping, visit friends or simply relax for a while from their responsibilities. The Trust also provided a remarkable piece of bone-uniting equipment (Bi-Osteogen) to be used in the Dunfermline and West Fife Hospital. Through electrical stimulation of the bone tissue, new bone growth is encouraged where previously a broken bone had failed to knit together; the apparatus can be used at home, with only periodic check-ups at the hospital—this saves valuable hospital beds.

Carnegie was particularly anxious that the Trust should see to the needs of the children of Dunfermline. Having provided more than £20,000 during the 1970s to help set up an educational television service, the Trust pursued this theme in 1981 by making further grants for video-tape recorders in secondary schools and for mini-computers in several primary schools; more money was set aside the next year for providing micro-computers in every primary school and for extra computing equipment in each of the five secondary schools. Many other small grants were made for educational use.

But it was not only the children who could benefit from new technology. Prestel—the computer-linked information service—was installed in the Carnegie Library in 1980, and in 1982, at a cost of £10,000, the Trust sponsored an infra-red aerial heat-loss survey of Dunfermline, with the aim of showing how much heat was lost as the result of poor insulation in houses and other buildings. The survey was followed by a major exhibition attended by local authorities, government departments, industries, banks and commercial insulation firms, all promoting ways of conserving energy and saving money. It has been difficult to judge the success of the venture but it was reported that in the first eight months of 1982 there were applications to the District Council for 2,000 insulation grants compared with 880 in the corresponding period the previous year.

During 1983-84, in addition to its unspectacular but valuable recurring activity, the Trust provided a special grant to mark the centenary of the Carnegie Library; put up half the funds needed to enable Dunfermline District Council to acquire a painting by a modern Scottish master; provided the last £4,000 needed by a voluntary organization to buy a mini-bus for taking long-term hospital patients for outings; purchased a set of handbells for use by school and adult groups; planned a third group of tapestries; issued a new edition of *My Own Story*, an abridgement primarily for young readers of Andrew Carnegie's autobiography; paid for an experimental computer network system in a secondary school and provided computer equipment for a retired headteacher to offer a liaison service for primary schools.

Three more projects perhaps call for further mention. The special place which Dunfermline Abbey had in the affections of Mr Carnegie influenced the Trustees—exceptionally—to make a grant of £10,000 to the restoration appeal. The Trust has also offered to contribute a large part of the cost of commissioning a design consultant to prepare plans for a new Country Park at nearby Townhill. In recent years the Trustees have followed the lead of the United Kingdom Trust in developing an interest in Interpretation. In 1980 they commissioned a special study of how the resident and visitor alike might be made more aware of Dunfermline's heritage and environment, and early in 1985 the Trust will be launching a new 'Dunfermline Heritage Scheme': orientation panels in the main car parks and market plaques on over 30 historic buildings will be supplemented by a brochure and booklet—and a special educational package for schools—in outlining three important aspects of the town's history—Royal Dunfermline, the industrial heritage, and of course the story of Andrew Carnegie. A course for would-be 'Heritage Guides' is also planned.

And yet much of the Trustees' thinking and resources in 1983 and 1984 has been concentrated on two special projects—a much-needed renovation of the Andrew Carnegie Birthplace Museum and plans for making the Andrew Carnegie sesquicentenary year of 1985 a memorable one for Dunfermline people. The Dunfermline Trust's share of the cost of redeveloping the Andrew Carnegie Birthplace Museum (which is dealt with elsewhere in this book) will come to over £30,000, while a fund of £75,000 has been built up to finance anniversary projects.

The main permanent 1985 project is one which would have been close to Carnegie's own heart, eloquently nostalgic as he was about Dunfermline Abbey and its curfew bell. The Trust is making a grant of about £40,000 to enable Dunfermline District Council to undertake a major extension of the present chime which was originally established to mark the centenary of Carnegie's birth. Ten new bells have been installed, bringing the present number up to 25; but a major part of the scheme has been the complete re-construction of the bell-frame which now has room to accommodate up to 48 bells. The obsolete control system also is being completely modernised so that the bells can be automatically operated by computer.

In addition, the Trust has commissioned from a leading Scottish playwright a one-man play about Andrew Carnegie which will be performed at the 1985 Edinburgh Festival. There will be an exhibition, to be shown in Scotland and the United States, of a commissioned photographic record of Dunfermline as it now is. A new account of Dunfermline in Carnegie's time will fill a gap in the local histories currently available. There will be a return visit to Pittencrieff Park of 'The Dancing Waters,' a spectacular display of fountains and cascades, imaginatively set to music and coloured lights. In the 'Carnegie Series' of concerts there will be performances by Scottish Opera, Scottish

Pittencrieff Park, Pavilion and Restaurant

Ballet, the King's Singers, and there will be a revival of *The Masque of Dunfermline*. Many local clubs and societies have eagerly responded to the Trust's suggestion that they should arrange special events or programmes during the anniversary year: a commemorative envelope will be sent out near the time of Carnegie's birthday, 25th November; a children's pageant of mediaeval music and drama from the time of Queen Margaret will be staged in Dunfermline Abbey; and a wild-life garden is being created in Pittencrieff Park.

It has never been easy for the Trustees to identify what is most needed, to pioneer what might become most successful, or to anticipate what is likely to prove a burden; above all, it has never been easy for them to remain flexible. Had they always been right, they must have had superhuman foresight—or were not far enough ahead of their times! The details of their efforts provide a brave record of experiment—a tradition which the Trustees are determined to maintain. But pioneering nowadays is more difficult than it was eighty years ago. Largely thanks to the foresight of previous generations of Trustees, Dunfermline now has its park, library, swimming baths, playing fields, community centres, museum and concert hall, the traditional means by which the whole community is benefited.

In 1910 the Trust's income at £37,500 almost matched the £45,000 which Dunfermline Town Council could command through the levy of burgh rates: in 1984 the Trust's budget of £200,000 paled in comparison with the £10,000,000 District Council budget. Local authorities too have much wider powers of using their resources for activities which were at one time the province of volunteers and charities. New schemes must not involve anything other than minimal running costs, since the Trust, the District Council, or even local societies, cannot contemplate recurring commitments. It took the State thirty-five years to catch up the Trust's health and welfare provision—but only two years to follow the Trust's example of putting a micro-computer in every primary school. The suggestion that the community's own initiative had been sapped by eighty years of Trust paternalism can hardly be sustained when the local newspaper in November 1984 reported that a £30,000 fund had been raised in two months to send one small boy to America for special hospital treatment, while in another part of the town another £15,000 has been raised for a similar appeal.

Carnegie Birthplace Memorial Fund and Museum
Founded: 1926

Purpose: To tell the story of Andrew Carnegie's humble beginnings and his remarkable achievements.

Finance:		*1984*
Original endowment (by Mrs Carnegie):	£10,000	
Supplements to endowments, and grants:		
Mrs Carnegie (1932):	£2,000	
Dunfermline Trust (1946-62):	£27,658	£36,000
Carnegie UK Trust (1969):	£5,000	£20,000
Institution of Washington (1969):	£2,086	£7,000
Carnegie Corporation (1969):	£6,270	£17,000
Endowment for International Peace (1969):	£1,257	
Universities of Scotland (1969):	£800	
Hero Fund Commission (over 10 years):	£1,000	
Hero Fund Trust/Dunfermline Trust (1969-83+):	£250-300 pa	
Mrs Margaret Carnegie-Miller (for 10 years+):	£2,000 pa	
Scottish Tourist Board:		£70,000
		£150,000

Current assets (end 1983):		£38,994
Annual monies in recent years:	*Income*	*Expenditure*
1983:	£7,772	£8,708
1984 (estimate):	£6,500	£10,000
1985 (estimate):	£7,500	£11,000

Number of visitors:
Per annum to 1983:   (approx) 6,000-9,000
  (With renovation and greater promotion, an increase is expected.)

Administration:
Chairman: James I. Scott
Secretary: Fred Mann, MA, LL.B
Staff: 1 full-time, 4 part-time.
Address: Andrew Carnegie Birthplace Museum, Moodie Street, Dunfermline
             KY12 7PL
             Office: c/o Carnegie Dunfermline Trust, Abbey Park House, Dunfermline
             KY12 7PB

The Andrew Carnegie Birthplace Fund—which is administered by the Carnegie Dunfermline Trustees—was established in 1926 with an endowment of £10,000 from Carnegie's widow, who wished to erect a 'Memorial Treasure House' in which to display her late husband's honours. A Memorial Hall was erected in 1928 next to the late-eighteenth-century weaver's cottage in which Carnegie had been born. Entry to the Museum has always been free, although the income from the original endowment has been severely devalued by inflation and has had to be supplemented by the Dunfermline and other Trusts and by Carnegie's daughter, Mrs Margaret Carnegie Miller.

The 'Treasure House' itself remained unchanged until the late 1960s, when extra capital made it possible to appoint for the first time a Museum Director, who made some progress in modernising the displays. However, it was only in 1983-84 that a comprehensive renovation could be undertaken with a fund of £150,000 raised with the help, again, of a number of other Carnegie Trusts and the Scottish Tourist Board. The renovated museum was reopened in the summer of 1984.

The tiny rooms of the Birthplace Cottage look much as Carnegie must have known them as a boy in the 1830s. The ground floor workshop has a Jacquard loom like the one his father used for weaving fine damask cloth; and among the period furnishings of the family living-room upstairs are the original wall beds typical of the time, and the very desk which the Carnegies left with the friend who lent them their passage money to America. Across the stairhead, the upper room of the adjoining house has now been brought into use to show the social and economic background to the Carnegie's decision to abandon the struggle for a decent living in trade-depressed Dunfermline and to set out, in 1848, for 'the land of promise' across the Atlantic.

In the Memorial Hall, new displays trace Carnegie's life in America and tell the story of how his millions are being used in a very different world through the range of Foundations. An imaginative new feature is a re-creation of Carnegie's private office, in which he is shown at his own desk surrounded by photographs of the friends and places he loved best. These and many other exhibits now on display for the first time came from Skibo Castle.

Among the Museum's many other unique treasures are the richly-worked caskets and ornamental scrolls he received with the Freedoms of more than fifty towns and cities all over Britain; the decorations kings gave him, the gold and silver medals he received from societies; university robes; and presentation mallets, trowels and keys, including the celebrated Laird's Key of Pittencrieff Park, Dunfermline, and a silver model of the Palace of Peace in The Hague.

Other important features are the Roll of Honour of the Carnegie Hero Fund Trust, which enshrines the names of 6,000 men, women and children honoured for saving human life; an audio-visual programme; and a hologram of Carnegie which was specially commissioned to commemorate the generosity to the Museum of his daughter.

Birthplace Museum, 1985

Mr Carnegie's office, Birthplace Museum

Freedom Caskets in the Birthplace Museum

135

CARNEGIE FOUNDATION FOR THE ADVANCEMENT OF TEACHING

Carnegie's first concerns in education had been to make it practical and more available to deserving students and the general public; he intended also to improve the quality of education by encouraging research. With his endowment of the Foundation in 1905, he added another dimension: he raised the status of teachers themselves in higher education by offering a free pension plan that brought vital new blood into the system. Very quickly, good teachers would work only in colleges that gave Carnegie pensions, and, since colleges and universities could only qualify for teacher pensions if they satisfied certain criteria established by the Foundation, the scheme served at the same time to raise the whole standard of education throughout the country.

It was an ingenious way to lead the educational establishments to an improvement of themselves; it made available a very tasty carrot to those who were prepared to reach out for it, reminiscent of the way in which Carnegie enticed communities into buying books by providing libraries in which to house them on condition that the people maintained them. Both approaches were in line with Carnegie's philosophy of helping those who helped themselves.

The scheme was so successful that there were quickly too many applicants for the available funds. In 1916, a new contributory pension scheme funded by the Corporation was devised, even more appropriate to the self-help principle. This was the Teachers Insurance and Annuity Association (TIAA), established in 1918, independent in 1938, and extended by the College Retirement Equities Fund (CREF) in 1952 (see page 148).

The Foundation continues to honour those free pensions offered before 1931 but after the closure of the list that year to individuals (it was closed to institutions in 1916) the Trustees were able to concentrate on a policy of sponsored research into education and standards. From 1967 to 1979, the principal activities of the Foundation were in support of the Carnegie Commission on Higher Education and the Carnegie Council on Policy Studies in Higher Education, both of which published a number of influential reports. Policy studies for education and the monitoring and analysis of higher education are now the principal responsibilities of the Foundation. They are responsibilities which the Foundation regard in a very practical way; the Trustees are concerned not simply with reports on what they find good or bad in the educational system but with making recommendations as to what should be done about it. They

136

also see their job as being to encourage open discussion of the standards and aims of education.

In eighty years, the Foundation has been responsible for at least 230 publications on all aspects of American higher education. Reports have been published on medical education, sport, science, computers in education, the arts, religious and ethnic minority groups, the education of women, the philosophy and economy of education, comparative studies with education in other countries, education and youth unemployment, the conflict between state and independent control of colleges and universities, and, most recently, a major report on the American high school, which is being followed up by practical financial support for certain schools that are implementing recommendations from the report.

There can be no doubt that the Foundation will go on worrying at the educational system until long after it is satisfied with what it sees—if it ever could be satisfied.

Carnegie Foundation for the Advancement of Teaching
Founded: 1905

Original purpose: 'To provide retiring pensions for the teachers of universities, colleges, and technical schools in our country, Canada and Newfoundland... without regard to race, sex, creed or color' (*from the Trust Deed*).

Current purpose: 'In general, to do and perform all things necessary to encourage, uphold, and dignify the profession of the teacher and the cause of higher education.'

Finance:		*Total*
Andrew Carnegie, original endowment:	$10,000,000	
For general support (1911-15):	$5,000,000	
For educational inquiry (1912):	$1,250,000	$16,250,000
Carnegie Corporation:		
Establish reserve fund (1912-19):	$4,487,831	
Assist pension payments (1912-34):	$13,747,285	
For operations (various years):	$16,411,603	$34,646,725
Capital Gains:		$17,930,971
Security Income, Grants, etc.:		$76,091,842
		$144,919,538
Expenditures (1905-1983):		
Pensions:	$85,973,698	
All other:	$30,257,531	$116,231,229
Fund Balance (June 30, 1983):		$28,688,309

Annual monies (1905-08):	*Income*	*Expenditure*	(Pensions)
1905-06:	$84,299	$99,391	($23,203)
1906-07:	$644,031	$198,792	($158,890)
1907-08:	$530,306	$287,072	($246,642)
Annual monies (1982-85):			
1982-83:	$3,862,310	$2,015,848	
1983-84 (estimated):	$3,391,645	$3,391,645	
1984-85 (estimated):	$2,741,860	$2,741,860	

Publications and research papers:

Bulletins and papers, 1907-1973:	56 approx.
Carnegie Commission, 1968-1973:	22 by staff
1968-1977:	65 sponsored studies
1970-1975:	20 technical reports
Carnegie Council, 1975-1980:	15 policy reports
	13 sponsored research reports
	30 technical reports
Publications and films, 1980-1983:	8 publications
	2 video films

Administration:

President:	Ernest L. Boyer (formerly Chancellor of the State University of New York, and former Commissioner of Education (U.S.)).
Secretary and Treasurer:	Jean Van Gorden
Staff:	3 officers, 3 administrative, 3 professional (to be increased for study of 4-year college), 8 support.
Address:	5 Ivy Lane, Princeton, New Jersey 08540
	1755 Massachusetts Avenue, N.W., Washington, DC 20036.

Carnegie Foundation for the Advancement of Teaching

It is said that Carnegie first became aware of the plight of teachers when he was invited to the Board of Cornell University in 1890. He was shocked to discover that a college professor might be earning less than a clerk in his own steel works. Such low rates of pay were apparent in all the academic institutions in America and resulted in a general impoverishment of the whole system.

Universities were unwilling to throw out ageing members who had no means of saving for retirement; cloisters were therefore crowded with men well over the decent age of retirement, and vital new blood, so badly needed to rejuvenate the system, was in consequence excluded. Able men hesitated to adopt teaching as a career. The scientific and technical faculties of the universities, so favoured by Carnegie, could not compete for young talent with the growing industries of engineering and chemistry, who could afford much better prospects.

It was fifteen years before Carnegie responded to the need to reinvigorate the academic system; meanwhile he had already set up a pension scheme for the employees of his own steel company. In 1904, on a visit to Carnegie's Scottish castle, Skibo, the President of the Massachusetts Institute of Technology, Henry S. Pritchett, persuaded Carnegie of the benefits of a pension scheme for university professors, that 'might count for a large influence in educational problems.' Carnegie responded a year later with an endowment for $10,000,000, 'to provide retiring pensions...without regard to racc, scx, creed or color'; in the same Deed, with typical farsightedness, Carnegie allowed for sufficient discretion on the part of the Trustees to enable them to adapt to the needs of a changing world—as, even within his own lifetime, they found it necessary to do.

Carnegie's biographer, Professor Wall, observed that,

inadvertently, Carnegie, with his pension plan, had done more in a year to advance the standards of higher education within the United States than probably any carefully conceived program to accomplish that goal could ever have done.

But Carnegie had been canny in guarding against the establishment of a general pension for *all* teachers in higher education, for that would have left his carefully selected Trustees little to do but administer the distribution of funds. As Professor Wall added,

It was Carnegie's strong bias against sectarianism, plus the phrase, in the Deed of Trust, 'under such conditions as you may adopt,' that enabled probably the ablest group of college administrators that could be selected at that time to set standards for higher education.

The Trustees were able to weed out the less desirable institutions from the vast field of potential clients. A questionnaire was sent to 627 colleges of higher education in the United States and Canada, asking for such details as the size of endowment, standards set for admission and graduation, size of the institute in relation to area served, and if it followed any sectarian preference. From the 421 replies, the Board was able to formulate a table of acceptable standards for entry into the pension fund. Only 52 colleges got in.

Not surprisingly, the critics had their field day. The fund was accused of being an intrusion of capitalism into the hallowed realms of academia, just as the fund for the Scottish universities had been accused, four years earlier. Colleges left out of the scheme moaned that the process of selectivity was unfair, while at the same time faculty members who belonged to colleges invited into the scheme but who were personally opposed to Carnegie's ideas howled with injured pride. At least one professor offered his resignation, declaring that, 'Our college cannot serve God and Mammon.' The college accepted his offer.

On the other hand, several colleges rejected their previous sectarian bias in order to qualify for admittance into the scheme, once they saw its advantages. Standards were raised in accordance with the Foundation's criteria, so that colleges belonging to the scheme were gradually able to attract the best young academics, who themselves selected only those colleges which offered the inducement of a pension scheme. The ripples spread with greatly beneficial results throughout the academic institutions.

The effect of higher standards went beyond the colleges; it permeated down to the high schools also. In due course, the Foundation declared that any college that wished to be eligible for acceptance into the pension fund must itself demand fourteen 'units' for entrance to the freshman year. The so-called 'Carnegie Unit' consequently became a commanding feature of every high school's programme; it was a standard, based on time, to measure high school work and so to avoid the confusion that existed among schools as to whether, for example, 'classics' meant ancient history twice at one school or Latin every day at another. A total of 120 hours in one subject (meeting four or five times a week, for forty to sixty minutes, for thirty-six to forty weeks a year) earned for the student one unit of high school credit. The system became a convenient, mechanical way to measure progress throughout the country; it remains the basis on which the school day, indeed the entire curriculum, is organized. Adding up Carnegie units, rather than concentrating on exactly what students should be learning, seems at some schools to be the main objective and an end in itself. The units certainly helped to transform the standards of American education but today, in very different circumstances, the Foundation urges that they be used with some caution.

The Trustees awarded their first 'retiring allowance' to William Harris, the 71-year-old U.S. Commissioner of Education; the word 'pension' was felt to be demeaning. The success of the enterprise, the rapid expansion of higher education and the increase in the number of eligible professors, had not been foreseen. Despite further grants of $5,000,000 between 1911 and 1915, there was simply not enough money to continue the provision of free pensions. Within a decade of its inception, the idea had to be abandoned. The list of institutions whose faculty were entitled to free Carnegie pensions was closed in 1916; although pensions already offered were to be honoured, their size was reduced.

In 1984, there were still 144 free pensions being paid out by the Foundation, from the original free pension list. In 1982-83, only five original free pensioners had died; the five professors were aged respectively 92, 93, 95, 101 and 104. It is anticipated that the Foundation will continue to be paying out free pensions from that list until the year 2001. Carnegie's scheme to give academics a ripe old age in retirement seems to have worked dramatically well! It had, however, already been pointed out that even when professors were poorly paid, in the earliest days of the pension scheme, there had been a problem of longevity; this was attributed by one observer to the inability of the impoverished men to afford carousals in the cities or even to indulge in strong drink or rich food at home.

Despite the closure of the free pensions in 1916, Pritchett, who had become President of the Board, was determined not to lose sight of the scheme altogether. He devised instead a contributory pension plan that would be open to all teachers in all institutions of higher education. The Teachers Insurance and Annuity Association (TIAA) was established in 1918 with an initial subsidy of one million dollars from the Carnegie Corporation. In 1938, TIAA became independent of the Corporation and, in 1952, it launched an affiliated company, the College Retirement Equities Fund (CREF), which offered the first variable annuities based upon the value of equity investments. At the end of 1983, the total assets of both organizations was thirty-one billion dollars; there were more than 3,600 cooperating educational institutions and more than 750,000 individual participants. Further information on TIAA and CREF appears on page ***.

Freed from the burden of the free pension scheme, the Foundation was able to develop the policy of educational studies already initiated by Pritchett before 1916 and for which Carnegie had provided an additional $1,250,000 in 1912. Reading back over the list of publications between 1910 and 1980, the Foundation's interests range through every possible concern of American education. One of the earliest and most influential projects was the Flexner Report on medical education, published in 1910. Abraham Flexner visited every medical school in the United States in order to assess standards and in almost every case he found grave deficiencies; his findings resulted in increased funding from the appropriate authorities and a notable raising of standards. His theme was extended in 1912 to 'Medical Education in Europe.' Six decades later, in 1976, there was a study of 'Progress and Problems in Medical and Dental Education.'

The theme of sport was pursued in 1929 with a study of 'American College Athletics' (including a topical section on the relation of the Press to College sport). 'Current Developments in American College Sport' were again being looked at two years later. Previously, in 1927, there had been a look abroad at 'Games and Sports in British Schools and Universities.' The Foundation has always taken an interest in what is going on outside the United States. In 1926, it studied 'Education in the Maritime Provinces of Canada.' In 1971, the Carnegie Commission was looking into 'Higher Education in Nine Countries.' 'Centers of Learning in Britain, France, Germany and the United States' were under scrutiny in 1977 and in the following year the Carnegie Council made some 'Observations on the Relations between Education and Work in the People's Republic of China.' In 1979 a report came out on 'Education and Youth Unemployment in Japan'; this was followed by similar studies in Mexico, Asia, West Germany, Belgium, Great Britain, Poland, Sweden and Denmark.

The education of minorities has been another continuing concern of the Foundation. In 1924, it was looking at 'Justice and the Poor.' In the 1970s, Carnegie Commission publications included *From Isolation to Mainstream: problems of colleges founded for negroes*; *Between Two Worlds: a profile of negro higher education*; *Escape from the Doll's House: women in graduate and professional school education*; *Women and the Power to Change*; *From Backwater to Mainstream: a profile of Catholic higher education*; *Education and Evangelism: a profile of Protestant colleges*; *The Academic Melting Pot: Catholics and Jews in higher education*.

Engineering was a subject for study in 1918. In 1972, attention turned to 'The Home of Science: the role of the university.' In 1973, there was a report on 'The Rise of the Arts on the American Campus.' And, not surprisingly, in 1975, the subject for discussion was 'Computers and the Learning Process in Higher Education.' The net was spread widely. 'The Student and his Knowledge' was studied in 1938. In the 1970s there were some tough investigations of 'The Great American Degree Machine' and 'Higher Education: who pays? who benefits? who should pay?.' Looking to the future, a report appeared on 'Preserving a Lost Generation: policies to assure a steady flow of young scholars until the year 2000.' One of the most eloquent titles of recent years was 'When Dreams and Heroes Died: a portrait of today's college student.'

Between the 1930s and the 1960s the Foundation went through a period of relative decline. There was a study of the relationship between secondary and higher education which resulted in the first widespread use of machine-scored tests and the work of the Graduate Record Office (1937-47) which developed tests for admission into graduate school. There was also, in 1947, the establishment of the Educational Testing Service, with funding from the Carnegie Corporation. These were not inconsequential achievements but it was in 1967 that the Foundation's activities were revitalized by the formation of the Carnegie Commission on Higher Education.

The job of the Commission was 'to study the future structure and finance of U.S. higher education.' It held thirty-three meetings in twenty-five cities and sponsored more than one hundred books and reports; it was disbanded in 1973 and succeeded by the Carnegie Council on Policy Studies in Higher Education. Between 1967 and 1979, the Foundation and the Corporation together spent roughly $12,000,000 to support both bodies. In *Private Power for the Public Good*, Lagemann wrote:

> If one considers the work of the two groups as continuous, that investment made possible what may have been the longest and broadest survey of higher education ever undertaken in the United States, or, for that matter, anywhere in the world.

On the occasion of the Foundation's seventy-fifth anniversary, Ernest Boyer, the President, considered future programmes and noted that higher education in America was suffering from 'a loss of overall direction, a nagging feeling that it is no longer at the vital center of the nation's work.' He added that, 'Many colleagues now face confusion over goals, reduced support, and an uncertain future.' In conclusion, Boyer's statement called upon American higher education to maintain its academic independence; ironically it was the destruction of that independence that was most feared when Carnegie first announced his plans for the Foundation. Independence, said Boyer, was vital, 'so that higher education's dual role as servant and critic of society may be vigorously protected and advanced.'

In pursuit of this aim, the Foundation published further reports in the 1980s that demonstrated its commitment not only to criticizing existing conditions but also to making specific recommendations for their improvement. 'A Quest for Common Learning' and civic illiteracy were two major issues in 1981. The next year, a report

Ernest L. Boyer, President of the Carnegie Foundation for the Advancement of Teaching

appeared on 'The Control of the Campus'; it proposed a new framework to encourage colleges and universities to govern themselves more effectively and it included forty-five recommendations aimed at protecting campus integrity while providing for public accountability. The report:

> discovered few heroes and few villains. We found few examples of public officials who tried overtly to control the essential functions of colleges and universities. We found stupidity. We found overzealousness. But only rarely did we find outright confrontation over the issues that matter most. In fact it is remarkable that so much public money has been channeled to the nation's public and private campuses with so little interference.... The important issue is where the line is to be drawn between the campus and the state. How can we distinguish trivial inconvenience from genuine interference with higher education's central mission?... Some of the most fearful threats to campus autonomy are found within the academy itself.

In the fall of 1983, the Foundation published its long-awaited *High School* report, by Ernest Boyer, the result of 'thirty months of extensive review, including 2000 hours of observations and interviews in high schools nationwide by a panel of 24 education

143

Headquarters of the Carnegie Foundation for the Advancement of Teaching,
Princeton, New Jersey, USA

advisers.' In the introduction, Boyer pointed to the demands made on the high school by Americans today:

> Today's High School is called upon to provide the services and transmit the values we used to expect from the community and the home and the church. And if they fail anywhere along the line they are condemned. What do the Americans want high schools to accomplish? Quite simply, we want it all.

Boyer noted that in 1982 the nation had invested $126.7 billion tax dollars to finance the biggest, most comprehensive system of public elementary and secondary education on earth; that there were now more people employed full-time in American colleges and universities than in agriculture; and that there were intrinsic dangers in the demographic trends rapidly overtaking the American population. These trends show that by the year 2000, only 34% of all Americans will be under 25 years old, while about 28% will be aged 50 and over. The implicit threat is that there will be less commitment to education when there ought to be more commitment.

This threat, added Boyer, is exacerbated because within the youth population the proportion of black and Hispanic Americans is increasing and it is in this section of the community that historically the education system has had less success. In 1980, slightly less than one-third of all white Americans were 19 years and under but 43% of all Hispanics and about 40% of all blacks fell into this youth category. In 1981 only 52% of all white families had school-age children under 18 years; in contrast, 71% of all black, and 75% of all Hispanic households, had children in this category. The effect of this contrast could be even less commitment by white Americans to the future of public school education. The result could be a further decline in standards. Boyer sees the danger clearly:

> Without good schools none of our problems can be solved. People who cannot communicate are powerless. People who know nothing of their past are culturally impoverished. People who cannot see beyond the confines of their own lives are ill-equipped to face the future. It is in the public school that this nation has chosen to pursue enlightened ends for all its people. And this is where the battle for the future of America will be won or lost.

After exhaustive study and the discovery that the majority of schools were uncertain of their own aims and the aims of education in general, the Report proposed four essential goals for high school education. These proposals were:

(1) To develop the capacity to think critically and communicate effectively through a mastery of the language.
(2) To help all students learn about themselves, the human heritage, and the interdependent world in which they live through a core curriculum based upon consequential human experiences common to all people.
(3) To prepare all students for work and further education through a program of electives that develop individual aptitudes and interests.
(4) To help all students fulfil their social and civic obligations through school and community service.

The common core proposed in (2) included language (English and one foreign language, preferably Spanish, rather than French), history, civics, science, mathematics, technology, health, seminars on work, and a senior independent project. Twelve key strategies were identified by the Report; they included these proposals, as well as clear goals, better teachers, improved instruction, effective use of technology, flexible school patterns, strong leadership, connections with colleges and with corporations, and a renewed public commitment to the nation's schools. Boyer summed up the importance of his message:

> The success or failure of the American high school will determine the quality of our democracy, the strength of our economy, the security of our defense, and the promise of our ideals.... If we value our country and our heritage, we must invest in our children.... James Agee once wrote: 'In every child who is born...the potentiality of the human race is born again.'

Determined to follow up the proposals by concrete action, the Foundation immediately sponsored a grants programme for high school improvement, administered by the National Association of High School Principals and funded by the Atlantic Richfield Foundation. In November 1983 applications were solicited from 16,000 high schools to redesign their curriculum based on the Carnegie recommendations. 'Clearly the time has come for action at the school level,' said Boyer. 'We do not need more education reports. We need principals and teachers, parents and concerned citizens, working together to build school quality and to help regain the nation's confidence in the public school enterprise.'

Nearly 1,700 schools applied for a Carnegie grant and about 200 received one, each of about $3,000, to a total of $575,414. Projects ranged from a new course to give students

Recent publications of the Carnegie Foundation for the Advancement of Teaching

credit for volunteer service, to a 'cadet' science teacher programme to train twenty-five students to assist in the teaching of elementary-level science lessons, to the first step toward the development of a foreign school exchange programme, to a study in depth of the USSR, and the preservation of history by the interviewing of participants in history. The Carnegie grants programme includes a second phase of larger grants, which began in the fall of 1984, to be used during a three-year period by a smaller group of high schools. These grants range from $35,000 to $50,000 each. 'Our grants,' said Boyer, 'will help advance school reform where it must take place to be successful—at the school and in the classroom.'

The Foundation continues to support projects and studies in higher education; it has also launched a major two year study of education at the undergraduate level. At the same time, it finds itself under increasing pressure to undertake studies of education in the early years of life, before secondary school. This extension down the age range is obviously of considerable importance to the healthy development of American education and will itself have an effect on secondary and higher education in the nation.

By creating the Foundation, Carnegie contributed to the dignity of the educational profession and hastened the time when retirement systems became virtually universal in American colleges and universities; by so doing, he also improved standards. At the same time, by supporting independent studies of American education practices and policies, Boyer considers that Carnegie launched a tradition that is now the earmark of the Foundation:

> We do not take this lightly. The Foundation is a unique institution. More than any other organization it is in a position to address education issues as an informed, concerned, and totally independent friend. In that position, we seek to confront significant policy issues in education, help share the debate, and enhance the quality of the nation's colleges and schools. This means that there will be debate and difference of opinion—as there always have been when the Foundation has tackled topics that really matter. At the same time, our position and our tradition impose on us an obligation to conduct our work carefully so that we can retain the trust we have come to enjoy through our illustrious 75-year history.

Boyer's conclusion is very practical. It reflects Carnegie's own concern with the practicality of education. But nothing in the down-to-earth philosophy of either man diminishes the high principles and hazardous future that are at stake. Boyer writes:

> Our policy also requires that we make a positive difference. Writing is not enough. We must become involved, or, as the trustees put it, we must move from thought to action. This means not only making studies and reporting our conclusions, but making sure that our findings and suggestions find their way into the deliberations of those who are directly engaged in shaping policy. Nothing has changed our attitude toward this function—except, perhaps, that we are increasingly aware of the almost awesome responsibility it entails.

TEACHERS INSURANCE AND ANNUITY ASSOCIATION
(TIAA)
COLLEGE RETIREMENT EQUITIES FUND
(CREF)

Carnegie established the Carnegie Foundation for the Advancement of Teaching primarily to provide free pensions for professors at nearly one hundred American colleges and universities, in order 'to remove a source of deep and constant anxiety to the poorest paid and yet one of the highest of all professions.' This was the first private pension scheme to offer portable pensions that could be taken with the teacher from one employer to the next. When it became clear that the original $15,000,000 gift would quickly run out, the Foundation and the Carnegie Corporation established TIAA, in 1918, to create contributory pensions. The principle of Carnegie money providing the initiative for self-help was in line with his own philosophy as manifested in several of his other trusts.

After a period of slow growth during the Great Depression, and receipt from the Foundation and the Corporation of $17,000,000 in support over the first twenty years, TIAA became independent in 1938. Its great period of growth was after 1946, with the vast expansion of higher education in America. Before the war, there were 191 member colleges and universities; by 1949, ten years later, there were 366 cooperating institutions and $270,000,000 of assets. But the problems of inflation were eating into savings. To tackle this, CREF was created in 1952—the first variable annuity company.

Like TIAA, this was a non-profit company that provided exactly the same kind of portable, fully-funded, fully-vested, contractual annuities but the level of annuity income was based on the changing values and dividend income of common stocks. A teacher could thereby have part of his pension fund directly related to the state of the economy. There were those who complained at first that equities were 'too risky' for pension investments for college professors who did not have much leeway in their budgets; the answer was that bond and mortgage investments and fixed-dollar annuities had their own risks also—they could be seriously hurt by inflation. The new fund, allied to TIAA, offered investment diversification. In 1956-57, with the help of $5,000,000 from the Ford Foundation, TIAA added major medical and total disability insurance to its offerings; it now has a variety of 'packages' to offer for pension benefits.

The Carnegie pension plans proved to be leaders in their field. The imaginative action of the Corporation and the Foundation in establishing TIAA preceded the establishment of the Federal Social Security system by almost twenty years. Then again, in 1965, the President's Committee on Corporate Pension Funds and other Private Retirement and Welfare Programs recommended that principles similar to those provided by TIAA for nearly fifty years should be incorporated into all private pension plans in business and industry. TIAA and CREF are still in the vanguard of pension development. Federal laws are forcing private pensions toward the TIAA-CREF pattern, and corporations and governments are voluntarily moving in that direction. Retired chairman William Greenough comments that 'We are, during the late 1980s, moving strongly towards retirement security in the United States and around the world for all working people.'

In the last year of his life, in 1919, Carnegie asked often about the progress of his 'little insurance company.' Arising from the free pension scheme of the Foundation, TIAA and CREF have now grown into what is probably the largest single private pension system in the world, with total assets at the end of 1983 of thirty-one billion dollars, with more than 3,600 cooperating educational institutions, and with more than 750,000 participants accumulating annuity benefits and another 128,000 receiving annuity income benefits. Both TIAA and CREF have been doubling in size every four-and-a-half years; it appears that they will continue to do for some time to come.

There is, meanwhile, another perspective on TIAA-CREF, beyond the provision of benefits to members of educational institutions. William Greenough views that other aspect with a simple question and provides the answer:

Where in the world will TIAA invest the huge funds being saved for college staff member retirements? Perhaps the phrasing of the question answers itself—in the world. More than $1.5 billion of CREF's $14.7 billion in assets is now invested in fourteen countries overseas, including Great Britain and other western countries, and Japan, Australia, and other Pacific basin countries. Very little of TIAA's funds are so invested at present, but coming years should see increasing international investments. Meanwhile TIAA has become one of the top two or three shopping center investors, as well as a large investor in downtown real estate property in America. It has been especially active in direct-placement loans to medium-sized businesses. TIAA and CREF's huge size and rapid growth will produce a great challenge for future investments.

Carnegie established his original pension plan from the profits of American steel; it is curious to speculate whether he could ever have envisaged that the subsequent capital would be so vastly greater than his own fortune or that it would be reinvested to such an extent not only in the economy of the United States but also in the economy of the world to help boost quite different industries. Carnegie was well aware of the changing nature of society and the continual need for flexibility, so the answer might well be that he would, at least, not have been at all surprised.

Teachers Insurance and Annuity Association (TIAA)
College Retirement Equities Fund (CREF)

Founded: 1918 (TIAA) and 1952 (CREF); independent 1938

Purpose: The provision of contributory pension plans for institutions of higher education, private schools, and related non profit scientific and research organizations; in addition, TIAA provides individual life insurance to employees of these organizations, and group insurance plans for educational employers including total disability benefits, major medical expenses and collective life insurance.

Finance:

Original grant from Carnegie Corporation:	$1,000,000
Additional funds by CFAT and Corporation:	$17,000,000
Current assets, to end 1983, TIAA:	$16,143,856,346
CREF:	$14,717,626,810
Income, 1983 (premiums and investment), TIAA:	$4,042,789,693
CREF:	$1,433,180,957
Distribution, 1983, TIAA:	
Benefits and dividends:	$1,502,420,911
Set aside for future benefits:	$2,486,434,841
Distribution, 1983, CREF:	
Benefits:	$193,199,144
CREF-TIAA transfers:	$311,382,599
*Total benefits and Dividends paid, 1918-83, TIAA:	$8,704,500,000
1952-83, CREF:	$1,175,800,000
	$9,880,300,000

* Aggregate total in then-current dollars; not adjusted for inflation over the years.

Beneficiaries (TIAA and CREF):

Institutions with TIAA-CREF retirement plans:	3,500
Participants accumulating future retirement income:	750,000
Participants currently receiving annuity income:	128,000

Administration:
Chairman and Chief Executive Officer: James G. Macdonald
President: Walter G. Ehlers
Employees (TIAA and CREF): 2,200
Address: 730 Third Avenue, New York, NY 10017

CARNEGIE CORPORATION OF NEW YORK

Carnegie's enthusiasm for education, whether social or scholarly, scientific or popular, for research or recreation, was largely expended by the end of 1905 but his fortune was not. For the next few years he turned his attention increasingly to plans for peace and the education of policymakers and the public in this direction (see page 213) but his rate of giving slowed down below the rate at which interest on his capital accrued; he still had more than $150,000,000 remaining by 1910 and he was getting weary. In 1911, he set up a general trust that was intended to relieve him of the responsibility for distributing his own wealth—in fact he ran it, essentially single-handed; at the same time it gave him the satisfaction of seeing his money put to good use during his lifetime. The Carnegie Corporation was ultimately endowed with more than $135,000,000.

It was founded to 'promote the advancement and diffusion of knowledge and understanding among the people of the United States (and subsequently among specific countries that were British Colonies) by aiding technical schools, institutions of higher lerning (*sic*), libraries, scientific research, hero funds, useful publications, and by such other agencies and means as shall from time to time be found appropriate.' These aims have mostly been adhered to, though good use has been made of the freedom and flexibility allowed by the charter to adapt to each generation's most important educational needs.

Large sums of Corporation money have in the past gone to support most of the other major American Carnegie foundations and the Corporation still helps occasionally to finance other Carnegie programmes but this is not a prime purpose. It has now evolved into a specialist source of funding for research and education throughout the United States and much of the English-speaking world. Certain projects originate from the Corporation but many grants are made in response to proposals submitted by universities and other institutions and organizations in line with the current priorities established by the foundation.

Projects supported range from J. K. Galbraith's *The Affluent Society* to the present *Second Carnegie Inquiry into Poverty and Development in Southern Africa*. In recent years, the Corporation has concerned itself particularly with the education and welfare of children and minority groups. The highly successful *Sesame Street* programme; a 'Defense Fund' for the rights of children to education, welfare and health; a report on family pressures and their effect on children; advocacy for children in New York; the educational rights of Navajo Indians and Puerto Ricans—all these have been supported by the Corporation, along with equal rights for women in education, government and the unions, and the education of blacks and whites on their legal rights and the administration of the law in South Africa.

The Corporation's current programme concentrates on four issues: the avoidance of nuclear war, education in science and technology, the prevention of damage to children, and the strengthening of human resources in developing countries. The President of the

151

Corporation sums up his aims as follows: 'to foster conditions under which young people everywhere may get a decent start in life, to deepen understanding of the rapidly changing world we live in, and to advance the cause of peaceful international relations.' This work represents an imaginative and practical development of Carnegie's central themes.

Carnegie Corporation of New York

Founded: 1911

Purpose: The advancement and diffusion of knowledge and understanding among the people of the United States and of the British Dominions and Colonies.

Finance:

Original endowment:	$25,000,000
Additional endowments: January 1912:	$75,000,000
October 1912:	$25,000,000
From Carnegie's will, 1919:	$10,336,867.89
	$135,336,867.89

Current portfolio value (September 1984): $500,000,000

Annual monies in recent years:	*Income*	*Expenditure*
1983:	$27,170,000	$17,153,000
1984:	$30,986,000	$23,766,000
1985 (estimated):	$33,000,000	$27,500,000

Total portfolio income, 1911-1983/84:	$660,115,484
Total portfolio gains, 1911-1983/84:	$272,638,078
Total appropriations, less cancellations:	$561,751,749
Other gifts (such as, to CFAT and TIAA):	$37,603,957

Expenditure on educational endeavours in some of the countries that are or have been members of the British overseas Commonwealth: approx 7.4% of total expenditure.

Programme expenditures, 1983-84

Avoiding Nuclear War:	$4,972,771
Education: Science, Technology and the Economy:	$4,193,020
Prevention of Damage to Children:	$2,565,650
Strengthening Human Resources in Developing Countries:	$1,359,895
Higher Education:	$2,095,150
Public Affairs:	$2,597,000
Miscellaneous:	$2,170,850
	$19,954,336

Carnegie Corporation of New York

How to rid oneself of money is not a problem many of us face but, after ten years of philanthropic energy, Andrew Carnegie was running out of ideas and enthusiasm. By 1910, he had already established eight major institutions and a number of smaller ones; he had given away $180,000,000 but the interest on his bonds at a healthy five percent, which brought him in anything between $10 and $15 million a year, kept gaining on the dispersal of those bonds and by 1910 he had at least $150,000,000 left. He had been working fast but not fast enough in handing out his fortune.

'You have had the best run for your money I have ever known,' said his friend, Secretary of State Elihu Root, when Carnegie was feeling at his lowest. Carnegie replied that he would die in disgrace, for he could not possibly get rid of all his wealth in the few years that were left to him. Root had a simple solution. He advised Carnegie to transfer the bulk of his fortune into a single fund for others to distribute, so that he could die happy and in a state of grace.

It was thus that the Corporation came into being—the largest single permanent philanthropic trust ever recorded at that time, with a capital endowment of $125,000,000 and a further $10,000,000 to come under the terms of Carnegie's will. It became one of the most successful and prestigious foundations of its kind, and it now has a portfolio that is greater than the sum of the total sale of the original Carnegie Company; the amount of money it has expended since its inception is $100,000,000 *more* than that sale.

Established for 'the advancement and diffusion of knowledge and understanding among the peoples of the United States,' the Charter of the Corporation included Canada and what were the British Colonies in 1917. The portion of the endowment that could be used for the latter was subsequently fixed at 7.4%. For the first eight years, Carnegie himself was President; five of the Trustees were the presidents of the five other major trusts founded by Carnegie in the United States. The Charter makes provision for a flexible approach to the Corporation's task but in its early years Carnegie's own views naturally shaped its programme; gifts for the construction of public libraries and the purchase of church organs were just such features.

The Board of the Carnegie Corporation at its founding in 1911
with Mrs Carnegie and her daughter Margaret

The concept of change was important, however. It was Carnegie's express wish that the endowment should not be hidebound by any unnecessary strictures and he was well aware that changing social conditions would necessitate corresponding changes in the way in which the Corporation would be administered:

> I give my trustees full authority [he wrote] to change policy or causes hitherto aided, from time to time, when this, in their opinion becomes necessary or desirable. They shall best conform to my wishes by using their own judgment.

He concluded his Trust Deed with these words:

> My chief happiness as I write these lines lies in the thot that even after I pass away the welth that came to me to administer as a sacred trust for the good of my fellow men is to continue to benefit humanity for generations untold.

The Corporation established the pattern of its support for educational and scientific research in the 1920s, when it also began to publish the work of professional and scholarly societies and associations. Since then, J. K. Galbraith's *The Affluent Society* and

154

Andrew Carnegie from a portrait by F. Luis Mora. Reproductions
of this portrait in colour were distributed to Carnegie Libraries as
part of the Centenary celebrations, November 25, 1935.

Riesman's *The Lonely Crowd* have both arisen from Corporation grants, as did Gunnar Myrdal's celebrated study of the American Negro in the 1930s, which resulted in the famous book, *An American Dilemma*. More recent publications have included such titles as *Race Discrimination in South Africa* and *The Teaching of Ethics in the Military*, or *Building Self-Esteem through the Writing Process* and *Out of the Bleachers—Writings on Women in Sport*, or *A World of Children* and *Quangos in Britain*.

In 1924, the Corporation began a series of surveys to discover what educational opportunities existed for adults; the American Association for Adult Education was set up with a supporting grant from the Corporation. Grants were made to the American Federation of Arts to encourage community art programmes. Help was given to such organizations as the National Academy of Design, the Art Students' League, the Community Arts Association, the American Institute of Architects, the Federated Council on Art Education, and the American Academy in Rome. Support was also given to national music organizations and a scheme was funded to provide materials for the study of music in colleges.

In its early days, the Corporation gave support to several major institutions that were pursuing programmes related to the aims of the Corporation itself: the National Academy of Sciences, the New York Academy of Medicine, the Brookings Institution of Washington, the American Law Institute, the California Institute of Technology and the Food Research Institute at Stanford University were among the recipients of Carnegie money. The Corporation has also assisted the other Carnegie foundations when funds have proved insufficient to their needs; some of this assistance has been in the form of single grants of substantial size, in other cases it has been in the form of long-term support. The Institute in Pittsburgh, the original Institute of Technology (now Carnegie-Mellon University), the Endowment for International Peace, the Institution of Washington, the Foundation for the Advancement of Teaching, have all received funds from the Corporation.

Between 1911 and the late 1920s, the Corporation spent $10,000,000 throughout the British Empire (more than half of that sum in Canada). Help was given to colleges and universities, libraries, museums, scientific institutions and special research projects, such as the study of the 'Poor White' problem in South Africa (published in 1932) and the study of insect pests in the British West Indies, or the publication of archive material in British Honduras and surveys of public education in the West Indies.

In 1959, John Gardner, then President of the Corporation, looked back after nearly fifty years of varied work and changes and tried to assess the problems that such a foundation naturally encountered and the contributions it could make to society. The fundamental purpose of such a foundation, he wrote, was 'to attack the causes of mankind's woes rather than providing the immediate relief of the trouble.' He referred particularly to the concept of 'venture capital' wherewith such foundations can afford to risk money on the gifted mind which may come up with new solutions to old or immediate problems. He recognized that the Corporation was in a peculiarly good position to take such risks, because it was not under constant pressure to produce urgent, tangible results in the way that a government agency has to produce them, nor were its funds committed to important long-term operations in the way that college and university funds are often committed.

The problem for the Corporation was how best to spend its relatively few dollars (at that time, about one-tenth of one percent of the total annual American philanthropic giving) to accomplish the greatest possible long-term benefit. It was obvious that, within the field of education, to which the Corporation was devoted, there had to be some emphasis on particular aspects of that enormous field; at the same time, it was sensible, as Carnegie had allowed, for the Corporation to shift that emphasis from time to time. The length of support in any area can vary considerably, from weeks to years.

Gardner stressed the importance of the individual. He wrote:

> The important advances in knowledge, the significant improvements in practice, the kinds of innovation which ought to interest foundations are made by individuals.

Grants, he added, should be based upon the quality of the individual. 'Find the good men and back them!' was the epitome of Carnegie's own philosophy. But the Corporation sought to support the individual usually through programmes administered by organizations in the various fields. The bulk of Corporation money is spent through colleges and universities. Staff members seeking to assess requests for grants (there are twenty times more requests each year than the Corporation can satisfy) must keep in touch with the academic world as well as the practical world, 'to identify the critical issues in any one field, the significant new ideas, the promising young people,' and for this the staff need 'a close and frank relationship with the ablest individuals in that field.' Corporation support for the reshaping of the mathematics curriculum in secondary schools in the 1950s was the result of exactly this kind of forward analysis and identification of a growing concern for such a need among academics and teachers, carefully researched by staff members.

Another former President, Frederick Keppel, summed up his own view of the ideal circumstances in which a foundation like the Corporation could take action; it would need, he said:

> To have the idea, the man, and the setting, in perfect conjunction: the idea, vital and timely; the scholar or executive, at the peak of his powers; and the organization at flood tide.

Keppel called these circumstances 'a favourable conjunction of the stars.' Commenting on this, Gardner said, 'What we pray for is the good luck to encounter such circumstances and the good sense to recognize them when we do.'

Freedom and flexibility have always been of fundamental importance to the Corporation. The principal intention of the endowment was that it should be a 'liquid asset' for each generation. This is one of the main answers to those who say that it would do better to give its money to something like cancer research. If it did that, its funds would be committed, like any conventional non-profit institution; nothing would be left for experiment and for new paths. Instead, the Corporation keeps 'free funds' for just this purpose, to act quickly and imaginatively to support individuals and ideas. Inevitably, this involves some risk and must leave many worthwhile things undone. As Gardner wrote:

> The bright new idea may prove to have more novelty than validity; the 'pioneering' venture may bog down; the research program may yield negative results, but foundations which engage in support of such efforts must be prepared to take these chances. It is in this sense that they regard their funds as 'venture capital.'

Not surprisingly, the Corporation has sometimes been accused of taking too much risk and sometimes of not taking enough risk, but all in all Gardner's conclusion was that:

> If one bets on able men and women, it is surprising how often genuinely significant and constructive results occur either in the short or long run.

To strengthen and extend these 'bets,' there have been a number of recent changes in the Corporation. For example, since 1969, foundations in the United States have been able to make programme-related investments (PRI). This method of funding, in the form of a loan, loan guarantee, or equity investment, can be used to support a philanthropic undertaking that may generate income in the future. In 1978, the Trustees approved a plan to make PRIs for institutions or projects that might otherwise qualify for a direct grant. Another change has been that, in 1971, the Corporation changed its charter to permit expenditure of accumulated capital gains in order to conform with federal tax laws; until then, only the income from the fund could be used for grants and administrative expenses, while the value of the fund grew to about $300,000,000 in that year.

There is less change in the way in which the grants are given. The majority still go to academic institutions which in turn administer them for individual projects. A large proportion of the staff of the Corporation are therefore recruited from these institutions. Once a proposal has been accepted initially, a formal document is discussed among the Corporation staff and its intrinsic value is compared and assessed in relation to programmes already in hand. Grants of $25,000 or less may be made at staff level, 'at the discretion of the President,' but others are taken before the Trustees. Once a grant is given, reports on progress are required by the Corporation.

A Program Development and Evaluation Fund provides a source with which staff officers can explore potential new programmes and call for outside evaluations of projects supported by the Corporation. The fund also allows them to follow up grant commitments with objective reviews of what has been learned. A Dissemination Fund exists to provide for the completion of books and other publications that emerge from projects and to ensure their widespread promotion and distribution, making the most of the Corporation's 'investment.'

What is the Corporation betting on today, with its 'venture capital'? In the 1983 Annual Report, Corporation President David Hamburg described the new programme

Sesame Street's cast of human and muppet favourites

directions and reiterated the Corporation's fundamental commitment to 'education, peace and social justice.' In identifying these areas of concern, Hamburg reinforced and developed themes already given substantial support by his predecessor, Alan Pifer, who is also a former President of the Carnegie Foundation for the Advancement of Teaching. These themes readily become apparent, taking just a few examples of grant-funding over the last ten years or so.

In the educational field, perhaps the Corporation's most spectacular success has been through its backing of the Children's Television Workshop, creator of *Sesame Street*, a programme for pre-school children that is now world famous. It was in 1966 that the Corporation enabled Mrs Joan Ganz Cooney to undertake a feasibility study for a television programme to teach some simple and some more complex cognitive skills to pre-schoolers; the Corporation also made larger grants later for research and production. In 1968, CTW undertook its experiment in using mass media technologies and techniques to reach and teach large segments of the pre-school population.

The initial target audience was the twelve million American pre-school children between the ages of three and six; the purpose was 'to teach them the beginnings of language and reading, numerical skills, reasoning and problem-solving, awareness of self and the world around, and social, moral and effective development.' These aims were the result of identifying several urgent needs: the importance of early learning; the poor schooling available in many disadvantaged areas; the knowledge that for poor children television is most often their only continuing window on the world. Initial assessment of the first *Sesame Street* programmes in 1970 showed that they were achieving their aims—the more children watched, the more they learned. CTW estimated that it cost less than a penny per child per day to show *Sesame Street*—something of a bargain!

Fifteen years on, the programme remains the focus of the now incorporated CTW's production efforts, with two showings daily on more than 300 stations in the United States. Gradually the curriculum has been expanded to include a number of skills, cultures and life-styles; regular inclusion of themes relating to disabled children has broadened the character, sensitivity and effectiveness of the programme. Safety messages, print literacy, preparation for school, listening and following directions, sound-pattern discrimination, pre-reading, computers, fire safety, writing, vocabulary and death have all been added to the curriculum list in the last five years. The series has built and maintains a regular audience of more than nine million children under the age of six. Many of its first viewers have now graduated from high school and are working or in college. Big Bird and Cookie Monster are moving toward a second generation of fans.

Sesame Street is often called 'the longest street in the world,' for since 1970 it has been shown in more than ninety countries and territories, either in its original English language form or in one of a dozen locally produced foreign language versions which are individually tailored to the needs and interests of viewers and which reflect the flavour and culture of each country. The first US-China co-production, which was broadcast in the US on primetime by NBC-TV and also seen throughout China on the national network, was a ninety-minute special starring *Big Bird in China*.

The Electric Company followed CTW's first success up the age range; it was designed to help teach certain reading skills to seven-to-ten year olds. Production on the series ended in 1977 after 780 half-hour episodes had been made, but the series is still being broadcast and is now in its fourteenth year; it remains the most widely viewed TV series in US classrooms. A large number of pre-schoolers watch the show as well. A study in 1983 by the Corporation for Public Broadcasting estimated that more than 100,000 teachers use the series and that more than 3,000,000 students watch it in school.

Road shows and concerts, computer software and community education services reinforce the messages of CTW. Product licensing and magazine publishing help to finance new projects. In 1984, CTW's operating budget was more then $57,000,000. One of its latest projects is a magazine, *Enter*, about computers for the ten-to-sixteen age market; more important is the production of forty new half-hour episodes of *3-2-1 Contact*, the second season of a daily series which introduces science and technology to the eight-to-twelve age range at home and in school. Preliminary development is also in hand on a proposed new daily series on mathematics for eight-to-twelve year olds.

Television has received attention from the Corporation in another way through support for ACT, *Action for Children's Television*. Credit for ACT goes to Peggy Charren, who in 1968 invited some neighbours to her home to discuss what they might do to cut down on what she described as 'wall-to-wall monster cartoons.' Her youngest daughter was three years old and she figured she had two years to fix up television before her daughter went to school and she went back to work. The statistics she produced are depressing: pre-schoolers spend more waking hours watching television than on any other activity; by the time they reach eighteen, they will have logged 15,000 hours in front of television compared to 11,000 hours in school. Much of the credit must go to Charren and her colleagues for the vigour and resourcefulness with which groups around the country began work to improve children's television and, in the process, to educate parents to its negative and positive power over the young.

A third television scheme given support by the Corporation, in 1982-83, has been *Twin Cities Public Television* in Minneapolis and St Paul, and the development of a series of seven documentary programmes entitled *Your Children, My Children* for national broadcast. The programmes examine important questions concerning children and their relationships with society, their parents and each other, to be followed by local and regional radio call-ins; a book is also released with the series. The aim is to help parents become active on their children's behalf in their own communities.

The pre-school field has been important for the Corporation in a number of ways. For example, grant aid was given to the *Mother-Child Home Program*, begun in the late 1960s and continued successfully throughout the 1970s. This home-based programme was developed with low-income, mainly welfare families by a psychologist and her staff at the Verbal Interaction Project (VIP) in Freeport, Long Island, using incentives to build on the emotional bond between mother and child to encourage their verbal interaction at a very early stage. Significant IQ gains for educationally disadvantaged children and higher academic achievement scores in school were among the proven results of the project. The director of the project also identified an interesting outcome of the programme:

> The child who is interested and ready to learn gets a better response from the school system. In that way, we can say that the child who has been through our program influences the behaviour of the teacher. It is only human to pay attention to the child who is responding to you.

The children's school performance and the performance of the school have therefore both improved side by side.

The Children's Foundation was founded in 1969, only shortly after MCHP, 'to develop, implement, and monitor food programs for children and their mothers living in poverty.' Recently it has expanded its activities to encompass related issues such as the need for day care and other support services for households headed by women. In 1983, the Corporation provided a grant for the foundation's family day-care project—officially, 'non-residential child care provided in a private home other than the child's own,' which distinguishes it from day care in a centre, nursery school or other family group. There are more than 20,000,000 children in the United States who spend from ten to thirty hours per week in family day-care homes, and there is a pressing need to upgrade family day-care and to reform regulations that tend to limit its availability.

Pre-school Corporation support in 1983 also went to the *Children's Museum* in Boston, which since 1913 has been a pioneering learning centre for children and their families. The museum has used previous Corporation support to install *Playspace*, an environment that encourages parents to observe their pre-school children in a variety of activities, provides opportunities to discuss their observations with other parents and staff, and offers resources for further learning about children and their development. Hospitals, clinics, prisons and other museums have expressed interest in the model, and a handbook is being produced by the organisers. The latest Corporation grant was to enable *Playspace* to be replicated in four locations within the United States, and for information about it to be widely disseminated.

With concern for working mothers of young children, a grant went to the *Conference Board*, an international business research organization, to assist it in forming a 'Work and Family Information Center,' to involve employers in solving the problems faced by working parents. Concern for the children likewise persuaded the Corporation to provide a three-year grant of $1,000,000 to the *Children's Defense Fund* (CDF). This fund is dedicated to helping policymakers, social agencies and other institutions understand and address the various conditions surrounding the lives of American children: the right to education, child health, child welfare, child care and family support, housing for families with children, and mental health. In each of these six areas, CDF has documented problems affecting large numbers of children, outlined remedies, and worked with the media, with networks of advocacy groups, and with government officials to place the needs of children and their families higher on the nation's public policy agenda. Among CDF's new projects are state and local action kits designed to assist individuals and organizations concerned with children in dealing with the effects of federal budget cuts on programmes in their communities.

The Corporation had already made grants totalling $2,100,000 for CDF activities since 1969. The need for a fund to 'defend' children grew out of the pervasive discrimination and shortcomings of the schools, out of statistics on children's health and infant mortality, out of the arbitrary and self-defeating practices of the juvenile justice system, and out of the wholly inadequate and limited day-care facilities, all of which told a story most people did not want to hear and certainly did not wish to act upon. The Fund's first report, *Children Out of School in America*, shattered the prevailing belief in 1973 that all children who ought to go to school were in fact in school. CDF's second report looked at school suspension and revealed how education, an essential ingredient for success in this society, was arbitrarily denied many children. The report stated that more than 1,000,000 children were suspended one or more times during the 1972-73 school year in school districts which enrolled better than half the nation's students. That represented one out of every twenty-four students; for black secondary-school children, the suspension rate was one out of eight students.

The Carnegie Council on Children, established in 1972 as an independent study group to explore what American society was doing to and for its young, produced in 1977 a publication entitled *All Our Children: the American Family Under Pressure*, which investigated the social, financial, working, health and legal pressures, among others, on the family, and the effect on the children. The book picked up many alarming statistics: for example, four out of every ten children born in the 1970s spent part of their childhood in a one-parent family, usually with their mother as head of the household. More than that, the book pinpointed 'the sense of not being in control as parents, and the widespread sense of personal guilt for what seems to be going awry.' As the Council expressed it in 1977:

> American parents today are worried and uncertain about how to bring up children. They feel unclear about the proper balance between permissiveness and firmness. They fear they are neglecting their children, yet sometimes resent the demands their children make. Americans wonder whether they are doing a good job as parents, yet are unable to define what a good job is. In droves, they seek expert advice. And many parents wonder whether they ought to have children at all.

Probing beyond the family, into the realm of education and social justice, the Corporation has made grants to a number of minority interests in recent years. Between 1979 and 1984, nearly $450,000 has gone to *Advocates for Children in New York* (AFC), to provide training and advocacy to safeguard the educational rights of handicapped or disadvantaged children in the New York City school system. In Colorado, Corporation support helped the *Chicano Education Project* in Denver, which started on a shoestring in 1973 and grew rapidly in its efforts to bring about equal education for Mexican-American children. The project developed in protest at the complete and complacent discrimination against Colorado's 83,000 Spanish-speaking public school children (about 15% of the total enrolment), which was causing widespread misery and a drop-out rate of 34%, or double the rate for Anglo-Americans.

Teachers in Colorado invariably found ways to humiliate the Chicanos. One was reported to have stood at the classroom door and sprayed Chicano children with perfume, 'because they smell,' as she explained to a visitor. Another made a girl stand in the corner for saying something in Spanish; the girl had only said, 'I don't understand.' Similar discrimination was practised against Navajo Indian children, with equally disastrous results both for their education and for their culture.

Reports indicated that many Indian children growing up in the 1950s and 1960s suffered from the official policy of the government which was still to 'acculturate' Native American life, using education as a weapon against Indian culture. Between 1967 and 1977, the Corporation gave grant aid of nearly $2,000,000 for projects planned and run mostly by Indians themselves, primarily to improve the education of Native Americans and to develop the field of Indian law. In 1983, the Corporation was still giving grants to the *Native American Rights Fund* to protect tribal resources, promote human rights, ensure the accountability of government to Native Americans and advance Indian law.

Continuing this theme, another 1983 grant went to the *Puerto Rican Legal Defense and Education Fund*, established in 1972 to protect the civil rights of the 2,000,000 Puerto Ricans then living in the continental United States and to increase the number of Puerto Rican attorneys in the country. Four previous Corporation grants to a total of nearly $1,000,000 have assisted the fund and have contributed to a project dedicated to ensuring that schools fulfil their responsibility to Hispanic students. Further grant aid for 1983-84 went to improve social, economic and political conditions for Puerto Ricans. Corporation support for minority law students was reflected in similar, earlier support to increase the number of black lawyers in the South, for which about $1,000,000 was given between 1968 and 1974.

Moving from race and colour to sex equality, the Corporation gave a two-year grant in mid-1977 to PEER, or the *Project on Equal Education Rights*, established to keep an eagle eye on enforcement of Title IX of the Federal Education Amendments 1972:

> No person in the United States shall, on the basis of sex be excluded from participation in, be denied the benefits of, or be subjected to discrimination under, any education program or activity receiving federal financial assistance.

This hard-won amendment made it illegal for public schools and most colleges and universities to discriminate against either sex in anything from admissions and athletic programmes to recruitment and benefits of janitors and teachers alike, but a 1977 report, aptly entitled *Stalled at the Start*, bluntly characterized the government's enforcement programme as 'lackadaisical' and its accomplishments in combatting sex bias as 'negligible.'

In 1982-83, a recoverable grant helped to pay for the first printing by the Feminist Press of *Everywoman's Guide to College and Universities*, a directory for prospective women students on topics ranging from academic programmes to the availability of day-care for children on or near the campus.

Taking women's rights a step further, another 1982-83 grant went to the *Center for Women in Government*, established in 1978 with the goal of improving the status of women in public employment; a grant was also given to the *Coalition of Labor Union Women*, founded in 1974, to increase participation by women in their unions. In 1981, one out of every four American union members was female but women held only seven to twelve percent of the elective and appointive positions within their unions. Grant aid also went to Rutgers University for the *Center for the American Woman and Politics*, for a national forum open to more than 1,000 women who now serve in state legislatures, to consider how they might organize themselves around issues of concern to women across state and party lines. *The National Council for Research on Women* also received support from the Corporation to help its programmes for improving conditions affecting women's lives. The desire to improve the rights and status of women has also been reflected in the Corporation's International Program, where grant aid has gone to a major research project on the conditions and experiences of women in the Caribbean.

Carnegie believed devoutly that peace and education go hand in hand, and more than one of his endowments stemmed from this faith. Special attention in recent years has been given to educational projects that support peaceful change in southern Africa. In the Republic of South Africa itself, the emphasis has been on developing and supporting black leadership, encouraging communication among racial groups, and increasing the protection of all citizens under the law. In Zimbabwe, priority has gone to educational needs accompanying the transition to majority rule.

An ambitious project in Kenya and Nigeria during the 1960s called for the creation of a worldwide network of research centres dedicated to the comparative study of child development. By setting up western patterns of child-rearing (and the social conditions which appear to produce them) in non-western cultures and then comparing the findings, anthropologists hoped to discover the universal principles of human behaviour, within which variations might be explained. After much hard work, the *Cross-Cultural Study in Child Psychology* came up against the insuperable difficulties presented by having such a diverse set of partners in the enterprise. 'In the end,' said Corporation President Alan Pifer, 'it is probably folly to think that outsiders can alone determine what another country needs—in scholarship or anything else.' On the other hand, the Kenyans are using the research experience they gained in the enterprise to improve the education system in their country—an important residual benefit.

Support in South Africa has gone to the *Centre for Applied Legal Studies*, to further education among blacks and whites on the way in which the law is being administered. 'Is there anything the law in South Africa can do for a person who is about to be evicted from his home or expelled from the city of Johannesburg because of his race, or who is detained incommunicado by the police without charge or trial?' By asking questions like this, the Centre aims to show that in fact the law, if justly administered, can sometimes be used to protect blacks from systematic oppression. The ultimate aim is to keep alive within the hearts and minds of South Africans the ideals of liberty and equality, and to build public support for the amelioration of repressive laws. In 1983 84, the Corporation provided another three years of grant aid for CALS' work in examining and monitoring South Africa's security laws.

Between 1928 and 1932, the Corporation financed the *Carnegie Commission on Poor Whites*, which reported on 'the process of impoverishment' that excluded many poor white South Africans from economic advancement. In 1982, a *Second Carnegie Inquiry into Poverty and Development in Southern Africa* was initiated, to examine the current causes and conditions of poverty for *all* racial groups, as well as issues related to the country's development. It is recognized that in the 1980s it is black Africans in rural areas who suffer most intensely from poverty. The knowledge and research of lawyers, doctors, economists, teachers, community leaders, social workers and religious workers, along with many others, are all being drawn on. The Inquiry is independent of all government bodies and political parties; it is financed wholly by the Corporation. Recommendations will be made, based on the Inquiry's findings, to develop strategies for dealing with the problems of poverty, and a broad education programme will be undertaken as a result.

Closer to home, one or two recent grants catch the eye. In 1983-84 the Corporation added its support to the computer project being developed between Carnegie-Mellon University and IBM (see page 77). The aim is for CMU students and faculty to have powerful personal computers, linked together and linked to a central computer, that will serve all of CMU's undergraduate and graduate education and also the continuing education of CMU alumni. Students will, for example, be able to use the system for writing and editing papers, searching the library's catalogues, and doing mathematical computations. The ultimate goal is to enable colleges and universities across the country to use the system and its educational applications. IBM is spending $20,000,000 to design the hardware and is providing the same again to CMU to manage the production of the software to operate the network. The Corporation made a three-year grant of more than one million dollars for a consortium of institutions to develop and test the educational software.

Looking even further into the future of American society, Lydia Bronte and Alan Pifer, now senior consultant to the Corporation, are investigating the *Public Policy Implications of an Ageing Society*. The unprecedented change in the age composition of the population is a concern also of Ernest Boyer, President of the Foundation for the Advancement of Teaching (see page 142) but Pifer's statistics are even more alarming in their implications—in terms of the workforce, social values, and equity between the generations. Pifer points out that the median age of the population is now thirty-one and rising; the number of persons below the age of fifteen has dropped by nearly 7,000,000 since 1970, while the number of adults aged twenty-five to thirty-four has grown by more than 13,000,000 and the number of the elderly has grown by more than 6,000,000; by the next century, twelve to fifteen percent of the population will be sixty-five years or older—the figure will rise to twenty percent by about the year 2035 (in

1900, the figure was about four percent over the age of sixty-five). There is of course a corresponding rise in the amount of money being spent on the elderly out of the federal budget, which in turn will cause social unrest in the younger, working generation.

These figures are warning signals, says Pifer, that society should make the most of the ever-smaller number of young workers in relation to the ever-increasing number of the elderly. Since the future of society is dependent upon the development of the young, and especially of children, major investment is needed in nutrition, health, decent housing and education for the poor and the affluent equally. This is not simply a matter of social justice but of practical necessity, concludes Pifer, concerned at the dismantling of social programmes.

Much of the health care, cultural activity, higher education, civic life, public advocacy and social services in America are provided by the private, non-profit organizations, and in 1982-83 the Corporation gave a grant to the *Urban Institute* to study how these organizations worked. Little is understood about their basic scope, direction and function, or about the extent to which they have become involved in the operation of public programmes. Taking this further, and linking with the sesquicentennial anniversary of Carnegie's birth, the Corporation allocated a modest grant to help pay for an Anglo-American conference in Dunfermline in 1985 on the importance of philanthropy in a changing world. This will take place alongside the representative gathering of Carnegie trusts.

Early in 1984, after his first year as Corporation President, David Hamburg announced his new programme directions:

> We live in a world transformed—and still in the process of transformation—but we see all around us the institutional lags which are so troublesome. Central among the issues of our time are the proliferation of devastating weapons in the absence of strong conflict-resolving mechanisms; the limitations of educational institutions to prepare young people adequately for the modern world; the wastage of talent, vigor, and health in early life by damage that is in principle preventable; and the persistence of ethnocentrism and prejudice.... To deal with them effectively, people everywhere must understand them better.

Hamburg's four main goals are: (1) avoidance of nuclear war and improvement in US-Soviet relations; (2) the education of all Americans, especially youth, for a scientifically and technologically based society; (3) prevention of damage to children and young adolescents; (4) strengthening of human resources in developing countries.

These programmes reflect Hamburg's concern with the inability of society to cope with the speed of change in the modern world. He sees the most remarkable feature of the Corporation being its freedom and flexibility 'to respond to important issues and to address problems the consequences of which can be only dimly perceived on the horizon.' Therefore the programmes combine fundamental values with the preparation of society for a very different future. Hamburg sums up the objectives as follows:

To foster conditions under which young people everywhere may get a decent start in life, to deepen understanding of the rapidly changing world we live in, and to advance the cause of peaceful international relations.

Turning first to the avoidance of nuclear war, the Corporation draws attention to the world's stockpile of nuclear weapons, the equivalent to three-and-a-half tons of TNT for every person on Earth; world military costs have risen to more than $1,000,000 per minute; more than $19,000 is spent on each soldier each year on average throughout the world while only $380 is spent on each school-age child for education; in thirty-two countries, governments spend more for military purposes than for education and health-care combined; in the first half-hour of a nuclear war, the US, the USSR and Europe might each suffer 100,000,000 deaths, while the possibility of a limited nuclear war is highly unlikely. The Soviet Union has inherited from its Czarist predecessors estrangement from and suspicion of other nations, as a result of a long history of foreign invasions, and the US and the USSR are now entering a new era of weapons development and deployment, with increased hostility. The continual international crisis imposes on top policymakers and their staffs cumulative emotional and physical fatigue; the penalty for human error in this kind of crisis management is obviously grotesque, as recent television films have suggested.

To counteract this threat, the Corporation is looking to replace crisis management by crisis prevention. It will be emphasising the health consequences of nuclear war as a potentially useful focus for public education programmes, and it will make every effort to spread accurate information equally in the US and the USSR. Some grants will be made to explore long-term improvements in the basic US-Soviet relationship, taking into account the Soviet view of the US as well as the US view of the Soviet Union, though it is admitted that 'to do this in a truly thoughtful and realistic way without romantic illusions will be very difficult.' Serious educational efforts will be made to build a broad, non-partisan interest in these issues. The Corporation will also explore what the behavioural sciences have to offer in near-term applied advice about negotiations, decision-making, and conflict-resolution—and in long-term understanding of human conflict and resolution. All information will be widely disseminated.

Turning next to the issue of education, and the scientific and technological needs of a modern economy, the Corporation will be asking how educational institutions can prepare people for change. Collaboration between classroom teachers, subject-matter experts (in physics, chemistry or biology, for example) and psychologists is seen as one way to improve education. Another, that takes the population trends into account, is to make the best use of available talent by providing ready access for minority-group members and women to high-quality education in science and technology. At the same time, there is concern that as much ingenuity will be required in adapting to the social dislocations brought about by technological change as was needed to invent the technologies and all their benefits in the first place. The Corporation is seeking practical answers to questions about the sort of cooperation needed among business, labour, education, science and government to build a more effective economy and a better educational system.

Turning thirdly to child development and the prevention of damage to children, the focus will be on tackling serious problems before they become permanently handicapping—problems that affect young people widely across different sectors of American society but that harm low-income and minority populations disproportionately. The programme will span from birth to age fifteen but will pay particular attention to the first few years and to early adolescence, from age ten to fifteen; these two formative periods are seen as crucial. It is recognised that during adolescence a significant number of young people from all social groups will drop out of school, commit crimes, become pregnant, become mentally ill, abuse drugs or alcohol, attempt suicide, or die from injuries.

Identifying the pressures and dangers to which the young are exposed, the programme picks out first the social and economic stresses that have characterized the changes in the American family in the past twenty years and it states the need, since 'today's more variegated family form seems likely to persist,' for the creation of a 'stable, dependable, supportive environment for child-rearing.' The programme picks out automobiles, computers and television as each presenting advantages and dangers to the young, in shaping or destroying their lives. It also points to prejudice, as one of the most ubiquitous and dangerous of all human attributes, despite the major shift in recent years that racial attitudes have undergone; prejudice, from either point of view, is greatly damaging—we cannot afford it in the world of the future. Recognizing the need to identify particular problems on which to work, the Corporation has selected for attention school failure, school-age pregnancy, substance abuse, and childhood injury.

On school-failure, the Corporation has already supported advocacy efforts to ensure the provision of quality education for low-income students. On school-age pregnancy, the programme is aware that young mothers tend to drop out of school with few skills to earn a living and so increase the problem. One in five of all children born today in America has a teenage mother, and teenagers account for half of all out-of-wedlock births; the pregnancy rate of girls under fifteen is increasing. There is a paradox that is largely responsible for this: the onset of puberty is earlier than it was by several years (enhanced nutrition and the control of infectious diseases) but adolescence ends a great deal later than it did. One serious effect of young motherhood on the next generation is that young mothers are far more likely to have low-birthweight babies who may die or suffer many serious health and developmental problems. Once again, it is the girls in low-income neighbourhoods (who may see no options other than adolescent motherhood) who are most at risk. The programme will seek to develop a clearer sense of alternative futures; it will explore the powerful rôles (both negative and positive) of peers and of the media in shaping adolescent development; it will emphasize the role of parents as sources of their children's education about sexuality.

As to substance abuse and addiction, though these are found in all social and economic groups, they exact their most devastating toll in minority communities, where, in addition to their obvious dangers, they can contribute to violence and injuries and to school failure in young people. Addiction has been called America's number one health problem; cigarette smoking, alcohol and drug abuse are common features of early adolescence. These are natural targets for programme study.

Following on from this, it is not widely appreciated, according to the Corporation, that the major health hazards for young American children stem not from disease any longer but from injuries—both accidental and intentional. Injuries account for half of all deaths in children and are an increasing source of long-term disability and serious health problems for children and adolescents. The death rate from accidental injury is twice as high for blacks as for whites and twice as high in pre-school children as in children of school age. The major unintentional injuries include falls, burns, poisonings, and motor vehicle accidents. Intentional injuries, or child abuse and neglect, can be physical, sexual or psychological; at least 60,000 serious injuries and 2,000 deaths among children are thought to be caused by abuse each year.

Turning finally to the strengthening of human resources in developing countries, it appears that the gaps between the developed and the developing nations are widening, not narrowing. In many developing countries, particularly in Africa, the high hopes generated at the time of independence have given way to pessimism. Much of the world's population today still cannot take for granted its ability to meet basic needs for food, water, shelter and other survival factors. The Rockefeller and Ford foundations have already contributed with their creative work on the 'green revolution,' on the great neglected tropical diseases, on nutritional improvement, on population problems and on economic development. The Carnegie programme will focus initially on mothers' and children's health, on nutrition and above all on basic education, especially for women and girls. Health studies have shown that the more educated are the mothers then the less likely are their children to die, regardless of differences in family income; education also helps delay marriage for women, partly by increasing their chances for employment. By giving children a decent start in life, this is the first way toward strengthening human resources.

Recognizing the interdependent nature of the world, the Corporation believes that America has a major contribution to make to the developed countries. Grants for three kinds of projects are planned: dialogues between experts and leaders from developing countries and the United States; technical and scientific cooperation; the assessment of lessons learned from experience in establishing effective programmes, and their applicability in other settings. While the perspective will be worldwide, priority will be given to sub-Saharan Africa and the Caribbean. Grants in the US will focus on Mexico.

Hamburg sees one theme that cuts across the new programmes: that is 'a precious resource in the great scientific community of the United States that can be brought to bear on these crucial problems.' With that in mind, he sees several rôles that the Corporation can play in all areas: to clarify and highlight what has already been done; to go beyond that in support of constructive innovation, models and demonstrations; to focus the attention of dynamic sectors of American society on critical needs and specific opportunities as they come to light; and to promote the cooperation of government, corporate, labour, and scientific and professional strengths in responding to these needs.

By pursuing these aims, Hamburg believes that the Corporation, seventy-five years old in 1986, will demonstrate that it continues to be guided by fundamental commitments to education, peace and social justice—to the enduring values so crucial to human survival and well-being.

CARNEGIE UNITED KINGDOM TRUST

The last endowment that bears Carnegie's name has also the widest brief of all his endowments: 'the well-being of the masses of the people of Great Britain and Ireland.' With the establishment of the Carnegie Corporation of New York in 1911, Carnegie's themes of academic and social education, research and the pursuit of international peace, had been drawn together and virtually exhausted. The United Kingdom Trust, founded in 1913 as an afterthought, developed the other side of Carnegie's concern—appreciation for the quality of life—taking into a broader and more varied community this aspect of his endowments in Pittsburgh and Dunfermline. The UK Trust has since extended its concern especially to the needs of the disabled and disadvantaged in the community.

In its early years, the Trust was largely occupied with meeting the grants already promised by the Corporation for church organs and library buildings in the United

Kingdom. Quite quickly, the Trustees used their considerable freedom of manoeuvre to seek out new community needs in which to pioneer projects of national scope. The UK Trust grew rapidly into a prestigious organization working on projects in the fields of child welfare, employment, housing and the arts, many of which had a major impact on society, especially through the troubled times of the 1930s. The Trust also published a number of influential reports on social welfare and educational subjects.

The Trustees have followed a policy of cooperation with government and voluntary bodies, although always maintaining impartial independence. Grants for village halls in cooperation with the National Council for Social Services, the provision of play areas in cooperation with the National Playing Fields Association, and, more recently, the unusual and spirited action of the disbursement of government funds for unemployed voluntary activities, are good examples of this approach. Inevitably, the progressive increase in government intervention in areas which hitherto had to rely on voluntary support has influenced the Trust's activities but it has succeeded outstandingly in involving itself in a great range of pioneering endeavours that have become household names.

Well-timed grants through the decades have supported the early progress of the Old Vic Theatre and Sadler's Wells Opera House, the National Youth Orchestra of Scotland and the Polka Children's Theatre in London, community drama and arts workshops for amateurs and disabled people. Grants have helped Age Concern and the Samaritans, pre-school playgroups and one-parent families, delinquency projects and a study of children in custody, widows and the care of the terminally ill. The Cheshire Homes for the Handicapped, the Disabled Living Foundation, the Physically Handicapped and Able-Bodied Clubs (PHAB) have each benefited from Trust aid. So have the National Councils of Social Service, the Women's Institutes, the Young Farmers Clubs, the Youth Hostel Association, the Village Clubs Association, the National Parks, rural projects, museums and countryside centres, projects in new estates, projects for the interpretation of local history and the national heritage and for nature conservation and wildlife. All these have been set on their feet with the help of the UK Trust.

This range of work continues today with the emphasis on three main areas: community services and family life; the improvement of amateur participation in the arts and especially by disabled people; heritage interpretation and its link with the arts through good design, and practical environmental schemes—all of which involve volunteers. The unemployed are also an important concern of the Trust, just as they were during the Depression of the 1930s. In all areas, the Trustees make the most of their independence and their ability to encourage new ideas; they can respond quickly to observed needs and act as a catalyst for positive action to improve the well-being of the community.

Carnegie United Kingdom Trust

Founded: 1913

Purpose: 'For the improvement of the well-being of the masses of the people of Great Britain and Ireland, by such means as...the Trustees might from time to time select as best fitted from age to age for securing these purposes, remembering that new needs are constantly arising as the masses advance.'

Finance:

Original endowment ($10 million):	£2,000,000
Additional funds (sale of Skibo Castle, 1984):	(approx) £600,000
Current assets, end 1983:	£6,692,104

	Income	*Expenditure*
Annual monies in early years:		
1913-14:	£146,435	£70,148
1915:	£107,664	£81,686
1916:	£121,136	£82,568
Annual monies in recent years:		
1983:	£686,064	£776,347*
1984:	£787,191	£852,336*
1985 (estimated):	£710,000	
Total monies, 1913-1983:	£13,556,248	£12,408,158

* Excess met from Reserve Fund

Main areas of expenditure, 1983-84:	*1983*	*1984*
The Arts:	£262,907	£247,741
Community Services:	£152,500	£186,000
Heritage:	£193,480	£167,929

Grants to organizations:

Grants in early years:

Trustees inherited from Carnegie and the Corporation obligations amounting to £212,443 for libraries, organs and some public baths. Though actual payment was spread over several years, other Trust initiatives were at first greatly restricted; the greater part of controllable income was directed at furthering the library movement.

Number of organizations *approved* for grant-aid in recent years:

1982:	62
1983:	52
1984:	65

(Total number of grants is greater, since a number of these represent allocation schemes, whereby the main organization distributes grants to branches for special developments).

Total number of organizations receiving grant-aid:

1913-1984:	More than 10,000

(Some organizations have received more than one grant and some grants represent an allocation scheme—therefore, the figure is much higher).

173

Percentage of total expenditure (1913-1983) allocated to main areas of interest:

Community and Youth Services:	39%
Non-grant, including advisory services:	19%
Arts and Education:	16%
Libraries:	13%
Countryside and Heritage:	10.5%
Museums:	2.5%

Administration:

Chairman:	Timothy J. Colman, JP, DCL.
Secretary and Treasurer:	Geoffrey Lord, MA, AIB, FRSA.
Staff:	Secretary and Treasurer; Administrative Assistant; 5 full- and 1 part-time office staff; 1 gardener/caretaker.
	Short-term contracts for specific projects (1984):
	4—Committee of Inquiry, Arts and Disabled People.
	2—Unemployed Voluntary Action Fund.
Address:	Comely Park House, Dunfermline, Fife KY12 7EJ.

Carnegie United Kingdom Trust

Andrew Carnegie's gift to the United Kingdom was a very personal one. He had to take $10,000,000 out of his own pocket from money he had put aside for private use; this was after he had given the remaining bulk of his fortune to the Carnegie Corporation. Up to 1913, he had stipulated that grants for the continuance of gifts for libraries and church organs outside the United States were to be made from a special fund in the Corporation but he then decided to transfer $10,000,000 from the Corporation to a trust for this purpose in the United Kingdom. To his chagrin, he was told that this would be illegal under the terms of the New York Trust he had signed for the Corporation. Not to be moved from his resolve, he produced the money himself.

In August 1913, Carnegie notified the Corporation that it was relieved of its responsibilities for library buildings and organs in Great Britain and Ireland. But the new UK Trust was not intended simply for those two purposes. Its charter was remarkable for the breadth of its mandate. There was only one notable restriction: Carnegie expressly cautioned the trustees against making grants for research into the development of implements or munitions of war and he prohibited them from using any part of their funds in any way which could lend countenance to war or warlike preparations.

The Trust was established in Dunfermline, but despite this firm grounding in Carnegie's Scottish birthplace, it quickly concerned itself with projects on a national scale. From the beginning, it attempted to pursue a consistent policy which would lead to the betterment of all classes of people through enterprises which would sooner or later become publicly supported, thus leaving the Trust free to pioneer in new fields. This concept of pioneering has always been an over-riding concern of the Trustees, throughout more than seventy years of grant-giving; the beneficial effects of this policy can clearly be seen in the following pages in the number and variety of endeavours that have borne fruit.

Another major consideration of the Trust has been the importance of good relations between itself and government and local authorities. Grants have often been made on a pound-for-pound basis. At the same time, the steady increase in statutory activity, whether central or local, and the marked changes in social attitudes over the decades have inevitably been reflected in the changing pattern of the Trust's grant-making policy. One constant contribution by the Trust has been the financing of investigations and reports on subjects of public interest and social significance; the most recent in a long line of such national inquiries are the Wolfenden Committee on Voluntary Organisations and the Attenborough Committee on the Arts and Disabled People.

Looking at the spread of Trust activity in its first fifty years, up to 1963, grants were paid amounting to £5,463,716. Slightly less than one-third of this sum was spent on public libraries. Of the rest, thirteen percent was spent on the arts, fifteen percent on village halls and social services, nine percent on youth organizations, playing fields and play centres, twelve percent on physical and mental welfare organizations, and ten percent on adult education, including museums. These overall figures contain an extraordinary amount of project activity throughout the country. It is not possible to review it all but some impression of the great range can be obtained by looking first at the main areas of interest up to and including the 1970s and then, because of a slight shift in emphasis, more specifically at the Trust's activities in the 1980s. The Trust follows a quinquennial policy in deciding its fields of interest, and the main areas of interest in each decade since 1913 can be seen at a glance in the following list.

Main areas of interest by decade, 1913-1985:

    1913-1920: Libraries
                  Church organs
                  Public baths
                  Music
    1921-1930: Libraries
                  Physical welfare
                  Hostels
                  Village halls, rural development and social service
                  Playing fields
                  Adult education
                  Music

1931-1940: Libraries
            Land settlement
            Village halls, rural development and social service
            Playing fields
            Youth services
            Hostels
            Adult education
            Music and drama
            Museums

1941-1950: Music and drama
            Community services and village halls
            Land settlement
            Libraries
            Museums
            Youth services

1951-1960: Music and drama
            Visual arts
            Museums
            Community services and family welfare
            Village halls and rural areas
            Libraries
            Education and field studies

1961-1970: Music and drama
            Visual arts
            Museums
            Community services and new communities
            Countryside
            Education and field studies
            Youth service

1971-1980: Music and drama
            Local history
            Community services
            Countryside
            Heritage and museums

1981-1985: Amateur participation in the arts
            Arts and disabled people
            Pipe organs in civic buildings
            Community services and volunteer action to enhance the
              quality of family life
            Heritage interpretation and environmental schemes

Libraries and church organs

At the outset, the Trust met its obligations in these two regards, bearing in mind Carnegie's words:

> My reason for selecting public libraries being my belief, as Carlyle has recorded, that 'the true university of these days is a collection of books,' and that thus such libraries are entitled to a first place as instruments for the elevation of the masses of the people.

Carnegie also gave his reasons for favouring organs. He cited:

> My own experience that the organ is one of the most elevating of voices, often causing me to murmur the words of Confucius as I listen to its peals, 'Music, sacred tongue of God, I hear thee calling and I come.'

Carnegie's endowments had already contributed about £50,000 to organ grants in the United Kingdom, and in 1913 outstanding grants amounted to roughly the same figure. The final organ grants were honoured after the First World War and the policy was thereafter discontinued. A total sum of £108,125 was spent on Carnegie grants for organs in the United Kingdom; nearly 3500 church organs benefited (see page 260).

Between 1890 and 1913, Carnegie's grants, ranging from £400 to £120,000, helped to finance 295 municipal libraries in the United Kingdom at a total cost of £1,750,000. This was more than half the total number of public libraries in existence in 1913. In 1914 a report commissioned by the UK Trust showed that about two-fifths of the population was still without a public library service. The report also gave examples of the poor maintenance of existing Carnegie libraries. An extreme case was that of a local authority which had received £10,000 in 1898 but which had spent only £1 on books in 1913. A subsequent report showed that the situation was even worse in Ireland, where several town libraries were found to be virtually derelict; others were used mainly as village halls; in one instance, the caretaker, who also acted as the librarian, had taken to burning the books in order to avoid being pestered by would-be readers.

The first report stressed the need for a service in rural areas, to which the Trust immediately responded. In 1915, for example, £5,000 was allocated for a library scheme for the Orkneys, the Shetlands and Lewis. Between 1915 and 1919, the Trust spent more than £200,000 on the founding of eighty county library schemes (see page 259). There can be no doubt that the success of the British library system, which many public libraries in other countries have attempted to emulate, is largely due to Carnegie and the UK Trust. Grants were also given to encourage libraries in youth clubs and other organizations.

Library spending formed a substantial part of the Trust's total expenditure up until 1936, by which time almost every person in the country was considered to have access to some form of public library facility, including travelling van libraries, but the Trust's task did not finally end until the 1950s, after the Public Libraries Act of 1947. A measure of the success of the scheme can be reckoned by the library membership figures. In 1924, there were 2,500,000 registered borrowers in England and Wales; by

1958, this had risen to 13,000,000; the number of books in stock over that period rose from thirteen to sixty million.

In 1933, King George V opened a new building in Bloomsbury, in London, to house the National Central Library, the cost of which was met by the Trust. The original function of the library was to act as a central source to provide books for adult education classes but it later became a resource for less popular or more expensive books that smaller libraries could not afford. As the King said at the opening: 'These buildings constitute a National University which all may attend and none need ever leave.'

Among other libraries to receive assistance before the Second World War were the Seafarers' Education Service and the British Sailor's Society, the London School of Hygiene and Tropical Medicine, the College of Nursing and the National Library for the Blind. The Trust was prominent in assisting the early breakthrough of the 'Lending Library for the Blind,' founded in 1882, into the National Library with its new headquarters. In 1953, the Trust made a substantial library commitment in contributing toward the rehousing of the Scottish Central Library, originally housed in the Trust office in Dunfermline and transferred to new accommodation in the Royal Mile, Edinburgh, at a cost of £94,000. This brought total expenditure on libraries to £1,500,000. An interesting and more recent grant was that to Trinity College Library, Dublin, for restoration of the mediaeval manuscript of *The Book of Kells*. In addition to libraries, the Trustees contributed to the general standard and status of librarianship as a profession through the Library Associations of England and Scotland and schools of librarianship.

Music, Drama and other Arts

With the conclusion of the organ scheme, the Trust was determined to pursue new ways in which to effect Carnegie's intentions that music should be a prime agency of improvement for the well-being of the people. Grants for Music Competition Festivals to encourage choral singing in rural areas, and for an Orchestral Loan Library to provide scores for amateur groups, and aid for a Village and County Town Concerts Fund were followed in 1916 by encouragement for music of the Elizabethan and Tudor periods resulting in the publication of *Tudor Church Music*, dedicated to H.M. King George V. The Trustees had been informed that a number of well-known students of music had begun the great task of recovering from the archives of cathedrals the sacred music composed in the sixteenth and seventeenth centuries. The edition in ten volumes supplemented by fifty works suitable for performance by choirs was a major undertaking. Then followed the publication each year of a limited number of works by living British composers; between 1916 and 1928, fifty-six new works were published, as the *Carnegie Collection of British Music*, at a cost of £25,000; they included Vaughan Williams's *London Symphony*, Granville Bantock's *Hebridean Symphony* and Gustav Holst's *The Hymn of Jesus*, as well as works by Bliss, Bridge, Howells and Stanford.

◄ Extracts from *The Book of Kells*, restored for Trinity College Library, Dublin, with grant-aid from the Trust

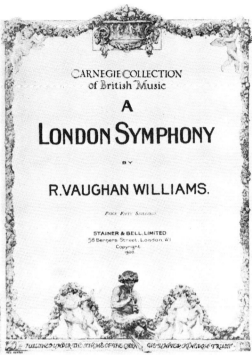

Two of the leading works in the Carnegie Collection of British Music, 1920

After 1922, the Trust moved away from the policy of founding original schemes for the encouragement of music, and concentrated its efforts toward helping established organizations. Guarantees against loss, for concert and drama tours, played a large part in this effort. One expensive experiment in 1924 cost the Trust £4,000 when it guaranteed the British National Opera Company against loss for one year. Ten years later, more than 130 music societies received guarantees in the first year of a new scheme which helped to establish the National Association of Music Festivals.

With drama as with music, assistance was given to help touring companies visit outlying districts. The most important drama grants were probably those given to the Old Vic (£15,000) and to the Sadler's Wells Theatre (£30,000); the latter involved complete rebuilding of the historic theatre, of which only the walls and stage remained. Between the wars, the English Folk Dance Society, the Lena Ashwell Players and the St Pancras People's Theatre all received grants; the Scottish Drama Association and the Scottish Children's Theatre were each given guarantees against loss.

Another unique provision is recalled by the 50th anniversary in 1984 of the founding of the Scottish Film Council. The Trust's interest in films as a developing art encouraged the Council's Film Library, which was to become the largest stock of educational and documentary films in Europe. There was also the fascinating Trust study of 'Children and Films' in 1954.

In 1938, a specially commissioned inquiry into the needs of non-commercial music in

Britain recommended that the Trust provide subsidies for touring opera companies and orchestras in return for their undertaking to give low-priced performances. The Trust made plans to implement this and other recommendations but shortly afterward the Pilgrim Trust began its own programme for support of the Arts; this programme led to the forerunner of the present Arts Council. The UK Trust was invited to participate but after lengthy negotiations declined to do so, eventually deciding to concentrate its support on the amateur in the arts. However, during the Second World War, the Trust support literally saved a number of important orchestras and organizations. Grants enabled the Hallé, the Liverpool and Scottish Orchestras, the London Symphony and Philharmonic and the Sadler's Wells Opera Company to undertake tours in the provinces during the blackout and bombing raids between 1941 and 1943, playing to large and enthusiastic audiences. It was at this time, too, that the Trust became involved in the development of voluntary county music and drama committees and the appointment of county music and drama advisers. This became the basis of the present state scheme which led to the introduction of music and drama nationally in schools and to appropriate teacher training courses.

The Trust continued to be involved, after the war, in a number of music schemes, including the formation in 1958 of an experimental music club in Liverpool, called 'The Music Box,' which proved so successful that it was later adopted by the local authority; similar schemes were subsequently run by a number of other authorities. Music groups for mentally handicapped children also received Trust support at this time. Several hundred local art societies and clubs were also given help in the early 1950s to enable them to hold short schools of expert instruction.

For thirty years after the war, the Trust gave long-term support to the educational provision of the Drama Board and the Associate of the Drama Board (ADB) award, inaugurated by the Trust. This is the only drama qualification for teachers in the United Kingdom. The Drama Board was closed in 1980 and its examinations were taken under the umbrella of the Royal Society of Arts.

Between 1960 and 1980, Trust support continued for music as well. A grant of £26,000 in 1976 was used to help more than one hundred local music festivals. Another grant helped toward a reference library of twentieth-century British music at the British Music Information Centre in London, the home of the Composers Guild. The National Youth Orchestra of Scotland received £20,000 when it started in 1978 and subsequently another £10,000 and an invested fund of £10,000 over a five-year period for bursaries. The orchestra completed a tour of the Northern Isles in its second year of operation. Bridging music and drama, grants were also given to the Lamp of Lothian for an experimental festival of music and theatre, with original composition and creative improvisation, supervised by the University of York and the Yehudi Menuhin School. The first study into music with disabled children was a seven-year study at Dartington College of Arts. This was under the auspices of the Standing Conference for Amateur Music (now the Amateur Music Association). It led to a report for teachers and a book by David Ward, *Hearts and Hands and Voices*.

An imaginative venture was the Glasgow Arts Centre, which in the late 1960s began to promote cultural activities for young people in large housing estates. In 1962, a limited guarantee against loss was given to a performance of the Coventry Mystery Plays at the dedication of Coventry Cathedral. In Hackney, London, money went to benefit the culture of people of African or West Indian origin. In Norwich, the Sewell Barn Theatre (a converted barn named after Anna Sewell of *Black Beauty* fame) received support for an extension for tuition and workshops for this community and family project; in Norwich also, the Da Silva Puppet Theatre was given £10,000 in 1980 toward the development of an octagonal workshop.

Drama activities stretched from Scotland to Devonshire. Theatre Workshop Edinburgh was helped with a scheme to introduce the arts to the mentally handicapped. The workshop combines pantomime, puppetry, drama and dance, with classes in mime and music. The Scottish Youth Theatre was given aid to develop drama workshops for young people from deprived areas. The Cumbernauld Theatre had a grant to develop a programme for ethnic groups, with dance, mime and drama workshops. In London, the Polka Children's Theatre was given money to create facilities for disabled children. In 1979, the Colway Theatre Trust, brainchild of playwright Ann Jellicoe, was launched in south-west England to develop community drama, with each play being written for and performed by the people of a particular locality. This has proved to be a marvellous exercise in bringing together a great variety of community interests with productions involving professionals and amateurs in a pioneering scheme—a plank for a future Trust policy.

Social Welfare and the Community

The Trust report, commissioned in 1917, on the *Physical Welfare of Mothers and Children* led to central welfare institutions being set up in London and Edinburgh and the creation of six 'model' clinics which helped toward a great deal of important work in the field of maternity and childcare and the formation in 1921 of the National Council for Maternity and Child Welfare.

Thirty years after that report, another, in 1947, on the *Employment and Training of Social Workers*, resulted in a grant of £20,000 for a new-style course in social studies at the London School of Economics. The report was recognized as a standard source of information on the problems of training social workers, and the new-style course gradually became standard practice with other universities.

A third report represented the largest investigation ever attempted in Britain into the relationship between health and diet. A survey of 1,300 families in Scotland and England, covering nearly 8,000 people selected from industrial and agricultural areas, was completed at the beginning of the Second World War, during which its findings were used by the government in developing its very successful war-time food policy based on the nutritional needs of the population. The report itself was finally published in 1955.

Less successful was the children's home 'Ponds,' which resulted from the UK Trust's involvement in 1938 with a Home Office Committee scheme to look into the problems of juvenile delinquency. After the war, the Trust made another attempt in this area by commissioning a report on *Delinquency and Human Nature*, which resulted in further information on existing agencies and activities. The conclusion was that:

> The main weakness in the environment of these youngsters...is in the most intimate and influential circle of all, the natural group of the family....Effort should be concentrated on understanding and counteracting the forces which are straining and weakening the family.

As a result, the Trust gave five-year grants to two organizations involved in family welfare: Family Service Units and the Family Welfare Association. In 1953, a substantial grant went to the Bristol Social Project to establish the means of tackling the stresses and strains which manifest themselves in the form of delinquency and other forms of disturbance. Two reports followed: *Difficult Housing Estates* (1963) and *Stress and Release in an Urban Estate* (1970). One interesting question was raised: 'In what sense and for whom are local centres of social involvement of importance?'

The advent of the Welfare State in the post-war years affected the nature of the Trust's work and saw it increase its rôle as a link between State bodies and voluntary organizations. The late 1950s and the early 1960s brought new problems to be solved in the community, as in Bristol, where council estates and tower block dwellings resulted in much social unrest. In the 1960s and 1970s, the Trust's concept of 'social welfare' adapted to new challenges in the form of 'community projects.' The elderly, the truant, the single-parent families, the abused child, parents with disabled children, immigrants, the lonely and the desperate—they all needed help and the Trust has played its part in helping them. Here are just a few of the projects given money in the 1960s and 1970s:

The After Care Trust needed help in 1965 to launch a range of hostels for alcoholics, the 'workshy' and those 'in transit.' Centrepoint set up an all-night shelter scheme for young people in London's Soho and Baron's Court in 1975. The City Farm Movement developed wasteland in towns and cities for mutual-help projects involving gardening, farm animals and, of course, people. The Girl Guides Association needed a review of its work and aims in the 1960s. Gingerbread began helping one-parent families. The National Council for One-Parent Families and the National Council for the Single Woman and Her Dependants both received substantial grants.

The Organization for Parents Under Stress (OPUS) was helped with training in 1979. The Pakistan Welfare and Information Centre was established to aid the integration of immigrants into the community. The Pre-School Playgroups Associations throughout the United Kingdom and Ireland received grants throughout the 1970s and special aid for training courses and integration work with handicapped children and children from ethnic minorities. The Samaritans needed new premises for new branches for their work with the lonely and desperate. Shelter Housing Aid Centre set up a 'one call' office to assist homeless London families to find a home and a job in another part of the country. The Widow's Advisory Trust established residential courses for widows who assist in local groups.

Aid for Disabled People

A large portion of the Trust's income in the early 1950s was absorbed by the Cheshire Foundation, for homes for the disabled. By 1963, there were thirty-four Cheshire Homes in Britain, and similar homes existed in at least six other countries, including India, Malaya and Nigeria. The Trust has also assisted many other organizations involved with the disabled, such as the National Association for Mental Health.

In 1954, information was collected on the nature of existing facilities to help home-based handicapped children. Surveys were subsequently commissioned on the whole range of physical and mental handicaps of about 600 children in Shropshire, Sheffield and Glasgow. In spite of the Health Service, there were important requirements that were not being met. As a direct result of the inquiry, in 1961 the Trust promised £30,000 to Glasgow for a child welfare centre, incorporating a normal child welfare clinic and an assessment clinic and day nursery for handicapped children. An assessment and advice centre was also set up in Shrewsbury, linked with the homes of the handicapped children by visiting counsellors.

In 1958, facilities and buildings in a light engineering course for blind adolescents in Birmingham were extended with Trust aid. An early endeavour in the period was to establish the first national residential centre for disabled students but, unfortunately, other Trusts and agencies did not have the same priorities or interests. However, Prospect Hall, in the Selly Oak area of Birmingham, was built with the largest-ever Trust grant of more than £250,000, and opened by Her Majesty the Queen Mother in 1977. Though it did not become a university resource, it is now administered by Birmingham City Council as a major residential centre for the training of disabled people and it is used by PHAB (Physically Handicapped and Able-Bodied Clubs) as a summer holiday resource. In sum, Prospect Hall produced a slightly disappointing result for the good intentions and hard work of the Trustees and the local committee but it remains a very useful resource to the community in the Midlands.

In 1966, help was given to improve an information service for the National Society for Autistic Children. From 1968 into the 1980s, a number of grants have been given to PHAB clubs. The Disabled Living Foundation has received several grants: one for a review of the problems of access to music; another for a scheme to train music teachers to work with the disabled; a third for a handbook on growing plants. Since 1979, Calibre has been given help to set up a voluntary postal lending library of recorded books for handicapped people.

The Partially Sighted Society was helped to acquire equipment for its large-print work, including the enlargement of sheet music for musicians and singers. The first DIAL (Disablement Information and Advice Line) was assisted as a result of a letter from an elderly widow in Derbyshire. Subsequent aid helped more than thirty new

Prospect Hall, Birmingham, opened by Her Majesty Queen Elizabeth the Queen Mother in 1970, as a rehabilitation centre for disabled people

groups in the expanding network and the formation of a United Kingdom headquarters. In fact, the Trust has assisted the establishment of every national information service of a social-service nature in the post-war era.

Playing Fields and Physical Health

Following the recommendations in the 1917 report on the *Physical Welfare of Mothers and Children* (see page 182), the Trust introduced grants up to £500 a time for layout and equipment to encourage local authorities who were willing to provide a site and future running costs for play grounds and play centres. Only fourteen grants were claimed in the first ten years. A national appeal was launched by the King in 1927 and further funds made available, with the result that one hundred grants for play centres were provided by the Trust between 1929 and 1931; by the time the programme came to an end in 1935, more than 1,030 schemes had received about £230,000 from the Trust, and the results of this work are still to be seen in towns and villages throughout Britain.

The Carnegie Physical Training College for Men was another contribution by the Trust to physical health and education. This was presented to Leeds Education Authority in 1933, with places for sixty students. It had been suggested that there was a need for people who would 'look at their work through the eyes of teachers rather than drill sergeants.' The initial plan was for two centres, one in the north and one in the south, each comprising a hostel and gymnasium, but finally the Trust provided £30,000 for the construction of a single college in Leeds. It was opened officially by Lord Irwin, who noted:

> In teaching control of the body, physical training helps that poise and balance of spirit which is so important in these days of fidgetiness and nervous strain, crowded cities and inescapable noise.

The College was occupied by the military during the war but in the post-war years it had a leading reputation for physical training and the development of teachers. In 1967-68 it began to offer Bachelor of Education courses under a scheme of study with Leeds University. In 1976, the City of Leeds and Carnegie Colleges, together with the James Graham College, were amalgamated into the Leeds Polytechnic. Carnegie College, still sited at Carnegie Hall, became known as the Carnegie School of Physical Education and Human Movement Studies and celebrated its Silver Jubilee in 1983 with a relay-run from the Trust office in Dunfermline to Leeds by college staff and students.

Land Settlement

The provision of small-holdings and allotments for the unemployed was first seen by the Trust as a possible ease to long-term unemployment during the Depression. In 1934, Lord Elgin wrote:

It is essential in the nation's interest to encourage and enable more men and women to live on the land, or at least to occupy part of their (involuntary) leisure time in working on allotments and smallholdings.

Land Settlement was adopted as a major element of Trust policy from 1936 to 1940 but the experiment was not encouraging. By September 1939, little more than half the allocation of £150,000 had been claimed. At the outbreak of war, the Land Settlement Association had about 850 tenants; by Michaelmas 1947, it had only 661 smallholders. No further expansion was attempted, as it was agreed that the scheme could not be self-supporting. An official report did, however, claim that the scheme had some merits:

It has put new heart and life into many men who have been unemployed for years and had little hope for the future....Strong evidence of both physical and mental improvement makes us feel that here, at all events, land settlement is a success.

New Estates

Social problems associated with the creation of large new housing estates and the subsequent relocation of sections of the urban population became evident in the late 1920s. At Dagenham, for example, 60,000 people were relocated by the London County Council within a few years; there were no public buildings, no recreational facilities, and the local authority had no responsibility for providing the tenants with social services. Tenants' Associations sprang up spontaneously. In 1928, a joint committee, including the National Council of Social Service and the UK Trust, was formed to encourage community life at Dagenham. The Trust provided a three-year grant toward the salary and expenses of a full-time official to deal with the estate. Other estates also applied for grants. The Trust subsequently provided money for training people to run a number of community centres in England, Scotland and Wales.

In 1958, the Glasgow Society of Social Services was given a grant of £8,000 to provide a district headquarters where organizations on the estate, both voluntary and statutory workers, could meet. A similar scheme was set up in Liverpool. A Trust report in 1961, *New Communities in Britain: Achievements and Problems*, pointed out the need for small meeting places in the early stages of building a new estate or town; as a result of this, the Trust allocated £100,000 for community building schemes.

Rural Development and the National Council of Social Service (NCSS)

The Trust gave its first grant to the NCSS, a government funded agency, in 1921, to organize an adult education service in the Oxfordshire villages, including lectures, handicrafts, the cinema, music, drama, combined with an agricultural and horticultural campaign. Support was also given toward the setting up and running costs and to coordinate the work of the various organizations such as Village Clubs Associations, the YMCA and the Women's Institutes.

The Women's Institutes (WI) went on to receive more than £80,000 of grant aid from the Trust up to 1984. The first WI in England and Wales started in 1915 (the first in the world was in Canada), to improve the conditions of rural life and to provide a meeting point for all countrywomen regardless of class or creed. The Institutes rapidly became a remarkable force for social change in rural areas, a focus both for entertainment and outspoken intolerance of poor conditions. At its height, the organization had nearly half a million members in 9,000 or more institutes in every village in the country; it has its own College of Adult Education. Without doubt, it is Britain's greatest women's movement. The Associated Countrywomen of the World, to which the WI is affiliated, boasts eight or nine million members, though it is hard for member organizations to combine their potential strength.

The Trust also gave the NCSS aid for the establishment of a Central Unemployment Committee during the Depression of the 1930s. The purpose of the Committee was to help administer government aid for social services. This important work has an interesting parallel in one of the Trust's current projects, the administering of funds in Scotland for unemployed youth in the 1980s, on behalf of the government through an independent body of Trustees registered as the Unemployed Voluntary Action Fund (see page 203).

The Trust has supported all the national Councils of Social Service since their beginnings—not only in England but also in Wales, Scotland and Northern Ireland; it has also supported Foras Eireann in the Republic of Ireland. In particular, support has been given with grants for information and training services. The total of Trust grants to each Council has been as follows: Wales, over £79,000; Scotland, £96,000; Northern Ireland, £104,000; Republic of Ireland, £38,000; and the National Council in England, £245,000. Some Councils have now changed their names to reflect their changing responsibilities. For example, the NCSS is now the National Council for Voluntary Organizations (NCVO) and the CSS in Wales is now the Wales Council for Voluntary Action.

Village Halls

As the Trust's work developed, it became clear that for most rural communities the provision of a village hall was essential if useful voluntary work was to be carried out successfully; without a hall, most villages had no focal point from which to launch community activities. The government took the initiative in 1925 with a small sum for use in interest-free loans for the construction of halls; in 1930, the Trust allocated £10,000 for grants to village halls, increased to £35,000 by 1932, when the goverment cut its loan fund. In this way, the Trust provided a grant, the government a loan, and the local people raised the rest. Plans for expanding the programme after the war were curtailed through shortage of building materials and the difficulty of obtaining building permission. In 1956, a fund was set up for the even greater need to renovate halls built before the war. Demands on this fund were so great that, by the time the Trust's programme had come to an end in 1962, total UK Trust grants for village halls from 1930 to 1962 amounted to £375,000 and more than 660 communities had benefited. The construction of these halls played an important part in the social revival of many rural areas.

In 1983, the Trust received an invitation to attend a celebration of the fiftieth anniversary of the opening of Southminster Memorial Hall. The accompanying letter was a welcome vote of thanks:

> The Hall was opened in 1933 to serve the interest of the people of Southminster and District.... The Carnegie UK Trust gave the Hall a grant of £260 toward the £2,000 cost, a contribution which the parish was deeply grateful for. The grant made by the Trust has reaped a rich reward, in that we have a thriving, well used and maintained Village Hall (over 800 bookings per annum) which has contributed much to village life over the years.

Youth Services and Youth Hostels

The Trust has consistently been involved in various aspects of youth service, in libraries, play areas, drama, music, museums, village halls, and so on. Many organizations have received support, including Boys' Clubs, Girls' Clubs, the Boys' Brigade, the Church Lads' Brigade, the Girls' Friendly Societies and the Young Farmers' Clubs.

In 1920, the Trust made the first of several grants for the establishment of a successful Vocational Guidance Scheme but the other side of the picture was seen in a 1934-35 report which drew the Trust's attention to the high rate of unemployment in the 18-21 age group. The Trust provided £20,000 for a three-year study of educational and social problems of young men and women. One result was the Federation of Eighteen-plus clubs; another was a historical record of life in three industrial towns (Glasgow, Liverpool and Cardiff) in the years immediately before the Second World War. This report was entitled *Disinherited Youth*. Another report, *Youth and Leisure*, by the National Council of Girls' Clubs, was also produced for the Trust's information. By 1942, the increase in government support for youth clubs reduced the need for Trust support, though a further allocation of £100,000 was made in 1961 by the Trust.

In 1933, the birth of the Scottish Association of Youth Clubs was assisted with a grant of £250. In 1984, the Association received help with computerization for administration and training. Safety on waterways has also been a small but important new concern in this field, with encouragement going to a federation of youth clubs involved in boating and canoeing, such as the Pirate Club on the Regents Park Canal, in London, with its own castle as a base.

It was the NCSS, again, who prompted the birth of the Youth Hostel Association in 1930. The Trust provided £10,000 for development. Hostels were built in the Lake District, Northumberland, the Midlands and in Oxford and the Association gained greatly from the publicity surrounding the Trust's activities. Subsequently, the Trust helped the Scottish Association build a hostel in the Argyll Forest Park, in 1937, and gave further aid to the movement as a whole at the end of the war. In 1970, a grant helped to establish the Slimbridge Youth Hostel for YHA members and school parties to make use of the educational facilities of the Wildfowl Trust's reserve.

Adult Education

In this field, there was a great deal of Trust activity in the 1920s and 1930s, some of it in music and drama, some through organizations such as the Women's Institutes. One enterprise that met with initial success was the Bureau of Current Affairs.

The Bureau was set up with a five-year grant of £150,000 at the end of the Second World War to inform the public about training and other services; it was widely used by various government departments in this area. By June 1947, its publication, *Current Affairs*, had about 10,000 ordinary subscribers and a circulation in the armed forces of 42,000. By October 1948, however, it was still failing to make money. Service demand had fallen, as expected, but there had been no corresponding increase in civilian circulation. When the War Office announced that it would cease to buy the magazine, a year later, the Trust withdrew support and the Bureau went into voluntary liquidation in 1951. This scheme absorbed the greater part of the Trust's expenditure on adult education in the first five or six post-war years.

With greater foresight, and perhaps remembering the failure of Carnegie's own Simplified Spelling Board, the Trust declined to give a grant in 1944 to the playwright Bernard Shaw for an educational scheme of great originality but little future. Shaw wrote the same letter to a number of funding bodies:

> I am at present making my will....My particular fad is the saving of labour by the establishment of a fit British alphabet containing at least 42 letters, and thereby capable of noting with sufficient accuracy for recognition all the sounds of spoken English without having to use more than one letter for each sound.

Arguing that 'Shakespear might have written two or three more plays in the time it took him to spell his name with eleven letters instead of seven,' Shaw proposed to leave his residuary estate to defray the cost of introducing a British alphabet and transliterating the masterpieces of English literature and school reading books. The Trust was not alone in rejecting Shaw's proposal that it should administer his fund; he wrote, acknowledging his failure: 'The need has not been questioned; but the replies are to the same effect: try elsewhere: it is not our job.' The British public was saved!

Breaking completely new ground in adult education, the Trust found greater success with a grant in 1945 to the Council for the Promotion of Field Studies, at Flatford Mill in Suffolk:

> To provide facilities for every aspect of field work at first hand and to set up for this

purpose residential field-study and research centres, distributed throughout the country in localities selected for the richness and variety of their ecological features, geological and geographical interest and archaeological and historical importance.

The project provided scope for amateur nature lovers, which appealed to the Trustees; it was followed by a grant to the Severn Wildfowl Trust, and this aspect of Trust activity was continued in the 1970s under the Trust's combined Heritage programme (see page 203).

In 1957, the Trust allocated £9,000 for amateur science, with the aim of encouraging amateur societies in botany, zoology, archaeology, geology and horticulture and of narrowing the gap between the trained scientist and the amateur. The money was spent on existing field centres, on local field work school, and on a new directory of amateur scientific societies.

The following year, the Trust gave a grant to start a Conservation Corps to improve nature reserves; the scheme also provided for new youth opportunities for leisure and education. Response from young members of the public was unexpectedly good and further grants were given. In 1970, the Conservation Corps became the British Trust for Conservation Volunteers. One subsidiary project given support between 1974 and 1980 was a series of practical handbooks, including *Drystone Walling* and *Footpaths*.

Museums

A report on *Public Museums* published by the Trust in 1928 accused them of being dull, criticised the curators for lack of imagination, and decried the lack of public money and interest (national museums were not included in the report). The report recommended that museums cooperate so that exhibits might be varied and brought to the attention of a wider public. The Trust offered a number of grants and also provided the Museums Association with an annual grant for general expenses.

A second report on the effectiveness of this policy was published ten years later; it confirmed the dire view taken by the first report and recommended an official inquiry but this did not get under way until 1960. Meanwhile, the Trust gave grants for training museum curators and for reorganizing the museums themselves, with little overall success. Between 1951 and 1955, the cost of the Museum scheme rose to £50,000 with much of the additional expenditure being used for the modernisation of Taunton Castle Museum and £24,000 being shared between fifty-one small museums. Another £95,000 was voted for museum schemes between 1956 and 1965. The Trust continued its support throughout the 1960s, providing in all more than £300,000 between 1931 and 1970. Final grants were made in 1975 of £75,339, though some further individual grants have been made relating to the Heritage programme. The continuing grants policy and expert reports over a forty-year period, and aid to the Museums Association for its professional and educational work, undoubtedly helped the museums' service set the basis of standards for which they are respected today.

National Parks

The Trust was caught by surprise when its involvement in the Parks became a subject of contention. In 1954, the Chairman of the Trust, David Marshall, proposed a grant for appropriate buildings to be used as vantage points and rest places, particularly for the elderly, to increase their enjoyment of the areas. Discussions with the Forestry Commission in Scotland came to nothing but agreement was reached with the Peak Park Authority for the Trust to give £36,000 for a suitable natural stone building at Eaglestone Flats.

When the Press reported the offer in July 1955, the building was unfortunately referred to as a 'tea pavilion.' There was a storm of protest at the image of a roadside cafe with advertising hoardings and mountains of litter. The Council for the Preservation of Rural England commented: 'It is wild country to look at and it is wild to enjoy. This cafe could destroy that very thing.' The final blow came when the District Council refused to sell the site to the Park. Not to be defeated, the Trust proceeded with another scheme which fully vindicated its original concept. The David Marshall Pavilion was built at a cost to the Trust of £50,000 in the Queen Elizabeth Forest Park in Perthshire. It has recently been refurbished by its new owners, the Forestry Commission, and is a highly successful vantage point.

In Wales, the Mountain Centre in the Brecon Beacons National Park was built with grants from the Welsh Office, the National Parks Commission and £25,000 from the Trust (total cost £47,000) to act as a focus for visitors and as a place of rest and relaxation. The Centre gained the 1966 premier award of the British Travel Association.

Both these schemes were assessed as important field experiments at the Duke of Edinburgh's Second Conference on 'The Countryside in 1970.' The Trustees' Countryside policy for the masses which had found expression in many ways, such as county libraries, village halls, rural community councils, county committees for music and drama, the Women's Institute movement, Young Farmers' Clubs, projects for remote communities in the Highlands and Islands, was now moving into the enjoyment of the countryside through the National Parks development and linked field studies centres. More recent environmental projects of a similar nature come under the Trust's Heritage scheme.

Ireland

The Society of United Irishwomen received a grant in 1916-17 to help raise the standard of living among the women in the countryside. Early grants were also made for the development of the county library service; this was especially needed where such a high proportion of the population was rural. The foundation in 1921 of the Irish Free State did not affect the eligibility of the southern Irish counties for Trust money, since Carnegie's Deed applied to the whole of the British Isles regardless of political changes, but very little could be done while the country was in the throes of civil war. An

David Marshall Lodge at Aberfoyle, the first countryside visitor centre assisted
by the Trust, 1960

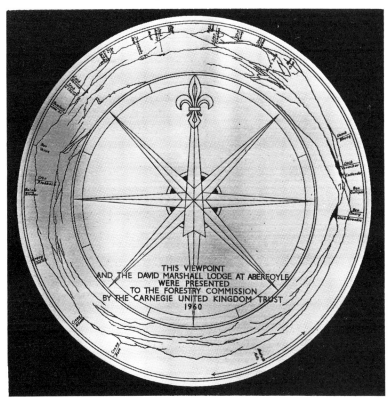

attempt to treat Ireland as a whole through a committee in Dublin collapsed over a religious dispute wholly unconnected with the work of the Trust.

In Northern Ireland, Trust activities were largely channelled through the Rural Development Council, supported entirely by Trust funds from 1931 to 1945. The Council was responsible for the creation of Women's Institutes, the Youth Hostel Association, Young Farmers' Clubs and other similar organizations during this period. Its work was subsequently taken over by the Council for Social Service, which arrived in 1938. The nearest equivalent in the South was Foras Eireann, a conference of national voluntary organizations concerned with cultural, social and economic problems, especially in rural areas. Voluntary social work was less common in the South than in England and there were relatively fewer sources of private funds. Since 1956, Foras Eireann has received a Trust grant for its general administration.

Ireland remained virtually outside the Trust's music and drama policy until the mid-1950s, mainly because the policy was based on the work of county committees which did not exist in Ireland, north or south. In 1957, Foras Eireann conducted a survey of existing amateur music activities with a Trust grant and the Trust also agreed to meet part of the cost of maintaining Foras Eireann's national music advisory service.

Ireland has remained a concern of the Trust but the number of difficulties and differences have limited the assistance it can give. There are exceptions. A well-attended conference in Dublin in 1981 introduced ideas for Heritage Interpretation; recent grants have included an apprenticeship to help maintain the craft of the Irish (Uilleann) Bagpipes; the development of a piping and music centre in Dublin and pre-school playgroup developments throughout the Republic have also been supported. In the North, special emerging voluntary activities, such as the 'Home Start' scheme to support families in distress, continue to attract aid. Regular contact is maintained with the Northern Ireland Council of Social Service to ensure a reliable stream of information. A representative from Northern Ireland, who is blind, sits on the current national Committee of Inquiry into the Arts and Disabled People and is helping with its findings. The recommendations of the Inquiry will encourage new and needed developments in Northern Ireland.

Changing Rôles in the 1970s and 1980s

The post-war years saw the Trust continuing many of its pre-war themes, in music and drama, adult education, youth services, museums, new estates, and so on. Some of those themes have been seen to run through into the 1960s and 1970s. At the same time, the Trust was seeking new areas of endeavour after the restrictions of the war. Community services, field studies, local history, interpreting the environment, renewed emphasis on amateur participation in the arts, volunteer action to enhance the quality of family life, arts for disabled people—these have been some of the themes that have emerged during the 1970s and 1980s.

These themes show that the Trust is maintaining its traditional rôle alongside developments to meet the new needs of society. Its avowed intent is to pioneer in new areas of need and to fill some of the important gaps left by other services. Its immediate aim is to identify the imaginative projects that will make a real contribution to family and community life. It is working where social concern is greatest—for the family and the community under threat, for the care of disabled people and the quality of their life, for the pressures of increased leisure through unemployment and shorter working hours. Operating under its quinquennial policy, the Trust has confined itself during the late 1970s and the first half of the 1980s to three main areas of operation, covering both old and new challenges. These areas have been the arts, community services and heritage interpretation.

THE ARTS

In outlining its current programme for the arts, the Trust has tried to encourage amateur participation especially by providing assistance from professional artists in order to raise standards. Drama, music, creative writing and effective speech have all been of interest, so have the less developed arts such as mime and puppetry. Special interest has been taken in schemes which help the disabled and the disadvantaged, particularly where such a scheme, when developed, could have national implications. Arts workshops have provided a positive framework for encouraging, involving and assisting disabled people.

The 1980s opened with a great deal of activity on this front, due mainly to the initiative of the Trust's Secretary. SCAD, the Scottish Committee on Arts and Disability, was set up in 1980 with Trust aid, in association with the Royal Bank of Scotland and the Scottish Arts Council. Among several multi-sponsored activities, and a donation from the Chevron Oil Company, was a series of Scottish Baroque Ensemble concerts and a composition, *Sonata with Some Pine-trees*. The national inquiry into the Arts and Disabled People, initiated by the Trust and chaired by Sir Richard Attenborough, delivers its report in 1985.

One of the most successful of recent Trust-aided ventures has been the Shape organization in London and its network of independent 'Artlink' organizations throughout the country. Shape was established to provide arts activities for people with disabilities: professional artists of all kinds perform and participate in hospitals, day centres, prisons and communities of every kind where the disabled and the disadvantaged might not normally have access to the arts and might benefit particularly from arts activities. Gina Levete, who started Shape, has subsequently formed an international organization for the exchange of artists; it is called 'Interlink.' By 1984, the Shape organizations had received more then £250,000 from the Trust. As with the Pre-school Playgroup Network, Carnegie is the only Trust in the United Kingdom to have aided the overall movement over a number of years. This support to the development of a theme, an organization or an activity over a period of time is a notable and distinctive feature of the Trust's work.

The Winged Fellowship Trust received a grant in 1981 to provide holiday centres for the severely disabled with a two weeks' drama course in conjunction with the Highway Theatre Company. The year before, the Lincoln Diocesan Deaf Association received support for a drama centre in a converted church, with the emphasis on puppets, mime and a religious drama group. In Brighton, Carousel has been supported in the use of drama, song, movement and play to create a rich environment for children and adults who have disabilities; its work with the mentally handicapped is being paid special attention by the Trust. Theatre Workshop in Edinburgh has already been seen at work; its continuing aim is to effect an interchange by inviting the community into the centre and by taking the arts into the community. Support has been given for several years to work with disabled children, involving parents and teachers.

Recent grants have also gone to support tutor training for the deaf in drama: Pat Keysell, initiator of the Theatre for the Deaf and the National Festival of Mime, is directing this scheme and has been the first-ever appointment for a Mime Artist in Residence at a major Arts Centre. Another teacher supported by the Trust has been Veronica Sherborne, whose films have shown how movement experience can contribute to the progress of severely handicapped people in self-image and in building relationships, and who wanted her work to be studied. Drama for the Blind and adult education courses in Talking with Confidence have also received recent Trust aid.

The Polka Children's Theatre has also been seen in action in the 1970s. More than 10,000 children visited in the first four years of this marvellous puppet theatre. Parents of disabled children are encouraged to bring them into workshops which also attract young people who want to work with the handicapped. In Somerset, a 'live' theatre company is used by Children's World to demonstrate the benefits of creative activities for enjoyment and education in special schools, ordinary schools and festivals. One headmaster commented:

> The children have learnt to express themselves naturally through movement and dialogue, and the valuable experience gained has greatly improved the quality of their written English. The less able and more reserved pupils have blossomed out and the more outgoing children have matured considerably as a result of the communication skills that have developed.

Meanwhile, the Colway Theatre Trust is continuing to put on a new community drama each year involving local inhabitants from particular towns in the South and West; the Cumbernauld Theatre in Scotland is also using community drama to create an alternative approach to education whether in a special school or with unemployed young people. The Children's Music Theatre is putting zest and professionalism into productions for large casts of talented young. The British Theatre Association, founded in 1919 and the only national organization to bring together professionals and amateurs interested in drama, has agreed to administer a special Trust allocation of £40,000 to provide new technical equipment to local amateur theatre groups, under the title of 'Money for New Rope.' Because of its success, further money is to be allocated up to

1987. This form of grant-aid by arrangement with a national body to assist their local groups is special and has been very successfully promoted by the Trustees. They welcome their aid getting to the 'grass roots' in practical action, whether by the provision of modern equipment or, as with a scheme through the British Federation of Music Festivals, to encourage new classes and improved management techniques.

In Belfast, Neighbourhood Open Workshops have been encouraging people to share their ideas through music and drama and to collaborate in 'weaving a tapestry about the island of their dreams' in an effort to combine social services with exploration of particular themes. In Dublin, Na Piobairi Uilleann, the Society of Irish Pipers, has received support for its new headquarters with an archive of Irish pipe music and a music studio. Meanwhile, in Britain, Carnegie would have been pleased to learn that the Trust has been reviving its connection with organs by assisting with the restoration of fine pipe organs in civic buildings, though it is not part of the current Trust policy to make grants for church organs. Some £200,000 has now been allocated to the restoration of thirteen important pipe organs, including a grant to the largest of them all

Rochdale Town Hall, 1913. J. J. Binns Organ, the first to be restored with Trust grant in 1978

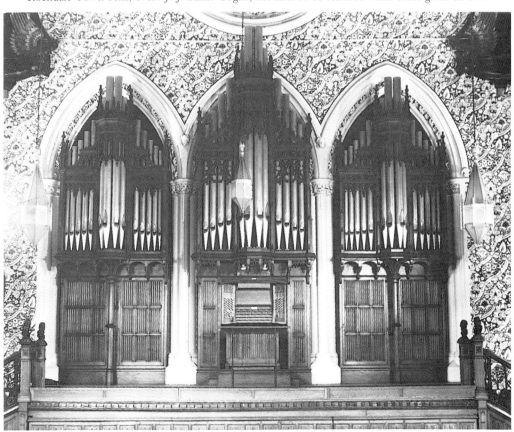

Kidderminster Town Hall, 1854. William Hill Organ restored in 1982

at the Royal Albert Hall, London, and to a smaller Schulze organ originally provided by Andrew Carnegie in a Durham church and now restored at Ellesmere College Arts Centre. Another welcome restoration in 1984 has been for the organ belonging to the Royal National Institute for the Blind.

An unusual grant was to the Seafarers' Education Service to provide a film collection for free loan to ships at sea, an art tutor on board ship and then for the commissioning of a symphony by one Jack Hawkins on a container ship in the South Atlantic.

Grants in 1984 ranged from the development of Shape throughout the United Kingdom to that of the dramatic work of the York, Orkney and Scottish Youth Theatres, the Colway Trust in Dorset, the music of the National Youth Brass Band and National Youth Orchestra of Scotland, and the Scottish National Orchestra Junior and Youth Choirs; a residential music course for the disabled and a special arts festival in Northern Ireland to arts for disabled people in Wales and the special educational tasks of the Disabled Living Foundation. The Guildhall School of Music, in London, has started a course for fourth-year students, inspired by Peter Renshaw, former Principal of the Yehudi Menuhin School, to involve them musically in disability centres and special schools and so widen the students' understanding of audiences and the way music can be presented. The aim is 'to eliminate the capital C in culture.' The Trust is evidently keeping in mind the full geographical range of its responsibilities as well as the needs of many different people in amateur art forms.

COMMUNITY SERVICES

The Trust is concerned with the improvement and care of family life, especially where there is substantial involvement by volunteers. Small, cost-effective schemes in neighbourhoods have had preference, and those which have encouraged participation and integration into a community and an improvement in the quality of life have been readily supported. One of the main aims of the Trust has been to encourage active cooperation between statutory and voluntary agencies; in many ways this can be seen as a development of the Trust's original social welfare and community work. *The Future of Voluntary Organisations* was the report of the Committee headed by Lord Wolfenden, a former Chairman of the Trust, and established in cooperation with and administered by the Joseph Rowntree Memorial Trust. Its task was to inquire into the rôle and functions of voluntary organizations in the last quarter of the 20th century, which led to a new momentum in voluntary work.

The Pre-school Playgroups Association (PPA) has, for example, continued to be extremely successful in the 1980s. In 1978, the Trust allocated £36,000 to 130 groups in England and Wales for special activities, including special equipment for groups with handicapped children and multi-racial groups. A further allocation of £30,000 was made for 1982-84, for a continuation of these and other activities.

Comparable grants were made to the Scottish, Northern Ireland and the Irish PPA for training and educational work. The aid in Scotland helped to promote a new and challenging 'Stepping Stones' concept in family centres. Carnegie is the only Trust to have assisted all PPAs throughout the United Kingdom and Ireland. The Trust Secretary, Geoffrey Lord, says that the movement is one of, if not *the*, most significant of post-war voluntary developments.

At the other end of life's scale, the Lifeskills project from Age Concern enables retired elderly people to make a contribution to the community through the skills they have acquired during their working lives. In between the young and the old, Family Forum has received total grants of £45,000 over three years to be a focus for the exchange of information between government and local authorities and organizations concerned with the family and its needs, to monitor the impact of policies, to educate and inform the public, and to stimulate the interest of those who are instrumental in making policy on issues of particular relevance to families.

NEWPIN, the New Parent Infant Network, aims to provide friends for new mothers to help them to avoid the risk of depression and to have a happy, healthy baby; it was formed in London largely because of concern for the causes of child abuse and prenatal mortality. Growing Up in Scotland received £10,000 in 1980-81 for the formation of self-help groups for parents of children aged five to twelve. Cope aims to develop family groups in several towns as a means of support for parents who are vulnerable or 'at risk'

Playgroup activity in Northern Ireland

because of isolation; Cope offers a chance for men, women and children of all ages and races to enjoy developing basic educational and social skills. Other training courses for One-Parent Families attempt to make more understandable the complex rules about benefits, maintenance and tax—in Britain, one in eight families have single parents; this represents more than 900,000 lone parents bringing up more than one-and-a-half million children.

The Family Welfare Association of Manchester received a total of £39,200 to help it to develop specialized services to families experiencing the effects of disability. A scheme in York, known as PACT, or Parents and Children Together, aims to encourage links between families with handicapped children and volunteers willing to care for them within their own families at special times. In Liverpool, the Personal Service Society is concerned with care for the terminally ill in their own homes and with support for their families; the aim is to enable those, for example, who are suffering from cancer to die with dignity, with as little suffering as possible and among relatives. The Breakthrough Trust helps to integrate deaf and hearing people in social opportunities by regular contact with each other, described as a 'deafinite' approach to the problems of communication! The National Bureau for Handicapped Students meanwhile aims to inform and influence those in educational circles on the needs for opportunities for all disabled students to allow them equal access to education.

The PHAB clubs were already receiving Trust support in the 1970s. There are already about 300 of these groups in the United Kingdom (and more than 1,500 volunteers) aimed at bringing together the physically handicapped and the able-bodied on an equal basis in club activities. Recently, the Trust has assisted the new and important development of the PHAB clubs in Scotland. In slight contrast, Contact a Family has tackled another aspect of isolation by assisting families with handicapped children to talk to others. A major grant has also gone recently for a peripatetic teacher, or parent counsellor, to provide special help for the National Association for Deaf-Blind and Rubella Handicapped, to encourage parents to work with their very handicapped children to lessen the effect of their problem and to lay the foundations for some form of communication. In the same vein, the Association for All Speech Impaired Children received £10,000 to help with activity day courses in the regions; and help was given for pre-school work and a teacher at the National Centre for Cued Speech for the Deaf. Cued Speech uses a combination of sign language and lip reading.

Unemployment is another community concern. The Trust has supported the National Association of Youth Clubs, which has 750,000 members in 6,500 affiliated clubs in the United Kingdom, to provide a 'Dayspace' scheme for services for those leaders working with unemployed young people. 'City Challenge,' an urban outward-bound activity, and the more unconventional 'Youth Call,' promoting the concept and need of a nationwide community-service scheme, are both endeavours backed by the Trust to help youth in the community and to develop leadership potential. In Wiltshire, the Shaw Trust was launched with Trust aid in 1981 to provide employment opportunities for disabled people near their homes. Another recent involvement for the

Contact-a-Family working with disabled children—street fun

202

Trust is a study of Children in Custody, aimed at finding alternative strategies of care and discipline.

Perhaps the most interesting recent involvement of the Trust in unemployment, reflecting back on its work during the Depression, has been with the Unemployed Voluntary Action Fund. Late in 1981, the Secretary of State for Scotland invited the Trustees to administer grant-in-aid to be made available by the government for 'opportunities for volunteering' in Scotland. This was an unusual request and a highly innovative step for both government and the Trust. The object was to stimulate volunteer projects in the fields of health, social work, community education and community development, with special reference to the unemployed and the young unemployed. During the first year, 1982-83, about £400,000 was allocated to forty-four organizations; further grant-in-aid of £540,000 was provided by the government for 1983-84, and the scheme, because of its success, is to continue for at least three more years.

HERITAGE

In the early 1970s, the Trust set up a working party to review the development of open-air museums in the United Kingdom. One outcome was a decision to unite under one umbrella the concepts of conservation, the development of museums, and the enjoyment of the countryside within a policy of Heritage Interpretation. The Trust programme now falls into four main categories: these are heritage centres, interpretative display schemes, education and training, and environmental schemes. The Centre for Environmental Interpretation in Manchester was established to create a philosophy, training programmes and guidelines for organizations, for residents and for visitors. One theme drew the various strands of the Trust's programme together: 'Through interpretation—understanding; through understanding—appreciation; through appreciation—participation; through participation—protection.'

The first regional scheme in the United Kingdom was the Carnegie Norfolk Project, interpreting at different sites in the county various themes such as 'Water and Transport,' and 'Food from the Land.' Started in 1973, it is still receiving Trust support, although not fully accepted by the local councils despite comparable and successful schemes in other regions, such as Pennine Heritage.

As with libraries and museums, support has been given to the professional body, the Society for the Interpretation of Britain's Heritage (SIBH), to improve contacts and standards; 1984 brought the introduction of the Carnegie Interpret Britain awards—fifteen made in the first year—to assist local heritage through adjudication and assessment.

Among other centres given support in recent years have been a Nature Centre at Loch Leven and a Centre at Ness on the Isle of Lewis to tell the story of the crofters and their lifestyle, their fishing, their trade, their battles, whisky stills, courtship and customs, their Special Constables and Truant Officers. The old silk industry in Essex is celebrated through the Braintree and Bocking Heritage Trust. Canal walkers and

Amberley Chalk Pits Museum, volunteers at work:
ABOVE Removal of water-pump from Gatwick, Sussex 1983
BELOW Restoration of 1935 Austin Van

Quarry Bank Mill Trust, Styal, Cheshire:
ABOVE LEFT The Mill in its woodland setting ABOVE RIGHT Village cottages
BELOW An impression of life in the Apprentice House before 1847

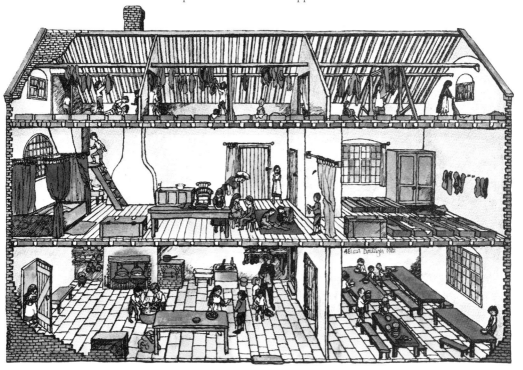

205

waterway users find enlightenment through the Kennet and Avon Canal Trust. The Chalk Pits Museum in West Sussex provides nature and geology trails in between its massive old lime kilns. A first-floor tenement flat in the heart of Glasgow has been restored by the National Trust for Scotland, complete with its original box and recess beds, closed range, 'jawbox' kitchen sink and coal box. An historic fishing vessel is being restored at Anstruther Fisheries Museum in Fife. In New Lanark, it is an eighteenth-century cotton-mill village, the testing ground for Robert Owen's social reforms, that has received support. A comparable village at Styal, near Macclesfield, has an industrial scheme tracing the cotton revolution through the life of Samuel Greg, an Irishman who introduced apprenticeships.

The polar explorer, Wally Herbert, has been investigating the possibility for a future Explorers' Museum, initially at Sir Francis Drake's home in Devon and more recently in London's Tower Bridge area. In Canterbury, there is a Centre to help visitors explore this ancient mediaeval and cathedral city. The Grasmere and Wordsworth Museum, undeterred by the knowledge that Wordsworth himself was not enthusiastic about museums, has created a local environmental display with a reproduction of a farm kitchen interior of the 1880s and representations of the poet's own life and work. On the Medway, a Heritage Centre tells the story of this river from the time that the Ancient Britons settled on its banks, through the sixteenth century and the Royal Dockyards, to the present-day container ports. In Macclesfield, a Heritage Centre has been based on a former Sunday School, erected in 1813, which in its heyday housed 2,500 children and played an important part in the education and enlightenment of the working people in this former 'silk town.' Other new Heritage Centres are found at Faversham, apparently the first in Britain, and from Crail to Eastbourne, from Lichfield to Torfaen and at Morwellham in Devon. At the old Willsbridge Mills near Bristol, built in 1712 for the rolling and splitting of hoop iron and steel manufacture and later for flour milling, the Avon Wildlife Trust has created the country's first wildlife and countryside centre.

The Trust has added grants to provide a travelling curator for private museums in Scotland; for a folk-museum in the Orkneys; for a film on Mountain Rescue; for the only available taxidermy course and apprenticeship in the country; for a marvellous collection of natural history books, put together by a doctor and endowed to the Scottish Natural History Library; and for a display about the Romans, Saxons, saints and legends, pilgrims and romantics associated with Hadrian's Wall in Northumberland. In the new town of Milton Keynes, an imaginative scheme encourages people to look at their townscape more closely; it draws attention to the scenery of the built-up landscape. In contrast, in Exeter Forest, an ingenious Beginner's Way, created by a young sculptor, takes a mile walk over a rope bridge, across a drawbridge, through a tunnel, over stepping stones, between the trees and past innumerable hidden delights to draw out all kinds of moods. The walk has delighted a huge variety of 'explorers,' especially the young and the mentally handicapped. One response was that it 'massages parts of us that are usually completely ignored'; another

The Wordsworth Museum at Grasmere:
ABOVE Dove Cottage with the converted coach-house museum to the rear
BELOW The domestic scene in the old museum

Scottish Conservation Projects Trust:
     ABOVE Youngsters working on an urban woodland in Glasgow
     BELOW Drystane dyking in Aberdeenshire
     OPPOSITE Building a footbridge on the Southern Upland Way in Dumfriesshire

'beginner' admitted that, 'I found it a bit terrifying—I saw a lot of things about my life that I'd been trying to hide from myself.' The talents of the young artist are to be supported in 1985 in the Crathes district through the interest of the National Trust for Scotland under a theme of 'The Wonderings of Bennachie.'

Between 1969 and 1981, more than £100,000 has gone to the Royal Society for Nature Conservation, for interpretative schemes and conservation or education officers. In addition, the Trust has continued its support for the British Trust for Conservation Volunteers (formerly, the Conservation Corps, see page 191). In one recent year alone, nearly 4,000 volunteers completed nearly 50,000 work days in the national scheme and more than 15,000 volunteers were engaged in practical conservation tasks in the 300 or more local groups. In 1982, the Trust gave a grant toward a training centre at BTCV's new national headquarters near Reading, the most important development since the Volunteers began. The Trust has also helped the newly-independent Scottish Conservation Projects Trust to pioneer work where unemployed people are encouraged to take part in voluntary tasks to improve the urban environment. The breadth and scope are exceptional and all develop the techniques of interpretation of the environment which should contribute to better understanding and action for the conservation of Britain's unique heritage.

Looking forward

The Trust has a number of schemes to celebrate Carnegie's anniversary in 1985. These include a newly commissioned work for brass band and choir by Peter Maxwell Davies; a new work for orchestra by John McCabe, to be performed by the National Youth Orchestra of Scotland during their European tour for European Music Year; a new concerto for organ, strings and percussion by Dr Francis Jackson; a United Kingdom organ competition for a new work comprising six *études* in the style of J. S. Bach, Handel and Scarlatti, the tercentenary of whose birth occurs in 1985; and a series of organ recitals on a number of famous organs in civic buildings which the Trust has helped to restore: 'Bach plus 300' will be performed at Perth, Rochdale, Norwich, Swansea and London.

Regarding its current philosophy in a recent report, the Trust recalled some of its main objectives and particular abilities:

> To think and plan ahead, to be sensitive to change and to examine and select areas of potential concern, and by the creative use of income to support experiment and new developments of particular flair and influence. It may decide to concentrate its resources in certain policies or 'prime the pump.' It may complement the aims and work of other agencies, and seek to lead opinion in new directions. Occasionally there will be inspired and practical projects which break the rules and may lead to new challenges for future policies. Part of the Trust's work is to seek out rewarding areas of interest, and bring together on neutral ground people with ideas from different disciplines and from the ensuing discussions distil the essence of new thoughts for new policies.

Looking ahead in this manner, the Trustees are considering possible policies for the 1986-1990 quinquennial period. The main area of interest is likely to be in opportunities for informal learning and participation, perhaps through three grant committees, on arts, the environment, and community service. The special policy on the Arts and Disabled People will continue and the Trust will be considering the recommendations that arise from their current Committee of Inquiry on the subject.

Summing up his own impressions of the Trust's work, the Chairman, Timothy Colman, suggests certain features. These include:

> Total independence from government at all levels. The ability and the incentive to pioneer. The ability to respond to new situations, perhaps faster than government can find it possible to respond. The ability to act as a catalyst between different people or voluntary organizations who may be working far apart on similar lines but have not yet come into contact.

Geoffrey Lord adds an essential ingredient to this list of assets: the support of talented and enterprising individuals who themselves should preferably have the backing of a dynamic and forward-looking organization. He believes that three important factors make the Trust different from most other philanthropic foundations: the wish to grip a

THE FUTURE OF VOLUNTARY ORGANISATIONS

REPORT OF THE WOLFENDEN COMMITTEE

Interpretation of the Environment
– a Bibliography

Carnegie United Kingdom Trust

The Arts and Disabilities

A Creative Response
to Social Handicap

Edited by
GEOFFREY LORD

Foreword by
His Royal Highness
·The PRINCE of WALES·

Milestone in Education for Social Work

The Carnegie Experiment
1954–1958

ALMA E. HARTSHORN

THE CARNEGIE
UNITED KINGDOM TRUST

Four recent publications by the Trust

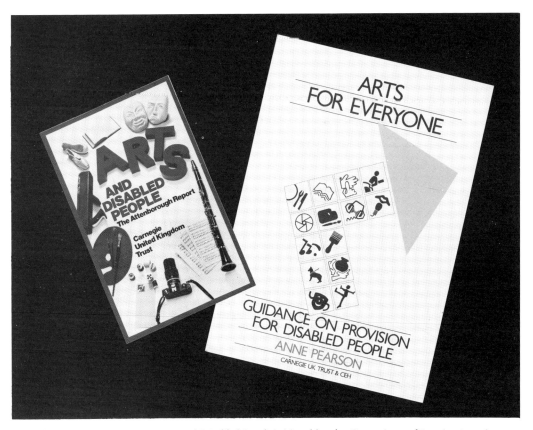

The most recent reports: *Arts and Disabled People* initiated by the Committee of Inquiry into the Arts and Disabled People chaired by Sir Richard Attenborough, and *Arts for Everyone*, a joint project with the Centre on Environment for the Handicapped

theme and support its development, and the people and organizations contributing to that theme, until success is evident; the careful examination of issues leading up to the selection of a policy; and the important conditions of grant-aid, including the submission of reports. Lord also emphasizes that all Trust policies have an overall educational impact to bring pleasure and enjoyment. In this, he echoes a key theme from a speech by Sir Hector Hetherington, a Trustee, in 1963, on the occasion of the 50th anniversary of the Trust: 'The all-important thing is that our every major policy has had a clear educational intention.'

This general view would be shared by all the Carnegie organizations and, of course, by Andrew Carnegie himself. It emphasizes the fundamental importance of the individual, and the value of independence, innovation and flexibility of response. The United Kingdom Trust has given ample evidence of all these ingredients in action over an extraordinarily varied canvas.

The Search for Peace

Peace was Carnegie's main pursuit in the later years of his life, when he was running out of ideas and enthusiasm for further educational projects. Between 1904 and 1919, he gave more than $25,000,000 to fund a number of 'Temples of Peace' and major foundations concerned with peace and the 'heroes of peace.'

It was his involvement in the early stages of the conflict between the Union and the Confederacy that gave Carnegie his first-hand experience of what modern warfare might entail, though it did not appear to mark him to any great degree; he quickly returned from the defence of Washington against the Southerners to his expanding commercial interests in the North. He expressed his desire to abolish war but as late as 1900 he was still opposed to any involvement in peace movements. 'We already have Peace Societies and Arbitration Societies,' he wrote to W. T. Stead, editor of *The Review of Reviews*. 'I do not see that it is wise to devote our efforts to creating another organization.' Under pressure from Stead and other friends to take positive action, Carnegie declared with good sense, 'There is nothing that robs a righteous cause of its strength more than a millionaire's money.'

Carnegie's straightforward character seldom allowed for sudden changes of mind, either in the world of business or in his private life, so his abrupt turn-around from something of a jingoist to become a 'peace at any price' man may seem at first a little surprising. But he was in increasing contact with men of power and influence whose views on the wider world encouraged Carnegie to mellow both as a man and a humanist. He was also looking for a mission, as Professor Wall points out, 'spurred on by the vast wealth that the selling of his Company had brought him.' He found the pursuit of peace to be that mission.

Carnegie's was a personal brand of pacifism, curiously insensitive to the complex moral and social questions raised by some others; it sprang from the mind of a man of great wealth who lived in a country of great power. Carnegie was accustomed to putting a price on what he wanted, on his own terms; he wanted peace and believed that it might somehow be purchased. It was an uncompromising view that did not endear him to many outside the United States; even those within the States viewed his ideas with some alarm. Nevertheless, the prospect of so much financial aid drew the world's leaders inexorably toward Carnegie, while friends and eager acquaintances acted as go-betweens. It was in this atmosphere of conflicting ideals and mutual regard that Carnegie's first endowments for peace were made.

He started with a fund for civilian heroes and followed this with support for simplified spelling throughout the English speaking world. No one could quite see how these were going to further the cause of international peace, except for Carnegie, but there was more to come: ten more national funds for the 'heroes of peace'; three buildings, or 'peace palaces,' dedicated to dialogue and justice between nations; a Church Peace Union to rally men of all religions to pursue international brotherhood; and the Carnegie Endowment for International Peace, the largest and most active of Carnegie's efforts in this field and still deeply involved in discussions about world affairs.

Whatever the success or failure of Carnegie's endeavours, his dedication to the pursuit of peace cannot be doubted; it was his closest and most genuine concern for more than a decade, and so it was ironic that the world's bloodiest and most terrible conflict should have punctuated his last years.

Carnegie Peace Foundations and Buildings

Hero Funds
Eleven funds established between 1904 and 1911 in America, Britain, France, Germany, Norway, Switzerland, the Netherlands, Sweden, Denmark, Belgium and Italy.

Total endowment:	$10,540,000

The Simplified Spelling Board
Established in 1906

Contributions from Carnegie:	$170,000
Contributions from Carnegie Corporation:	$110,000

Carnegie Endowment for International Peace
Founded in 1910

Endowment:	$10,000,000

Temples of Peace
The International Court of Justice at The Hague
Founded in 1903; dedicated in 1913

Endowment:	$1,500,000

The Central American Court of Justice
Gifts in 1908 and 1910 (after destruction)

Total gifts:	$200,000

The Pan American Union Building
Gift proposed in 1907; dedication in 1910

Total gifts:	$850,000

The Church Peace Union
Founded in 1914

Endowment from Carnegie Corporation:	$2,000,000
	$25,370,000

CARNEGIE HERO FUND COMMISSION

In January 1904, the lives of 178 men and boys were lost in the Harwick mine disaster, near Pittsburgh. Among the victims was a former mine superintendent who went into the collapsed workings in an attempt to rescue others. It was this tragedy that directly led Carnegie to institute the Hero Fund Commission, with the intention of honouring those 'heroes of civilization' who are injured or killed when trying to save their fellows.

Those eligible for an award are civilians who voluntarily risk their lives to an extraordinary degree in saving or attempting to save the life of another. Excluded are members of the armed services and other persons whose vocations or duties require them to risk their lives. The act 'must have been performed in the United States, Canada or the waters thereof and must be brought to the attention of the Commission within two years of the date of the rescue.'

Acts of heroism are brought to the attention of the Commission through media reports or by individual notification. Each recommended act is carefully investigated by Commission staff. If the act is recognized by the Commission, then a Carnegie Medal and a cash sum are awarded and, as appropriate, a continuing grant toward living costs and education. Up to 1980, medals of gold, silver or bronze were given, according to merit, but now there is only a single medal. In those cases where those honoured have sacrificed their lives in their attempt to rescue another, the medal and the monetary benefit are given to the dependants. The medal bears this inscription: 'Greater love hath no man than this, that a man lay down his life for his friends.'

Carnegie Hero Fund Commission
Founded: 1904

Purpose: To honour civilians who risk their lives saving or attempting to save the lives of other persons, and to provide financial assistance to disabled heroes and to the dependants of heroes who lose their lives in the performance of the rescue acts.

Finance:

Original endowment:		$5,000,000
Additional endowments:		$750,000
Additional funds from Carnegie Corporation:		$100,000
Current assets, March 1984:		$12,421,000
Annual monies in early years:	*Income*	*Expenditure*
1904:	$127,000	$47,100
1905:	$256,000	$20,000
1906:	$264,000	$92,000

Annual monies in recent years:

1983:	$984,000	$910,000
1984 (estimated):	$1,000,000	$950,000
1985 (estimated):	$1,000,000	$950,000
Total monies, 1904-1984 (estimated):	$19,324,000	$18,210,000
Total monetary awards, 1904-1983:		$15,003,944

Grants and awards:

Number of grants, 1905-1907:	126
Number of grants (approx), 1982-1984:	294
Total grants, 1904-1984:	6,875

Latest annual figure, 1983:

Medals awarded:	97
Posthumous awards:	20
Grants made:	$441,508

Projected totals, 1904 to June 1985:

Total cases considered:	60,750
Total awards:	6,900
Posthumous awards:	1,420

Major categories of rescue acts:
  Rescue from drowning
  Rescue from burning structure
  Automobile accidents
  Industrial accidents
  Acts of civil violence

Two special awards, gold medals mounted on bronze tablets, were made in honour of heroes of the steamship *Titanic*, lost off Newfoundland, 15th April 1912, and of the mine disaster at Springhill, Nova Scotia, 23rd October 1958.

Administration:
President: Robert W. Off.
Vice-President and Secretary: Walter F. Toerge.
Full-time staff: 9.
Address: 606 Oliver Building, Pittsburgh, PA 15222.

Carnegie Hero Fund Commission

Of all his endowments, this was closest to Carnegie's heart; in some ways, too, it represents his best side—direct and straightforward in intention, a little ingenuous some would say, but humane. Whereas most of his other trusts were suggested to him, he took particular pride that this was his own idea, his personal contribution to the abolition of war. As far back as 1885, he had pointed out in the *New York Tribune* that noble things are done in peace as well as war.

Many scorned the Fund for seeking publicly to reward those whose actions were beyond the call of human duty and thus above consideration of reward. Newspapers and journals at first showed little sympathy for the scheme; it was easy for the cynical to suggest that the thought of reward would stimulate would-be heroes into precipitate action. Carnegie replied firmly:

> I do not expect to stimulate or create heroism by this fund, knowing well that heroic action is impulsive; but I do believe that, if the hero is injured in his bold attempt to serve or save his fellows, he and those dependent upon him should not suffer pecuniarily.

Recognizing the reality that heroes and their families often did suffer as a result of such deeds, Carnegie not only wished to reward heroism but also to provide financial help in cases where hardship resulted from death or injury to the hero. There was no Welfare State to compensate for such a loss; to lose a bread-winner was, for many families, a disaster from which they never recovered.

It was the Harwick mine disaster and the heroic action of the mine superintendent that determined Carnegie to establish a permanent fund to help in such cases. The community raised $40,000 for the bereaved. Carnegie matched this sum with a donation of his own and then sat down to write the opening paragraph of a Deed of Trust:

> We live in an heroic age. Not seldom are we thrilled by deeds of heroism where men or women are injured or lose their lives in attempting to preserve or rescue their fellows; such the heroes of civilization. The heroes of barbarism maimed or killed theirs.

His conclusion was simple: why should not the heroes of peace be rewarded, just as the heroes of war were traditionally praised? He was delighted with what he had done. He called the Fund 'my ain bairn.' It appealed to his idealism: 'I don't believe there's a nobler fund in all the world,' he wrote.

In fulfilling its brief, the Commission has always been equally enthusiastic but it has also been cautious; its criteria have necessarily been strict. A team of field investigators is employed to look minutely into the facts of each case that is brought to its attention. These investigators often go to extraordinary lengths to establish the real worth of a reported action; it is unlikely that any bogus claim would get much further than the Commission's wastepaper basket. Only ten percent of recommended acts receive final recognition.

If the case looks promising, the investigator will visit the scene, interview witnesses and the rescuer and rescued if they are still alive, and anyone else acquainted with the circumstances or with the individuals; he takes measurements and maps the area, fills in forms for specific categories of problems, and finally interviews the dependants to discover the degree of their need. This demands great tact and objectivity in a highly

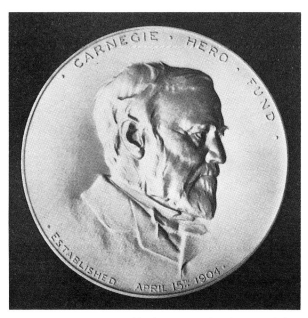

Andrew Carnegie's profile dominates the obverse of the
American Carnegie Medal, which is struck in bronze and
is three inches in diameter

emotional circumstance; it is also necessary to recognize unintentional exaggeration in a witness's report as well as genuine reluctance on the part of many people to be seen as heroic. Sometimes the investigators are rebuffed but not often. In many cases, people are only too glad of someone who is taking a genuine interest.

Some investigations make considerable demands in terms of travel and research; indeed, the Carnegie investigation has been called more thorough than many conducted by government agencies. There was, for example, the time when Walter Rutkowski had to fly to the Yukon, charter a truck and drive into the tundra to verify an act of valour in which a gold-miner held off a bear with an axe while trying to save a Canadian college student from being killed.

Other investigations end in failure. Jim Rethi had a candidate whose body was found lying next to that of a small boy inside a house that had been destroyed by fire. The man had been nominated for an award because he had been observed running back into the burning building that housed his apartment; it looked as if he might have been trying to save the boy. But Rethi found that the man had bought a new television set that day, and then he found that the man's blood alcohol level was very high. 'Even though it seemed apparent at first that the man went in to save the little boy,' said Rethi, 'it could not be established beyond a reasonable doubt.' No medal was awarded.

The investigators are probably in the best position to assess why people perform heroic deeds. People are seldom heroic before crowds, they say; potential rescuers often think that someone more capable will take over or that they will look foolish. Yet

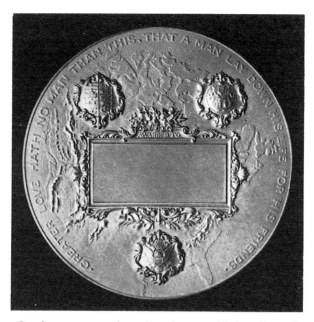

On the reverse are the seals and geographical outlines of the United States and Canada. The cartouche carries the awardee's name and a brief description of the heroic act.

when the same person faces a situation alone, he or she is impelled to action because of the knowledge that no one else is there to help. On the whole, heroism is an impulsive act, as Carnegie himself realized. 'I don't know why I did it,' said one rescuer. 'If I had stopped to think I couldn't have gone through with it,' said another. That was probably true of a case quoted by Rethi of a man who rescued a little girl from a burning building:

> Once inside the building, the man found to his dismay that the girl's mother was a deputy sheriff and that her ammunition was starting to explode in the heat. Dodging bullets all the while, the man high-stepped his way through the thick smoke with the girl cradled in his arms. He lifted his feet so high, in fact, that he stepped right through an open window and tumbled to the ground.

At one time, there was a staff of seventeen. During the Second World War, only one remained. Today, there is a staff of nine including three field representatives. When, on the basis of their reports, the Commission recognizes an act of heroism, a citation is prepared and a medal is presented. Every attempt is made to provide the necessary financial award as quickly as possible. The case is not then abandoned. Great effort is made to follow up cases to ascertain the extent of further need and the progress of any children in school. This personal concern is considered by the Commission to be as important in their work as the initial award.

The reports of cases which appear in the Commission's *Yearbook* are written in a bland, unembroidered style that often helps to emphasize the bleak reality that must often accompany each heroic act. There is little in those reports that smacks of derring-do, yet they readily conjure up the selfless qualities of true heroism. Here are three examples taken at random:

Carnegie Medal awarded to Thomas Peter Yuskus, who saved Robert P. Allen, Jr. from drowning, Glenwood, Illinois, June 13, 1981. Robert, 12, and a friend were swept from their bicycles into floodwaters covering Arquilla Park, which was inundated by Thorn Creek after two days of heavy rain. Irregular currents moved Robert into eight-foot deep water, where he shouted for help. Yuskus, 38, quality control inspector, swam 240 feet to Robert, who struggled with him and caused him to swallow water, which was contaminated. Despite the swift undercurrent and Robert's struggling, Yuskus swam 120 feet with Robert to a partially submerged tree, where they rested. A man with an inner tube arrived and took Robert to safety. Before leaving the flooded area, Yuskus searched unsuccessfully for Robert's friend, who drowned.   6649

Carnegie Medal awarded to James Young McDaniel, who died as a result of his efforts to save an indeterminate number of persons from being shot, Daingerfield, Texas, June 22, 1980. When a man armed with four weapons entered the nave of a church, fired at the worshipers, and was forced into the foyer by a member of the congregation, McDaniel, aged 53, railroad shop foreman, followed them into the foyer, where the two men had fallen to the floor. McDaniel grabbed the assailant and, struggling with him, pushed him through the front door of the church to the outside. During the struggle, McDaniel was wounded. Another man who then sought to subdue the assailant also was shot. McDaniel and the other wounded man died, as did three of the persons wounded in the initial gunfire.   6516

Bronze Medal awarded to Ethel H. Kline, who saved Prudence Marmurowicz and Kimberly Mueller from being struck by an automobile, West Allis, Wisc., December 16, 1977. Mrs. Kline, aged 60, was standing on the sidewalk at an intersection with Prudence, aged 11, and Kimberly, aged 6, when an automobile became involved in a collision at the crossing and then veered toward them. Mrs. Kline pushed each girl in a different direction, removing them from danger; but she was unable to move out of the path of the oncoming vehicle before it struck her. Mrs. Kline, who was dragged some distance by the automobile, required hospitalization for her injuries.   6375

The pattern of rescue acts has changed over the years. Where there used to be animal attacks and runaway horse teams, there are now crashed and burning vehicles, and industrial accidents. Ironically, in view of Carnegie's own connections, railway accidents were also prominent in earlier reports. Rescues from water and fire have consistently appeared in the reports. In a typical year in which eighty-one medals were awarded, twenty of those involved rescue from fire, and twenty-eight were attempts to save people from drowning. Increased leisure time accounts to some extent for the growing accidents in water sports and similar pursuits. The age range of rescuers has remained wide always. The proportion of heroines has also kept fairly constant—at about five percent of the total.

What is most pleasing to the Commission is when a letter is received recalling an award long after the event. For example, in 1907, Frank Omner, foreman, climbed down to save a fifty-eight-year-old labourer from suffocation by gas at the bottom of an eleven-foot sewer manhole. The labourer survived; Omner died at the bottom of the sewer. In 1975, counsellors representing Omner's son and daughter wrote to the Commission, reminding the officers of the funds provided by the Commission for support and welfare of the family sixty-eight years before and explaining that their clients wished to leave the family home in New Orleans to the Commission following their own deaths. Legal difficulties in executing this offer did not mar its generosity.

In 1917, Walter Wood, aged fourteen, saved two women from drowning and received a medal and $1,600 for his education. In 1971, he wrote to the Commission, describing his hard struggle during the Depression to get himself through medical school and the eventual success of his practice:

> I feel the least I can do is to bring to your attention that your efforts and kindness were not entirely wasted. I am retiring far from a rich man financially, but rich in the feeling that I have helped many people physically, emotionally and financially and have in those ways, I hope, helped repay my debt to the Commission. This, I am sure, is the spirit of the repayment which you seek in your awards.

A third example throws another light on the awards. In 1982, John Lee received the Carnegie Medal for rescuing an elderly neighbour from her burning bathroom. At the first attempt, he was forced back by thick smoke and intense heat. He had to go in a second time to drag her out. The woman required extensive hospitalization for her burns; her left foot and right toes were amputated. Two years later, the Commission received a letter from Lee:

> It has been difficult for me to find the words to say thank you. The year and a few months that passed between the fire and your award had been a very difficult time for me. I went to the aid of Mrs Davis only because I could not have lived with myself knowing I had not made any effort to assist her while fire took her life. My failed first attempt still leaves me with a guilt I had hoped to avoid. Your award, however, has left me with a new assurance. . . .

Lee's point of view is understood by Walter Toerge, at the Commission, when he notes that:

> Here in America, as in Britain and elsewhere, the importance of our financial assistance to our beneficiaries is somewhat diminished relative to the aid available from the state. But the continuing moral and psychological support we try to extend continues to serve good purposes beyond the strictly monetary help.

Toerge goes on to express confidence in the future:

In the words of the popular song of a few years ago, 'the fundamental things apply as time goes by'. Man's nature has not changed noticeably since 1904. Fear and self-preservation are still fundamental to mankind. The 'heroes of civilization' continue to ignore and contradict those basic impulses.

Commission President Robert Off reflects that confidence. Writing on the Commission's seventy-fifth anniversary, he remarked that the average eighty-five awards each year were only a tiny sampling representative of a much larger group of people who would respond with courage and selflessness if they were ever put to the test. He added that:

There seems to be a feeling abroad in the land today that people do not care as much as they once did; that people are 'different' now; that our values and our mores, wrought by social revolution and four devastating wars, have changed radically in seven and one-half decades. We do not share the negative view. We have more than ample evidence to the contrary, supporting our conviction that people *are* just as concerned as they ever were. Hundreds of rescue acts are called to our attention each year—just as many as there were early in this cataclysmic century. People still get into trouble, and other people still go to their rescue.

THE SIMPLIFIED SPELLING BOARD

Just as, in the Old Testament, God divided the pagan builders of the Tower of Babel, so Carnegie believed that mankind would remain disparate until a common language was spoken. He intended that the Simplified Spelling Board, by making English easier to read and write for the masses throughout the world, would facilitate a substantial move toward world peace.

There has been talk of spelling reform in America and London since the 1870s. Several conferences were held in New York to launch a more aggressive campaign in 1905. Carnegie was enthusiastic, encouraged by the celebrated Melvil Dewey, whose system of classification in libraries was later adopted worldwide. The Board was set up in 1906 and formally constituted in 1907 to administer an annual contribution by Carnegie of $25,000 designed 'gradually to substitute for our present caotic spelling, which is neither consistent nor etimologic, a simpler and more regular spelling.' Between 1907 and 1917, the Board received regular aid from Carnegie and the Corporation; a similar society in Great Britain was also aided by Carnegie during this period. A *Handbook of Simplified Spelling* and a quarterly bulletin were published.

Fifty distinguished Americans were approached who would agree to adopt the simplified spelling of several commonly used words, altho, catalog, decalog, demagog, pedagog, prolog, tho, thoro, thorofare, thru and thruout. An advisory council was formed of 250 educators, scholars, writers and men of affairs. Further main lines of attack included the dropping of the 'u' in such words as 'labor'; the dropping of the final 'e' if it did not indicate a long vowel, as in 'lov'; the substitution of 'f' for 'ph' where appropriate; and the phonetic rendering of 'gh' in such words as 'draught' or 'draft.'

The fifty distinguished names included leading men of business, politics and letters, including President Theodore Roosevelt, who ordered the adoption of the new spelling in all White House documents. Carnegie was delighted at this coup and wrote to Roosevelt:

> The reform of our language may seem a small task compared to the establishment of arbitration instead of war, and so it is, yet the former is no mean accomplishment.

For years, Carnegie used the new forms in his personal correspondence and, to the confusion of some of his associates, insisted that they be used in the early official minutes and records of the Carnegie Corporation. He also tried to persuade his other trusts to use them. The British trusts refused to do so. The Institution of Washington made an effort but reverted to standard spelling after a two-year experiment. On August 27th, 1906, the *Worcester Telegram*, in Massachusetts, was the first newspaper to use the new spellings.

The Board itself was fulsome in praise of Carnegie and passed a resolution that:

> Among the monuments which your love of your fellow men has built for you, this one will be not only the greatest and most enduring, but among those most significant of your generosity, in that it can never bear your honored name.

Cynics, however, heaped ridicule on the idea. A columnist in the *New York Times* suggested that, 'The Bored of Speling start with their own names: Androo Karnege....' Swinburne railed against the 'monstrous barbarous absurdity.' Samuel Clemens (Mark Twain) stated that even Torquemada, of the Spanish Inquisition, had never committed any crime comparable to 'St Andrew's treatment of the language.' He changed his mind later, when he admitted that his only regret was that the scheme 'won't make any hedway. I am sory as a dog. For I do lov revolutions and violens.'

The scheme was never a great success; perhaps it was not surprising. By 1915, some victories had been achieved—a number of newspapers, universities, state teachers' associations and education boards had agreed to try the new forms—but Carnegie considered that progress was too slow:

> A more useless body of men never came into association, judging from the effects they produce. I think I have been patient long enuf. I have much better use for twenty-five thousand dollars a year.

He withdrew further support, though the work of the Board continued for some time, as did Carnegie's own use of the new spelling—when he remembered.

SIMPLIFIED SPELLING BOARD

1 MADISON AVENUE, NEW YORK

S.S.

May 20, 1912.

Andrew Carnegie, Esq.,
2 East 91st street,
New York, N. Y.

Dear Mr. Carnegie: As you are about to go to Aberdeen to deliver your address as Lord Rector of the University, and perhaps to receiv the freedom of the city, an other degree, and other delicacies of the season, you may be interested to read what happend to Dr. Johnson, an other celebrated orthografer, who visited Aberdeen in 1773. I quote his observations from the original edition of his "Journey to the Western Islands of Scotland":

"We came to Aberdeen on Saturday August 21 [1773]. One Monday we were invited into the town-hall, where I had the freedom of the city given me by the Lord Provost. The honour conferred had all the decorations that politeness could add, and what I am afraid I should not have had to say of any city south of the Tweed, I found no petty officer bowing for a fee.

"The parchment containing the record of admission is, with the seal appending, fastened to a riband and worn for one day by the new citizen in his hat."

1775 DR. JOHNSON, Journey to the Western
Islands of Scotland, p. 34, 35.

As to the salary of the first "Lord Rector" Dr. Johnson says:

Letter from the Secretary of the Board to Mr Carnegie, 1912

224

A.C.--May 20, 1912.-- 2.

"In Old Aberdeen stands the King's College, of which the first president was Hector Boece, or Boethius, who may be justly reverenced [as] one of the revivers of elegent learning.***

"Boethius, as president of the university, enjoyed a revenue of forty Scottish marks, about two pounds four shillings and sixpence of sterling money. In the present age of trade and taxes, it is difficult for the imagination so to raise the value of money, or so to diminish the demands of life, as to suppose ~~four and~~ four and forty shillings a year, an honourable stipend; yet it was probably equal, not only to the needs, but to the rank of Boethius."

1775 DR. JOHNSON, Journey to the Western
Islands of Scotland, p.27, 29.

What would Dr. Johnson have said if he had known that one hundred thirty-nine years later the University of Aberdeen would have a Lord Rector whose ideas of orthografy would be so different from his ?

I wish you a plesant voyage, a cheerful summer, and a safe deliverance from all your rectorial and orthografical diversions.

Yours truly,

A.D.G. Scott

225

CARNEGIE HERO FUND TRUST

The Hero Fund Trust in Britain was set up by Carnegie in 1908 after the success of the Hero Fund Commission established in Pittsburgh four years earlier. Carnegie took great personal interest in both funds and did much to promote them. The $1,250,000 endowment was placed in the hands of the Carnegie Dunfermline Trustees. Subsequently, between 1909 and 1911, nine other European Hero Funds were established.

The Hero Fund Trust follows the pattern of the Commission in many particulars, though it does not employ paid field representatives; instead it relies mainly on local police forces to report on cases likely to be of interest. The Fund applies 'whenever heroism is displayed by man or woman in saving human life in peaceful pursuits,' but only those cases in which there is injury or loss are recognized and no cases involving rescue between husband and wife or parents and children are considered.

The names of all those whose heroism is recognized as falling within the scope of the Trust are inscribed on the Roll of Honour. Although watches of gold and silver and other mementoes were given in earlier years, the Trust now makes only two awards—a Certificate or a Bronze Medallion. The latter is reserved for 'outstanding cases,' usually involving repeated or sustained acts of heroism, and in just over 75 years only 166 medallions have been awarded. An immediate payment, generally of £200, is made together with most awards. In certain cases of severe injury or death, the injured or his or her dependants are provided with a regular allowance.

Continuing personal contact, friendly counsel and correspondence are an important part of the Trust's work—more important, some would say, than the financial help Every third year, each of the nearly 300 current beneficiaries is visited by a Trustee or the Secretary. In 75 years, 6,000 names have been inscribed on the Roll of Honour, and £1,600,000 has been paid out.

Carnegie Hero Fund Trust

Founded: 1908

Original purpose: 'To place those following peaceful vocations, who have been injured in heroic effort to save human life, in somewhat better positions pecuniarily than before, until again able to work; in case of death, the widow and children to be provided for.'

Current purpose: 'To give financial assistance if necessary to (*a*) the dependants of persons who have died (*b*) persons who have been injured (*c*) persons who have incurred appreciable financial loss, etc., through performing acts of heroism in peaceful pursuits.'

Finance:

Original endowment ($1¼ million):		£250,000
Current assets, 1983 (book value):		£855,342
(market value, approx):		£1,340,000

	Income	*Expenditure*
Annual monies in early years:		
1908/09:	£12,530	£1,614
1910:	£13,132	£3,259
1911:	£13,429	£4,113
Annual monies in recent years:		
1983:	£94,098	£91,699
1984 (estimated):	£100,000	£95,000
1985 (estimated):	£105,000	£100,000
Total monies, 1908-1983:	£2,171,418	£1,934,429
Total payments to beneficiaries, 1908-1983:		£1,601,602

Beneficiaries:

Number of Medallions, 1908-1984:	166
Register of beneficiaries in regular contact:	276

	Considered	*Roll of Honour*
Number of cases, 1908-1984 (August):		
1908-09:	208	147
1910-1919:	3,092	2,018
1920-1929:	2,092	1,112
1930-1939:	1,054	1,016
1940-1949:	751	975
1950-1959:	423	516
1960-1969:	147	92
1970-1979:	111	105
1980-1984 (December):	28	24
Total cases, 1908-1984 (August):	7,906	6,005

(The substantial drop between the 1910s and 1920s is because the Trust agreed not to make awards in non-injury cases which had already been recognized by other bodies, such as the Royal Humane Society. The reduced number of cases in more recent times was the result of the decision in 1959 (*a*) not to make awards in cases where the rescuer had not sustained any injury or loss; (*b*) to exclude cases of husbands rescuing wives and parents rescuing children, etc.)

Administration:

Chairman:	James I. Scott
Secretary:	Fred Mann, MA, LL.B
Staff:	Administration is shared with the staff of the Dunfermline Trust
Address:	Abbey Park House, Dunfermline KY12 7PB

Carnegie Hero Fund Trust

Carnegie's letter of gift to the Dunfermline Trustees for the endowment of the Hero Fund Trust began as follows:

> Gentleman: The success of the Hero Fund upon the North American Continent has been so great that I have decided to extend its benefits to my native land.

The immediate inspiration for the Hero Fund Commission in Pittsburgh had been the Harwick mine disaster in 1904, but Dunfermline itself did have some claim to be the original inspiration for Carnegie's idea. In 1886, a Townhill boy, William Hunter, lost his life in an attempt to save two Dunfermline boys from drowning in Townhill Loch. Carnegie heard of the incident and subscribed money toward the cost of raising a monument to Hunter's memory. Complete with sculpted urn draped in funeral cloth, the monument still stands in Dunfermline cemetery, and in 1978 the Trustees paid a modest sum toward the cost of cleaning it. The inscription, devised by Carnegie, lends support to the theory that it was here that the seeds of the Hero Funds were sown, for the words are close to those with which Carnegie endowed the Commission:

> The false heroes of barbarous man are those who can only boast of the destruction of their fellows. The true heroes of civilisation are those alone who save or greatly serve them. Young Hunter was one of those and deserves an enduring monument.

Carnegie corresponded with King Edward VII about the establishment of the Trust and was rewarded by a letter from Windsor Castle in November, 1908: 'I am anxious to tell you how warmly I recognize your most generous benefaction and the great services they are likely to confer upon the country.' Carnegie took great pride in the King's approval and included a specific instruction in his letter of gift: 'If his Majesty ever chooses to express a wish in these cases, it is to be your law.'

This instruction was addressed to the Trustees, for whose work Carnegie was openly appreciative:

> At our recent conference here, I stated that it was your admirable administration of the Dunfermline Fund 'for bringing into the lives of the toilers more of sweetness and light' that induced me to appeal to you to take this Fund also into your wise keeping.

With a degree of modesty, Carnegie added:

> While I only give money, many of you are giving yourselves freely to service for your fellows without compensation other than that all-sufficient reward of knowing you are thus performing a holy duty, since the highest worship of God is service to man.

Carnegie did, however, take the trouble to lay down certain guidelines for the Trustees. Perhaps he knew of some particular incidents that persuaded him, for example, to include the following caution:

> No grant is to be continued unless it is being soberly and properly used, and the

recipients remain respectable, well-behaved members of the community. No exception will be made to this rule; but heroes and heroines are to be given at first a fair trial, no matter what their antecedents. They deserve pardon and a fresh start.

In his letter of gift, Carnegie particularly recommended the heroic action of doctors and nurses who volunteered their services during epidemics; he also suggested that in some cases the Trust might be able to recognize the heroism of policemen and firemen. Carnegie had excluded those whose duty it was to rescue others, when he set up the Commission in the United States, but he said nothing about excluding them, when he established the British Hero Fund Trust. He also commended railroad employees as being 'remarkable for their heroism.'

In the early years, the Trust income easily met the demands of its beneficiaries. For its first fifty years, the Trust was prepared to recognize heroism even where there had been no loss or injury—and even obtained in 1931 a private Act of Parliament to confirm that it was entitled to do so. Inflation, however, took its toll and, for financial and other reasons, the Trust was forced in 1959 to make certain basic changes. The rules were revised to exclude cases where there was no injury or loss and cases of husbands and wives or parents and children; it was also decided that, where duty played a part in the rescue, some exceptional valour and severe injury would be required for recognition of a case. This served its purpose, to cut down the number of cases accepted. Care is taken not to duplicate awards by other bodies, such as the Royal Humane Society, the Society for the Protection of Life from Fire, or the Royal National Lifeboat Institute, who make a great number of the awards we read about in the papers each year. From time to time, however, the Trustees have given substantial contributions to national or local disaster funds.

The primary purpose of the Trust is to provide financial help, if needed, to those whose heroism has cost them or their families dear. Sometimes a relatively small grant to make up lost wages is all that is required, but in cases of serious injury or death the Trustees assume what will be a continuing interest in the welfare of those injured or of the dependants of a hero who has lost his or her life. Their names are added to a 'Register of Beneficiaries' and—according to individual circumstances and need—the Trustees provide regular financial help. About 130 regular allowances are made, currently ranging from a nominal £1 to £12 a week: over 100 grants are given each year for special needs, and at Christmas time gift cheques and calendars are sent to all beneficiaries. The circumstances of every family are reviewed at least once a year. At present there are on the Register about 270 individual names, representing about 180 families; and the 'senior beneficiary,' now 94, has been associated with the Trust since August 1920.

This kind of continuing interest—discreet, unobtrusive, and friendly—is an important part of the Trust's work—some would say almost as valuable as its financial help. The Trust has always tried to build up a relationship of mutual confidence with its beneficiaries, and to instil a feeling that it can be called upon for help and advice in time

Extract from the Roll of Honour of the Carnegie Hero Fund Trust

of trouble. Each family is asked to choose a 'correspondent' from among local friends—perhaps a minister or lawyer—who can provide on-the-spot guidance and advise the Trust of any special concerns. But, to supplement the exchange of correspondence between beneficiary families and the Trust Office, the Trustees also place great emphasis on personal contact. The Chairman and Secretary usually travel to ceremonies at which Trust Certificates are presented in order to give a new family a chance to put faces to an otherwise impersonal-sounding organization, and every third year each beneficiary family is visited by a Trustee or the Secretary. Thus when the Committee is considering a report suggesting, say, that a holiday grant might be made to Mrs Jones, there are likely to be three or four Committee members who have actually visited her home and know about her and her family—and her dog. Just as important, over the years Mrs Jones herself will have come to realize that the 'Trust' is not simply a faceless body but a group of people who take a sympathetic and genuine interest in her doings. The Trustees too are always pleased to welcome to Dunfermline families who come to see the name of husband or father on the Roll of Honour, kept on display in the Andrew Carnegie Birthplace Museum. On his recent visits to the United States, the Secretary of the Trust sent back postcards to every family on the Register, a small gesture which was very much appreciated.

A high percentage of early cases were Scotsmen—not surprisingly, since the communications of the media were not so comprehensive then. Today, through police reports, newspaper clippings, television and radio, Trust awards go to cases all over the British Isles. Beneficiaries even include one family in Pakistan, another in Turkey and a third in Germany, the dependants of a factory worker and two sailors who were killed in Britain. In the beginning, cases included rescues from drowning, shipwreck, runaway horses, motor vehicles, coal mines, fire and gas accidents. The number of rescues from drowning have remained high: in 1912, it was 74% of the total; in 1958, it was 51%; in 1978, it was 54%. Other types of incident have almost disappeared: in 1912, there were fifteen rescues from runaway horses; there was only one such case in 1958, and today such cases are hardly heard of. Incidents involving trains have also declined, though rescue from fires appears to have increased. Rescues involving acts of violence show an increase, reflecting a disturbing trend in society.

The cases that follow are taken from the years 1912, 1958 and 1978, to give a range of years and types of case. Consecutively listed in the Report for 1912, there is evidence of a positive landslide of heroic activity among the members of the Royal Irish Constabulary. Four separate incidents in that year by five members, each of whom received an honorary certificate and the sum of £5, involved an attempt 'at great personal risk, to stop a runaway horse, with cart attached, in Holywood Road, Belfast'; an injury 'while attempting to stop a pair of runaway horses in Shankhill Road, Belfast'; a risk to life 'in stopping two runaway horses at Cootehill, Cavan'; and the serious risk to two men who 'rescued a man from drowning in the sea at Letterfrack.'

A case from 1958 demonstrates that heroic acts are not the prerogative of men; it is a remarkable case of putting others before self, and it won the rescuer a rare medallion:

231

5718. Mrs. Shirley Alma Howard, 1 Herbert Street, Cardiff, although shortly expecting the birth of her baby, rescued a little boy from drowning in the West Dock, Cardiff, on 29th March 1958. A Police Constable and another man were standing talking when they saw a small boy on the quay wall and heard him shout that there was a boy in the Dock. The Dock, which accommodates small and medium sized shipping, is 4000 feet long, 200 feet wide and covers an area of 20 acres. A very fast running fresh water feeder enters the Dock and creates strong currents and undertow and at this point the water is between 15 and 20 feet deep. A ship was berthed on the dockside with the stern about 10 feet away from the quay wall and it was into this gap that the boy had fallen. Both men ran towards the Dock and, as they did so, they saw Mrs. Howard run along the quay wall, remove her shoes and, although in an advanced stage of pregnancy, jump, without hesitation, into the Dock. The woman grasped the boy, who was from 5 to 10 feet from the quay wall, and held him up. One of the men then jumped into the water to assist her and the second man, clinging to the mooring rope of a motor vessel, helped Mrs. Howard and the boy from the water. Both were suffering from shock but soon recovered. The rescuer, who gave birth to a child four days after the incident, was awarded a Medallion, which is the highest award of the Trust, and a sum of £25.   (Case 7570)

The example from 1978 provides an indication of the horrors of industrial accidents in modern Britain. David Sandiford (26), a die-caster, sustained serious injury on 18th November 1976, in rescuing a man whose clothing had caught fire in a foundry at Radcliffe, Manchester.

CITATION

In the foundry of Strebor-Diecasting Ltd., Hollind Green Works, Radcliffe, are 200-ton diecasting presses, operated hydraulically by oil which at the time of the accident was of flammable type. At 10 minutes to 1 on the morning of Thursday, 18th November 1976, a hydraulic feed-pipe ruptured and sprayed out flammable oil at a pressure of 1,200 lbs. per square inch. The oil was ignited by the red-hot metal of the pressings, and then ignited oil was sprayed on to a 27-year-old labourer, Terence Nelson, and to a lesser degree on to David Sandiford. Nelson's clothing and hair caught fire and he was screaming and running about the foundry. The back of Sandiford's own shirt was on fire, but although there were eleven other workers in the foundry it was he who, ignoring his own predicament, caught hold of Nelson, who was badly afire, and began to tear his clothes off. Although Nelson was very seriously burned, he survived; Sandiford himself was badly burned on the back, hands and arms.

Because of the injuries he received in performing this heroic act, Mr. Sandiford was not able to resume regular work for some six months and he was unable to take up his former employment. In recognition of his gallantry he has been awarded a Certificate of the Carnegie Hero Fund Trust, together with an immediate grant of £100 towards financial loss: his name will be inscribed on the Roll of Heroes of the Trust, and the Trustees will keep his welfare under review.

Obverse and reverse of bronze medallion of the Carnegie Hero Fund Trust

233

Triple presentation ceremony at which the Mayor of Scunthorpe and the Chairman of the Carnegie Hero Fund Trust, Mr James I. Scott, presented certificates to Malek Own, Jeffery Oughtibridge and the widow of Richard Simpson, heroes of a gassing tragedy in a steel plant

There have, of course, been many unusual cases, which are well-remembered by the Trust. One tragic case involved a widow whose second husband was only nineteen when he was drowned trying to save someone in a boating accident. He was a few years younger than she was, and the Trustees felt that they should see the marriage certificate. They were suitably chastened when the Police sent on the certificate as requested, with apologies for the fact that it was in poor condition because 'it had been in deceased's pocket when he was drowned.'

There is the Irish story about the bill for funeral expenses that was sent to the Trustees. It included twelve bottles of whiskey, a number of boiled hams, rather more bottles of beer, and twelve loaves. The list was read out to the Trustees, one of whom, ignoring the earlier items, asked in all seriousness: 'What were they doing with all that bread?'

There are more than thirty cases on record of men who received Trust awards for two or more separate acts of heroism—one man was honoured five times between 1912 and 1920. In another case, a father and son were both recognized for trying to save an old woman who had been swept away in a flash flood. And there is one case of a son who received a Hero Fund award years after his father had been similarly honoured when drowned in the Peterhead lifeboat.

In 1958, on the fiftieth anniversary of the Trust, two guineas were sent to each beneficiary, without intention to solicit a reply. The letters the Trust did receive in acknowledgement summed up the real value of its work. 'The sense of security has given me peace and happiness and opportunities of leading a useful life,' wrote one mother of five children, who had been getting a regular allowance. 'I can never tell you how much your friendly letters have meant to me, apart from the financial support,' wrote another beneficiary. 'My first thought was that the gift should be the other way round—from the annuitants as a thank offering for all the help given over the years and always so generously given too,' wrote a third. Many of them remembered Andrew Carnegie, too: 'There is no doubt that the lives of many people have been eased by the kind thought of Mr Carnegie in establishing the Carnegie Hero Trust Fund,' wrote one recipient. Carnegie would have wanted no better seal of approval.

Through the years, this refrain has been common: 'Your financial aid brought her relief; but your manner of giving it brought her happiness.' And again: 'It is not just the financial gifts that were made, although they were appreciated, it was the tremendous moral support that we were given.' One correspondent, writing on the death of her widowed mother said: 'She valued her independence so much and greatly appreciated your having given her this and, in particular, the way in which this was done. Everyone with whom she came into contact at Carnegie was so very kind and understanding.'

Concluding a recent report, the Trust had this to say:

Most heroes are modest: many would walk away anonymously. Some—perhaps the bravest—admit to having been afraid: others knew only a sense of urgency. Some say (if you can believe them) that they would not do it again: others say they would, no matter the cost.

Sometimes a heroic act is a lightning reaction: sometimes a grim weighing-up of the chances of survival. Sometimes an act of heroism is brushed aside: sometimes it has been the turning point in a man's knowledge of himself. The early critics thought Andrew Carnegie was trying to manufacture heroes, but it seems that the capacity for heroism lies within every man. Like gold, heroism is not made: it is uncovered.

EUROPEAN CARNEGIE HERO FUNDS

Britain	Carnegie Hero Fund Trust, 1908	$1,250,000
France	Fondation Carnegie, 1909	$1,000,000
Germany	Carnegie-Stiftung fur Lebensretter, 1910	$1,500,000
Norway	Carnegie Heltefond for Norge, 1911	$125,000
Switzerland	Fondation Carnegie pour les Sauveteurs, 1911	$130,000
Netherlands	Carnegie Heldenfonds, 1911	$200,000
Sweden	Carnegie Stiftelsens, 1911	$230,000
Denmark	Carnegie Belonningsfud for Heltemod, 1911	$125,000
Belgium	Fondation Carnegie, 1911	$230,000
Italy	Fondazione Carnegie, 1911	$750,000
		$5,540,000

It is difficult to assess precisely the reasoning that lay behind the different amounts Carnegie gave to each Hero Fund—except in the case of France. When he endowed the *Fondation Carnegie*, he felt it necessary to explain to Ambassador Henry White why it was that France received $250,000 less than Britain. 'Life is much more secure in France I think,' wrote Carnegie, 'even than in Britain with its enormous number of mines, an enormous amount of shipping, fruitful of accidents.' It was presumably because Carnegie felt that Germany was even more fruitful of accidents that he gave to that country $250,000 *more* than Britain! It has transpired that the German Fund alone has ceased to exist; the other Hero Funds gathered for the first time in Brussels in 1961 to discuss their procedures and problems. A reception was given by King Baudouin and Queen Fabiola. The Hero Funds are gathering again in 1985.

CARNEGIE ENDOWMENT FOR INTERNATIONAL PEACE

This was the most significant of Carnegie's endowments for peace. It was founded in 1910, after the Simplified Spelling Board and several of the Hero Funds had been established, with a professed aim 'to hasten the abolition of international war.' It remains one of the leading independent organizations whose interests and capabilities, through its staff, extend over a wide range of international issues concerning the maintenance and development of world peace.

The Endowment is based in Washington and conducts its own operations; it does not make grants. It employs currently more than two dozen professional staff, Senior and Resident Associates, whose expertise in foreign affairs reflects backgrounds in journalism, government and public affairs. Through writing, through public and media appearances, through liaison with kindred organizations, and through participation in conferences, the staff encourage discussion and the dissemination of information on areas of potential crisis in ways that are intended to reach both expert and general audiences. New interests and issues are brought to the fore by each member of staff being replaced after about two years with the Endowment.

The general aim is toward a greater understanding of world problems, wherever they might be, in Europe or Afghanistan, in Central America or Southern Africa, in the Middle East or the Far East. The Endowment's own quarterly magazine, *Foreign Policy*, plays an important part in providing a platform for the expression of independent views on world affairs. This independence is crucial to the integrity of all Endowment activities; it enables the Endowment freely to pursue what it sees as the central wisdom which contemporary policymakers most need, to clarify what is avoidable in world affairs and what is unavoidable.

Carnegie Endowment for International Peace

Founded: 1910

Original purpose: 'To hasten the abolition of international war, the foulest blot upon our civilization. . .and when war is discarded. . .the Trustees will pleas then consider what is the next most degrading remaining evil or evils whose banishment. . .would most advance the progress, elevation and happiness of man.'

Current purpose: The Endowment is an operating foundation, which conducts its own programmes of research, discussion, publication and education in international relations and U.S. foreign policy.

Finance:
Original endowment: $10,000,000
Current assets: $60,000,000

Annual monies in early years:

	Income	Expenditure
1912, year end 30 June:	$568,290	$450,985
1913, year end 30 June:	$513,735	$487,270
1914, year end 30 June:	$514,310	$646,605

Annual monies in recent years:

1983, year end 30 June:	$4,403,217	$4,858,535
1984 (estimated):	$4,449,000	$4,538,415
1985 (estimated):	$4,832,700	$4,692,900

Operating grants received:

(a) Substantial grants from Carnegie Corporation before 1945. Current grant of approx. $200,000 for multi-year project on nuclear non-proliferation is the only recent Corporation grant.

(b) Occasional small funds for special projects from other private foundations. In 1981-84, three grants, approx. total $100,000.

Foreign Policy magazine:

Founded:	1970
Published:	quarterly
Circulation, 1983:	25,000
Editor:	Charles William Maynes

Administration:

President: Thomas L. Hughes (former Minister and Deputy Chief of Mission, U.S. Embassy, London, 1969-70; Assistant Secretary, Dept. of State, 1963-69; Board of Trustees, Arms Control Association and International Institute of Strategic Studies)

Secretary: Larry L. Fabian (also Director, Middle East Program)

Staff:	Program:	21
	Administration:	6
	Secretarial:	22
	Interns:	5

Address: 11 Dupont Circle, N.W., Washington, D.C. 20036

Carnegie Endowment for International Peace

Carnegie's fears that a massive injection of cash would spell ruin for any peace movement were put to the test when he established a peace fund of his own, which he finally did in December 1910. The Trust Deed made clear his feelings about war:

Altho we no longer eat our fellow men nor torture prisoners, nor sack cities killing their inhabitants, we still kill each other in war like barbarians. Only wild beasts are excusable for doing that in this, the twentieth century of the Christian era, for the crime of war is inherent, since it decides not in favor of the right, but always of the strong.

In terms of policy, the purpose of the Endowment was to advance the cause of peace among nations; to hasten the renunciation of war as an instrument of national policy; to encourage and promote methods for the peaceful settlement of international differences and for the increase of international understanding and accord; and to aid the development of international law and the acceptance by all nations of the principles underlying such law.

For all these high ideals, the Endowment was, perhaps, never quite as close to Carnegie's heart as the Hero Funds were to be; indeed, but for the pressure exerted by his friends, among them Nicholas Murray Butler, President of Columbia University, the Endowment might never have been made. Butler claimed that it was he who finally persuaded Carnegie to take the plunge, but credit is more properly due to Carnegie's old friend, the ex-Secretary of State Elihu Root, who took on the Presidency of the Endowment.

It was quickly divided into several sub-agencies, including those of International Law, Economics and History, and Intercourse and Education—the latter attempted both to seek and to influence public opinion. Carnegie's friends and the influential men with whom he corresponded nurtured the hope that the general move toward peaceful cohabitation between the enlightened countries of Europe and the United States would grow strong with the help of public opinion. This ideal, perhaps naïvely conceived, was the first step in this century toward international cooperation between major powers. Had the move been strengthened in time, Carnegie's dream for the abolition of war might have been fulfilled: 'After the arbitration of international disputes is established, and war is abolished, as it certainly will be....' But it was already too late.

The Peace Palace at The Hague was opened on 28th August 1913. Carnegie had put $1,500,000 of his own money into this international court of arbitration and he ended his speech on that occasion with the words: 'One small spark often creates the flame. The German Emperor holds in his hand the torch.' He meant 'the torch of peace' but the dreadful irony of this remark became clear less than a year later when, on 1st August 1914, the German Army marched into Belgium and, three days later, Britain entered into a war in which millions were to be sacrificed on the altar of nationalism.

The outbreak of the war left the various peace organizations in a considerable quandary. While Britain and Germany drew battle lines across Europe, America hovered uncertainly in the background for three years. The international make-up of the Endowment, which in pre-war years had seemed so vital to its aims, now posed problems involving considerable diplomacy and tact. The entry of the United States into the war in 1917 came almost as a relief and resulted in an immediate flow of resolutions from the Board and Executive Committee of the Endowment, grateful at last to have a clear view of the conflict. On 19th April 1917, the Trustees resolved to declare:

their belief that the most effective means of promoting durable international peace is to prosecute the war against the Imperial German Government to final victory for democracy, in accordance with the policy declared by the President of the United States.

On 1st November 1917, the Executive Committee reaffirmed this policy:

in view of recent events, emphasized by the widespread intrigues of the German Government to deceive and mislead the peace-loving people of the world.... The path to durable international peace on which the liberty-loving nations of the world would so gladly enter, is now blocked by the blind reliance of Germany upon the invincibility of German military power and upon its effectiveness as an instrument of international policy. This reliance must be broken before any other effective steps can be taken to secure international peace. It can be broken only by defeat.

The Endowment promptly offered its services, its personnel and equipment directly to the government, 'for dealing with the pressure of international business incident to the war.' The offer was gratefully accepted by the Secretary of State.

Following the Armistice in 1918, the Endowment concentrated on the publication of a large number of works dealing with the effects of the recent war. The largest of these, by far, was the 155-volume *Economic and Social History of the War*. Many smaller, more esoteric titles followed: *Economic Effects of the War upon Women and Children in Great Britain*; *Hygiene and War: Suggestions for Makers of Textbooks for Use in Schools*; *Problems about War for Classes in Arithmetic*; *Epidemics Resulting from Wars*.

In 1925, Nicholas Murray Butler took over from Elihu Root as unsalaried President of the Endowment. It was largely through his influence that the course of the Endowment's work was greatly strengthened in the areas of international cooperation in business and politics; it was Butler, too, who was instrumental in fashioning the Kellog-Briand no-war pact of 1928. The Second World War confronted the Endowment with much the same problems as had the First. After the war, with Butler's retirement, the three divisions of the Endowment were incorporated under the direction of a full-time salaried President.

The new Chairman of the Board was John Foster Dulles, who had been senior United States adviser at the United Nations founding conference in 1945 and who was three times US delegate to the UN. As Secretary of State from 1953-59, under Eisenhower, it was Dulles who conceived the theory of 'brinkmanship'—that a statesman should, when necessary, take his country to the edge of war but not beyond. He earned himself a reputation for inflexibility in matters concerning the USSR and communist China. It was ironic, therefore, that Alger Hiss, who achieved notoriety in 1949 when convicted of perjury in denying communist affiliations, had been selected by Dulles as President of the Endowment in 1948. The case on his behalf is still being hotly argued.

For the next two decades, the Endowment conducted research and public education programmes on a broad range of issues, and during this time the Endowment's offices were located in New York and Geneva in order to provide closer links with the United

Through its quarterly journal of analysis and opinion, the Endowment facilitates debate about contemporary policy issues and ideas

Nations agencies there. These headquarters became the focal point for European and American dialogue on international issues but were closed in the 1970s because of increased financial pressure. In the same period, the Endowment provided for 250 young foreign service officers from emerging nations to be trained in diplomatic procedures; it also published a leading journal on international affairs, *International Conciliation*.

The rapidly changing face of international politics in the 1970s, bringing ever more dangerous conflicts into view, was met by radical changes within the Endowment itself. It reopened in Washington in 1971. Under its new President, Thomas L. Hughes, the Endowment elected to become an operating foundation, conducting operations itself rather than making grants to others. All grant-making activities were phased out and all income from the portfolio was allocated to internal projects and joint-venture programmes with organizations such as the Arms Control Organization. By this method, the Endowment sought to husband its resources and simultaneously to look for greater breadth of reach, in an effort to take a more prominent rôle in the fight for world peace and to meet the increasing complexities of world affairs.

The Endowment and the Arms Control Association devote major attention to issues involved in controlling the nuclear arms race

To remind himself of the original purpose of the Endowment, Hughes put up outside his office door a copy of a letter to one of his predecessors from Ramsay MacDonald (British Prime Minister in 1924 and from 1929 to 1935) resigning his Trusteeship of the Endowment on the grounds that it was dissipating its money on activities of which Mr Carnegie would not have approved. But Hughes was realistic about what the Endowment might seek to achieve. In 1974, he wrote:

> We have recognized that, whatever we do, our leverage will be modest at most. Since, therefore, we are serious about being relevant, we are trying, as actively, inventively, and imaginatively as possible, to achieve the highest intensity of useful involvement, deliberately choosing, whenever possible, operational situations of pertinence, combining pertinent people with pertinent subjects in pertinent places.

Vietnam posed one of the greatest problems in recent times, both for America and for the Endowment; it was a time when the clear vision of 'good' and 'bad' was both heightened and threatened. Hughes avoided impossible ideals, in the search for lasting values and workable approaches toward peace:

> The Endowment is called to work for peace publicly, accountably and with fairness at a time when differing champions of peace are very clear that peace is enlisted cleanly on one side of an issue only.... Those to whom instant insights occur will inevitably be disappointed in those of us who lag behind. More often than not, they will want to write off our obtuseness as a lack of moral keenness, and attribute it to years of double vision or to a chronic inability to make up our minds.

For critics and supporters alike, Hughes had some stirring words:

> We have experienced the discord among the high-minded, heard the dialogues of the deaf, and watched the defeatism of the disillusioned. In the process, we have discovered what should have been obvious to begin with: that there are more roads to peace than roads to Rome; that peace, like heaven, has many mansions; that peace, like man, has many seasons.

Six years later, entering the 1980s, Hughes was very aware of the effects of the aftermath of the Vietnam war and what isolationism might do to America's relations with the rest of the world and, in consequence, to the peace of the world. By encouraging discussion and an exchange of views, the Endowment tried to arrest the flight from foreign policy. Its policy has been to identify points of conflict among the world's disputing groups, networks and environments and to bring about dialogue with a purpose. In sum, the Endowment has tried to clarify what is avoidable in world affairs and what is unavoidable; according to Hughes, this is 'arguably the central wisdom which contemporary world policymakers most need.'

If it should appear that the Endowment is concerned only with talk and more talk, Hughes declares his hand firmly: 'We have an aversion to research for the shelf, to research without recommendations.' It has been a view expressed by a number of other Carnegie endowments, notably the Foundation for the Advancement of Teaching. Hughes's aim is to bring people together to talk about their differences, in the most practical sense. His staff are selected for their ability to make recommendations based on their professional experience of their particular field of responsibility.

Since it is the staff who are instrumental in carrying out the objects of the Endowment, it is necessary that the journalists and specialists who are brought in as staff members combine significant academic, governmental and operational experience and are recruited on a wide base across the United States and from abroad in an attempt to assure diversity of viewpoint. Appointments are normally for about two years, during which the member is given independence to pursue a particular interest and area of concern. New blood is then brought in and interests change. This period of independence to research and comment is of key importance to the staff and therefore to the Endowment which provides that independence. It is the individuals who are

Through the writings of its Associates, the Endowment deals with central international issues, as in these three books

fundamental to the work of the Endowment, as in many of Carnegie's other trusts. Hughes puts it like this:

> In the final analysis, programs are run by people, and their background, their thinking processes, their values and objectives—all will shape the programmatic consequences.

What potential problem areas were staff concentrating on during 1983-84, in their efforts to anticipate crises and provoke discussion before the situations worsened? There were the rising tensions in Southern Africa, the Namibian negotiations, and the Cuban and Savimbi factors in Angola. There was the Cuban factor in Nicaragua and El Salvador, and the impact of this on United States and Latin American relations. There were Indo-Soviet relations, and the question of India's potential for leadership of the non-aligned countries. There was the decline in relations between the United States and

Europe, and the conflict of perceptions on détente, arms control and East-West trade. There was Soviet foreign policy, its domestic sources and the Soviet world outlook. There were United States foreign policy and security interests in the Pacific; the impact of the Soviet occupation of Afghanistan; the politics of oil in East Asia; relations between China, Japan and Taiwan; and relations between India and Pakistan. In the Middle East, there was United States policy toward the Arab-Israeli negotiations; relations between Israel and the Palestinians and between Israel and Jordan; and the problems of West Bank and Gaza Strip developments. In Latin America, there was the subject of the international law of the sea and dispute settlement.

These are only some of the issues of possible confrontation on which staff were writing articles and bringing people together for discussion, to broaden awareness of the problems and seek constructive dialogue. One area to which particular attention is being paid during the Endowment's 75th anniversary, in 1985, coinciding with the 150th anniversary of Carnegie's birth, is Africa. Endowment staff are considering African trouble spots with special concern.

Face-to-face facilitates frequent dialogue at the Endowment among leading members of the foreign affairs community in Washington

One of the projects undertaken by the Endowment is the 'Face-to-Face' discussions of major foreign policy issues in Washington. This is a joint venture between the Endowment and the American Foreign Service Association, with informal dinner and luncheon meetings. A second project is the 'Foreign Policy Press Breakfasts,' sponsored by *Foreign Policy* magazine. These breakfasts are 'on-the-record' meetings between foreign policy makers and the international affairs Press. The third special project is the 'Mid-Atlantic Club,' a joint effort between the Endowment and the European Communities Delegation, to encourage discussion among private experts, former officials and current representatives of the United States and the European governmental, financial, economic and social organizations.

Foreign Policy magazine is an influential quarterly, owned and published by the Endowment. It has a circulation of about 25,000 and is committed to imaginative new writing on international issues. As with the Endowment, its independence is the key to its relevance. Three representative articles from the Spring 1984 issue demonstrate the range of its content. 'The War Over Water' identifies the constant struggle for the waters of the Jordan, Litani, Orontes, Yarmuk and other life-giving Middle East rivers; the article argues that this struggle is little understood outside the region, that it was a principal cause of the 1967 Arab-Israeli war, that it 'could help spark a new all-out conflict,' and that it is 'a major aspect of the Palestinian question and of the struggle over the future of the West Bank.'

The second article, entitled 'Who Needs the Sea Treaty?,' considers Reagan's rejection of the United Nations Convention on the Law of the Sea and the formulation of a new policy with the proclamation of a 200-nautical-mile exclusive zone for the United States. Thirdly, 'Europe's American Pacifier' makes this controversial claim: 'By sparing the West Europeans the necessity of autonomous choice in matters of defense, the United States removed the systematic cause of conflict that had underlain so many of Europe's past wars.'

It had best be said that the independent opinions expressed in the magazine do not necessarily represent the views of the Endowment. On the other hand, Hughes's sensible expectations do not prevent the Endowment from rolling up its sleeves and entering into the thick of the argument for world peace, just as Carnegie wished it to do.

PAN AMERICAN UNION BUILDING

Gift proposed:	1907
Dedication of building:	1910
Sum of gifts from Carnegie, 1907-11:	$850,000
Grants from Corporation, 1928-35:	$650,000

Carnegie's gifts toward the cost of an international home for 'the union of all the republics of this hemisphere' made possible the construction of the Pan American Union Building at 17th and B Streets, N.W. Washington, D.C. Carnegie was particularly gratified by President Roosevelt's 'hearty expressions of satisfaction.' The gift was made through the agency of Elihu Root, Secretary of State and Chairman of the Governing Board of the International Bureau of American Republics. On 1st January 1907, Carnegie wrote to Root:

> I have never felt more keenly than I do this New Year's morning how much more blessed it is to give than to receive, and I consider myself highly honored by being considered worthy to provide the forthcoming union home, where the accredited representatives of all the Republics are to meet and, I trust, to bind together their respective nations in the bonds of unbroken peace.

This was the first of Carnegie's gifts for 'temples of peace.' The Pan American Union subsequently became known as the Organization of American States.

CENTRAL AMERICAN COURT OF JUSTICE

Gift proposed:	1908
Building completed:	1910
Sum of gift from Carnegie:	$100,000
Additional gift from Carnegie for reconstruction:	$100,000

This gift, like that for the Pan American Union building, was prompted by a suggestion from Elihu Root, Secretary of State and Carnegie's friend. The suggestion was the result of the Central American Peace Conference in Washington, in December 1907, at which the five republics of Costa Rica, Guatemala, Honduras, Nicaragua and Salvador invited the United States and Mexico to participate. The aim was to provide a permanent court to house representatives of the five republics and to be a place in which they could sort out their differences.

Carnegie provided $100,000 for the project, to erect a courthouse in Cartago, Costa Rica, but shortly after its opening, in May 1910, the building was destroyed by an earthquake. Carnegie immediately provided another $100,000 for a second building at

San José. The Court was closed in 1917, upon the expiration of the Convention under which it had been established. The building was subsequently used by the Ministry of Foreign Affairs of the Government of Costa Rica.

INTERNATIONAL COURT OF JUSTICE, THE HAGUE

Trust founded for Court of Arbitration:	1903
Dedication of building:	1913
Endowment by Carnegie:	$1,500,000
Budget of Court for Biennium 1982-83:	$9,641,700
(including contribution to Carnegie Foundation: $537,000)	

Of the three buildings, or 'temples of peace' to which Carnegie subscribed, the Palace of Peace at The Hague was his favourite. Reluctant at first to fund such a project, he was eventually persuaded to contribute $250,000 for a library on international law for the use of the Permanent Court of Arbitration. This Court was established in 1900, as a result of the First Hague Peace Conference of 1899, which had greatly impressed Carnegie. The Court began operation in 1902.

It seemed, however, that Carnegie's offer was too large a sum for a library and not big enough for a building in which to house it, so he agreed to come up with a total of $1,500,000 'for the purpose of erecting and maintaining at The Hague a courthouse and library for the Permanent Court of Arbitration.' The Russian diplomat, Frederic de Martens, whose idea the Palace had originally been, heaped praise on his potential benefactor:

It would render the man who makes the gift a benefactor to every nation and to all mankind—acknowledged as such through all time.

Less high-flown but, in view of subsequent events, rather more ironic, the German Ambassador wrote to Carnegie:

The gift which fairly takes my breath away is your provision for the Temple of Peace. That will result undoubtedly in the saving of thousands of lives.

The cornerstone of the palace was laid in the summer of 1907, at the opening of the Second Hague International Conference. The four years between the 'stichting,' or endowment, and the beginning of construction were fraught with petty squabbles over design which Carnegie was often called upon to settle. In its finished form, the palace is not dissimilar to Carnegie's castle at Skibo—a masterpiece of neo-gothic committee planning. As one journalist commented at the grand opening on 28th August 1913, it was 'certainly unlike anything else in the world.'

All the great nations contributed gifts to the furnishings, as 'a symbol of the growing amity of the peoples of the world.' Among these gifts were a Gobelin tapestry from France, gates and railings from Germany, the site and seven windows from the Netherlands, marble from Italy, candelabra and vases from Austria-Hungary, a sculptured group representing 'Peace through Justice' from the United States, vases from China, silk cartoons from Japan, a desk for the President's room from Australia, a carpet from Turkey, iron-work gates from Belgium, granite from Sweden and Norway, clocks from Switzerland, onyx from Mexico, precious woods from Argentina, porcelain from Denmark and wood for the chamber of the Secretary from the Republic of Haiti.

The Permanent Court of Arbitration still exists; it has decided only twenty cases from 1900 to 1983. In 1920, the Permanent Court of International Justice was created, under the Covenant of the League of Nations; this dealt with twenty-nine contentious cases between 1922 and 1940. It was dissolved after the Second World War and replaced by the International Court of Justice, brought into being by the Charter of the United Nations to be the principal judicial organ of the UN. This court consists of fifteen judges, elected by the General Assembly and the Security Council of the UN; only States, not individuals, may be parties in cases before the Court. In 1983, forty-seven States accepted the compulsory jurisdiction of the Court, and between 1946 and 1983 the Court dealt with forty-eight contentious cases and seventeen requests for advisory opinions.

During the 1950s, there was an average of two or three cases submitted each year; this fell to one at most each year during the 1960s; from July 1962 to January 1967 no new case was brought forward. In a review of the rôle of the Court in 1974, it reaffirmed 'that recourse to judicial settlements of legal disputes, particularly referred to the Court, should not be considered as an unfriendly act between States.' A revised set of rules came into force in 1978 aimed at simplifying and accelerating proceedings, to the extent that this depended on the Court; it also aimed at introducing greater flexibility and at helping parties to keep down costs.

Among recent cases submitted to the Court has been the dispute in 1972 in which the United Kingdom and West Germany began proceedings against Iceland over the proposed extension of its exclusive fishing zone. Another was that in 1973 in which Australia and New Zealand each began proceedings against France over proposed tests of nuclear weapons in the South Pacific. In 1983, the Court was considering a dispute between Libya and Malta over their Continental Shelf, and the delimitation of the maritime boundary in the Gulf of Maine; the case of the United States diplomatic and consular staff in Tehran, following occupation of the US Embassy by Iranian militants in 1979, had recently been removed from the Court's list.

The Library of the Peace Palace is still administered by its own 'Carnegie Foundation' and is supported from the Court's budget. The public has access to this library, though there is another private library for the Court, which is housed in the same building.

COUNCIL ON RELIGION AND INTERNATIONAL AFFAIRS
(*formerly* CHURCH PEACE UNION)

The last of Carnegie's major endowments for peace was the Church Peace Union, founded in the belief that members of religious bodies would be particularly responsive toward a strong appeal to banish war. Carnegie did not have either the time or inclination to study theology but he recognized the common belief in God and he saw beyond the limitations that the Church of his day imposed on free-thinking men, toward a universal religion founded upon peace and understanding.

Like the charter for the Endowment for International Peace, four years earlier, that for the Church Peace Union looked forward to a time when its work would be completed:

> After the arbitration of international disputes is established and war abolished, as it certainly will be some day, and that sooner than expected, probably by the Teutonic nations, Germany, Britain and the United States first deciding to act in unison, other Powers joining later, the Trustees will divert the revenues of this fund to relieve the deserving poor and afflicted in their distress, especially those who have struggled long and earnestly against misfortunes and have not themselves to blame for their poverty.

Perhaps Carnegie felt that the Endowment for International Peace was likely to be rather more academic in outlook and that what he also needed was an organization that would in time concern itself with the ordinary man and woman in the street in the quest for peace and justice. He added in the Trust Deed:

> Members of the various churches will naturally know such members well, and can therefore be the better judge; but this does not debar them from going beyond membership when that is necessary or desirable. As a general rule, it is best to help those who help themselves, but there are unfortunates from whom this can not be expected.

The first work undertaken by the Union was a conference of the various churches of Europe and Asia in the first three days of August 1914, at Constance, in Germany. Sixty delegates went from the United States, twenty-five from Britain, and many others from a number of countries. The meetings were broken up by the preparations for war. After a day and a half at Constance, the delegates were offered seats on the last train out of Germany, and the conference was adjourned to London. Like the Endowment, the Union turned its attention to a flood of literature about the war, including pamphlets on *The Moral Aims of the War*, *A League of Nations*, *The Moral Values of a League of Nations*, *The Minister and his Preaching in this Time of War*, and *Program of the Church in this Time of War*.

Whatever his feelings of disappointment at the circumstances in which the Union began, Carnegie seemed pleased with the concept and with the ecumenical make-up of the Board of Trustees. 'I am so pleased at the union of the separate sects,' he wrote, 'Jews included.' After the war, the Union continued to further the cause of world peace by attempting to forge bonds between the various church groups in Europe and America; it also worked through association with similar agencies, such as the World Alliance for International Friendship. Publications, lectures, conferences, exchanges of ministers, and studies of current issues were the means by which the Union carried out its purpose. For four decades, it was active in promoting a variety of organizations of international cooperation, including the League of Nations and the United Nations.

In 1961, when church groups themselves had become increasingly active in international affairs, the Union took on a new name and new activities. As the Council on Religion and International Affairs (CRIA), it dedicated its efforts to examining the rôle of ethics in international relations; its ultimate goal remained the furtherance of world peace with justice. Its President, Robert Myers, believes that its insistence on examining the moral consequences of foreign policy decisions has added an important dimension to America's understanding of relations among nations.

The Council is independent, non-partisan and non-sectarian; it is interested in the ethics and values of all the world's principal religions and in the inevitable and integral part ethics play in any decision, whether in economics, politics or national security. As Myers explains:

> We try to 'demistify' the idea of ethics and explain it as a companion of our daily lives. George J. Stigler, Nobel laureate for economic science in 1982, confirms that 'the ethical questions are inescapable; one must have goals in judging (economic) policies, and these goals have ethical content, however well-concealed it may be.' It is this 'well-concealed' dimension that is revealed in CRIA discussions, seminars, consultations and publications.

It is through such practical means that CRIA conducts its various programmes, such as the Education and Study Program, which includes several current aspects. One is the development of a college-level curriculum that examines the rôle of ethics in the formulation of US foreign policy. The curriculum is being developed through a comprehensive series of lectures to be distributed among teachers and members of the religious and business communities: lectures include subjects such as 'Realism *v.* Idealism,' 'American Nationalism,' 'Justice and International Society,' 'The Ethical Dilemma of Immigration Policy,' and 'Culture and Victory in the Fiji Islands'; a series of lectures beginning in January 1985 focuses on the ethical dilemmas of nuclear weapons. The aim is to introduce future decision-makers to ethical problems.

A second concern of the Education Program is the plight of the world's refugees—the millions of people displaced by war, drought and famine. A three-year project funded by the Lilly Endowment is enabling CRIA to clarify the relationship between the wide-ranging overseas activities of church-sponsored voluntary organizations and US Government organizations, 'the better to plan more effective relief programs.' Concern to improve international awareness and observance of humanitarian law to protect the lives of the innocent in situations of crisis is the subject of a study by Thomas Boudreau, *Protecting the Innocent: Enhancing the Humanitarian Role of the UN in Natural Disasters and Other Disaster Situations* (1983). The study concludes that the present information-gathering capability of the UN in these circumstances is inadequate; it recommends more effective telecommunications and the replacement of the present UN 'shuttle diplomacy' in its international mediation efforts by more effective video conferences via satellite.

A third concern is the reform of the international economic system. Myers questions whether there is a separate set of standards for the borrowers and the lenders in the IMF decision-making process. He points out that it does matter whether foreign loans are repaid and at what rate money is loaned; and it matters whether such loans create jobs and contribute to the general welfare or are of benefit to foreign élites only. All such CRIA programmes examine not only the international but the domestic impact of economic policies. At present, CRIA is looking with special interest at the effects of US financial aid to East Asia and the Caribbean.

Also within the Education Program, the series of 'Values in Conflict' conferences are bringing together businessmen, politicians, religious leaders and scholars from different countries and cultures to identify areas of mutual agreement and examine areas of difference. Recent discussions have concentrated on the competing visions of American and Korean social values, their legal and political traditions, and their economic systems. CRIA is also planning a survey of comparative religion and nationalism; the study will look at the impact of religion on the contemporary national consciousness of five nations—the Soviet Union, the United States, India, China and Japan. Another plan is for an inquiry into the rôle of the religious Press in the formulation of American foreign policy since 1945 and in shaping American attitudes toward nuclear weapons, the Middle East, world hunger, Vietnam, the United Nations, and world economic development.

The regular CRIA Conversations form a second programme. More than 400 corporate and individual Associates meet informally with select authorities and policy-makers from the US and abroad. Subjects range from 'US Shortsightedness toward Syria's Power in the Middle East' to 'International Terrorism.' Worldview Press Breakfasts provide another opportunity for similar subjects to be aired. Briefings for students on career opportunities in the Foreign Service and in international business are also part of this programme.

The Carnegie Leadership Program is designed to meet the needs of multi-national corporations, international business executives, community leaders and students and faculty at US universities and colleges; it provides a forum for the discussion of sound decision-making in foreign policy and global economic affairs. Seminars at universities and colleges are designed to help students understand how global events affect everyday life—the prices we pay for goods, job opportunities, wages and pensions. The seminars also provide rôle models for black students by inviting high-level black economists, academics, and corporate executives to discuss global economic concerns.

CRIA has its own monthly magazine, *Worldview*, which provides coverage and analysis of international affairs for a growing audience in the university, business, government, religious and professional communities. Recent articles include, 'Reconstructing Argentina,' 'Sorting out Lebanon,' and 'Cuba and the Caribbean.' There are also CRIA newsletters, pamphlets and books. One recent book concentrates on the close interdependence of religion and economics in India, Iran, Mexico, Japan and Nigeria.

As with each of Carnegie's endowments, independence is crucial to the Council's work. This was demonstrated, for example, in a recent venture in which the Council acted as 'honest broker' in trying to guide the governments of emergent countries and business corporations intending to establish branches there on how problems could be anticipated and solved. This was an obviously practical effort and it is by such practical means that CRIA tries to promote peace, bringing the high-flown arguments and principles down to the earthy considerations of business economics and basic human rights. There are many contending visions of peace with justice among the nations of the world. The Council attempts to draw these together, toward the development of universally acceptable standards of international conduct.

Council on Religion and International Affairs
(formerly *Church Peace Union*)

Founded: 1914; renamed 1961

Original purpose: 'To promote peace, through the rallying of men of all religions to supplant war by justice and international brotherhood.'

Current purpose: 'By promoting a greater understanding of the values and conditions that ensure peaceful relations among nations, CRIA hopes to contribute to a better life for people everywhere.'

Finance:

Original endowment (from Carnegie Corporation):		$2,000,000
Additional grant by Carnegie Corporation:		$500,000
Current assets, June 1984:		$10,064,471
Total expenditure, 1914-1984:		$17,168,548
(Total for Church Peace Union, 1914-60:	$6,061,118)	
(Total for CRIA, 1961-84:	$11,107,430)	
Operating budget, year end June 1984:		$891,035

(Investment income represents 61% of the budget; the remaining 39% is gathered from corporate associates, grants and contributions, membership fees, magazine subscription, and others).

Administration:
President: Robert J. Myers
Assistant: Ulrike Klopfer
Staff: 12 including President and Assistant
Address: Merrill House, 170 East 64th Street, New York, NY 10021

Carnegie Library,
Dunfermline, opened 1883
showing the 20th-century
extension

BELOW City Hall Square
and the Carnegie Library,
Allegheny, Pennsylvania,
1905

254

Other Carnegie Gifts and Buildings

CARNEGIE'S FREE PUBLIC LIBRARIES

Total number:	more than 2,500
Total cost of buildings:	more than $56,000,000

Carnegie is possibly most widely known for his library scheme, though less than one-third of the buildings he paid for bears his name; he liked to think of them not as 'Carnegie Libraries' but as 'Free Public Libraries.' They were among his favourite benefactions, because they involved two of his favourite themes—education and self-help.

His articulate Morrison background and Colonel Anderson's private Allegheny library, into which, as a boy, he had been allowed to delve, had left Carnegie with a passion for books and a dedication to the idea that ignorance was the cause of most human misery and injustice. He firmly believed that, by placing into the hands of every person what Matthew Arnold described as 'the best that has been thought and said,' the world would be a better place. In Britain, there was a long tradition of public libraries but not in America, where, in 1880, very few communities had a free public library.

Carnegie provided the initiative by donating a building on condition that the community provide a site, guarantee to stock the library and pledge an annual amount for maintenance. This was usually required to be ten percent of the amount that Carnegie had given; Carnegie's gift was approximately $2 per head of population. So, a city with a population of 50,000 might receive $100,000 from Carnegie provided it would furnish the library and guarantee $10,000 annually for upkeep. By this method, Carnegie saw himself providing the bait that would induce the community to perform its duty. His greatest delight was not so much in the money he himself gave but in the money that his gifts compelled others to produce for their own benefit. This, to his mind, was philanthropy at its best. In only three instances did he commit himself to an endowment for the maintenance of the library and in each case the community failed to provide any further money for upkeep; in consequence, those libraries struggled to keep going in the face of the gradual erosion of the value of their endowment—examples by converse of the wisdom of Carnegie's standard policy.

Children's Room in the Hazlewood Branch, Pittsburgh, 1907

Library Club work among the children, Soho
Hill, Pittsburgh, 1907

Travelling Library Wagon from the Washington
County Library, Hagerstown, Maryland, 1907

His first library gift was to Dunfermline, in 1881; it was his first important gift of any kind. Later in the same year he offered $250,000 to Pittsburgh for a library and was turned down; he gave the building instead to Allegheny. Pittsburgh subsequently accepted $1,000,000 for a library and music hall that became the basis for the facilities of the Carnegie Institute. His largest library gift was $5,000,000 for sixty-six branches of the New York Public Library; he was particularly delighted at thus twisting the arm of New York to produce $500,000 annually for upkeep. When the scheme really got going, requests came in at the rate of two or three a day. Some grants, for small American towns, were as low as $1,000. Indiana topped the league with about 140 library buildings, followed by California, Illinois, New York, Ohio and Iowa, each with about 100 or more libraries. Bottom of the league, with less than a handful each, were Arizona, Arkansas, Delaware, Hawaii, Nevada, New Mexico, Puerto Rico, Vermont and Virginia.

Carnegie's activities initiated the building of more than 2,500 free public libraries in the United States, Great Britain and the Commonwealth (estimates vary between 2,500 and 2,509) at a cost of more than $56,000,000. He paid more then $43 million of this sum out of his own coffers, leaving the other $13 million to be paid by the Carnegie Corporation of New York. In 1926, the Corporation embarked on its own large-scale expansion of its library programme, to strengthen the library profession by supporting the activities of the American Library Association and by improving training opportunities. Between 1926 and 1941, the Corporation spent an average of $830,000 a year on this area of work, equivalent to one-sixth of its available income. By 1961, in its first fifty years, the Corporation had spent a total of $33,457,142 to improve the library service and had been associated with every major development in library service in the United States and in most parts of the Commonwealth. This sum represented about eleven percent of the total of its grants in those fifty years.

Carnegie Library, Atlanta, Georgia

Cartoon satirising Carnegie's passion for building libraries

In Britain, the Corporation paid for and promised a number of library buildings before the creation of the Carnegie UK Trust in 1913; the UK Trust then met the remaining commitments. In all, there were 660 library buildings provided in the British Isles through the Carnegie scheme, and the UK Trust has spent about £1,665,000 on libraries and library activities of various kinds, most of this being in the early years but some of it over a number of decades. In the first forty years, during which the Trust was associated with the development of libraries, about thirty-five percent of its grant-aid went to this activity.

The figures in the table below indicate the approximate number of free public libraries financed by Carnegie himself and by the Carnegie Corporation of New York:

Country	Buildings		Appropriation
United States	1,681		$41,748,689
Canada	116	(125)	$2,559,660
Great Britain and Ireland	660		$11,849,457
New Zealand	18		$207,397
South Africa	12		$123,855
Caribbean	6		$97,355
Australia and Tasmania	4		$68,240
Seychelles	1		$9,740
Mauritius	1		$8,765
Fiji	1		$7,300
	2,500	(2,509)	$56,680,458

CARNEGIE ORGANS

Total number:	more than 7,600
Total contribution:	approx. $6,250,000

Carnegie believed that books would make better people; he also believed that music would help to humanize them. Carnegie Hall was a monument to his esteem for music; more precisely, it is a tribute to his wife's more cultivated taste, since Carnegie preferred an organ to an orchestra. The organ arouses the deeper nature of man, said Carnegie. There were organs in his homes in New York and Skibo, and it is the organ that dominates the Music Hall in the Carnegie Institute in Pittsburgh.

Carnegie's first organ gift was to the Swedenborgian Church in Allegheny, which had been attended by his father when the family first moved to America. Other gifts to other churches followed and the occasional request soon turned into a flood that had to be systematized. Any church might apply for a gift if it could raise half the cost of the organ itself and could answer some simple questions to satisfy Carnegie of its general attitudes. Very soon, organs began to appear in far greater quantities than libraries, throughout America and in various corners of the world; there were three times as many organs as library buildings donated by Carnegie, though at less than twelve percent of the cost.

It is hard to be completely accurate about the number of organs and the money spent, because of discrepancies between early promises and fulfilments. Estimates range from 7,629 to 7,689 organs and $6,220,647 to $6,248,312 spent by Carnegie. Of the lower estimate on cost, Carnegie himself paid out $4,492,669, leaving the Carnegie Corporation to pay out the remaining $1,727,978. Of the more then 4,000 organs built with Carnegie money in the United States, top of the league was Pennsylvania with 1,351 organs, followed by Ohio with 440, New York with 290 and Illinois with 207. Bottom of the league were Alaska, the Canal Zone, Hawaii and Puerto Rico, each with one organ only.

In Britain, the Carnegie UK Trust took over, in 1913, the commitments already entered into by the Carnegie Corporation, just as it did with the Corporation's library commitments. The Carnegie UK Trust paid out approximately £50,000 on outstanding promises, bringing the total Carnegie organs in the United Kingdom to 3,375; it then made promises amounting to another £50,000 for 300 more organs. The total spent by the Carnegie UK Trust on the original organ scheme was £108,125; the total number of organs built with Carnegie money in the UK was more than 3,600.

Church Organ appropriations (acc. Lester, *Forty Years of Carnegie Giving*)

Country	Number of organs	Amount
United States	4,043	$3,579,841
Canada	121	$116,116
England	2,119	$1,508,320
Scotland	1,005	$765,220
Ireland	219	$158,370
British West Indies	46	$33,015
Wales	32	$22,210
Africa	27	$16,100
Australia	6	$9,465
New Zealand	12	$8,240
Gibraltar	2	$2,125
India	1	$875
British Guiana	1	$750
	7,634	$6,220,647

HOME TRUST COMPANY—PENSIONS AND ANNUITIES

This amounted to a private bank, established by Carnegie in 1901, to handle his financial interests after his retirement. Major endowments, transfers of bonds, and smaller gifts were paid through this company by Carnegie's agent.

Among other activities, the Company became trustee and administrator of trust funds of $4,250,000 for payment of pensions to a number of Carnegie's former associates and subordinates; these included people who had served with him when he was Superintendent of the Western Division of the Pennsylvania Railroad from 1859 to 1863 and many individuals who for one personal reason or another he had placed on his private pension list. At the time of his death, 409 people were being provided with pensions out of this fund.

The Company also became executor of Carnegie's estate and trustee of a further fund of $6,782,000 for annuities to be paid to another forty-five people designated under his will. On the death of any recipient of one of the pensions or annuities, the capital from which the money was paid reverted to the Carnegie Corporation, which was the residual legatee of Carnegie's estate.

Among those receiving annuities under the terms of the will, through the Home Trust Company, were President Taft, Mrs Edith Roosevelt and Mrs Cleveland (subsequently, Mrs Thomas J. Preston). In 1912, Carnegie had requested that part of the income of the Corporation should be used to provide pensions for past Presidents and their widows, since the government failed to uphold their dignity by doing so. There was much public disapproval for Carnegie's proposal and he withdrew it; no such pensions were in fact voted by the Corporation.

CARNEGIE RELIEF FUND

One of Carnegie's first provisions upon retirement in 1901 was a fund of $4,000,000 for relief of, and pensions for, Carnegie Steel workers. In 1910, this was merged into the United States Steel and Carnegie Pensions Fund, for pensions to incapacitated employees of the steel company and its subsidiaries.

ENGINEERING SOCIETIES BUILDING

Carnegie provided $1,500,000 in 1904 to the United Engineering Trustees to finance a building in New York that would be a public meeting place for the national engineering societies of America, and would also house offices, scientific and publishing firms, and facilities for an extensive engineering library. This was in line with his passion for education in practical matters and his establishment of the Technical Schools in Pittsburgh.

AUTHORS CLUB—CARNEGIE FUND

Carnegie had discovered the power of the written word when, as an eighteen-year-old telegrapher, he wrote to the Pittsburgh *Dispatch* complaining about a charge being imposed in the hitherto free library of Colonel Anderson. He won his case and thereafter became a frequent contributor to newspapers and a keen author.

His first books were an account of a coaching trip in Britain and a round-the-world tour. At first these were printed for private circulation but they proved extremely popular when made available to the public. Later, he published books on politics, wealth, business, peace, and an autobiography. *Triumphant Democracy*, *The Empire of Business* and an article on *The Gospel of Wealth* are probably the best known of these. His books generally grew from articles published in the leading periodicals on both sides of the Atlantic.

It was not surprising that Carnegie cultivated authors such as Mark Twain and Matthew Arnold; he also provided financial help for some of them, both privately and through the Authors Club of New York. The Carnegie Fund was a charitable trust made up of a succession of gifts from 1890 to 1903 and from his will, for the relief of needy authors who were members of the Club, and for others whom the Club might consider worthy of aid. The sum of the trust was $250,000. In 1939, three legal trustees replaced the Club itself, in having responsibility for the distribution of the Fund.

The Authors Club was organised in 1892 and soon published its first *Liber Scriptorum* with 109 articles including 'Genius illustrated from Burns' by Carnegie. The second book by a further 109 authors, including 30 who had survived, was published in 1921 and the original presented to Carnegie's daughter. Each article in every limited-edition copy of the two books was signed by the author.

COLLEGES, UNIVERSITIES AND SCHOOLS

Estimates of the sum that Carnegie gave to a whole range of academic institutions vary from about $15,000,000 to about $20,000,000, depending largely on what is included. He gave money in more than forty American States, with more than $1,000,000 going to each of the following: Massachusetts, New Jersey, Ohio, Pennsylvania (excluding the Institute of Technology at Pittsburgh), Tennessee and Virginia; more than $2,000,000 went to New York State. In all, it is estimated that Carnegie gave to more than 500 colleges and universities.

Included in his will were bequests to the Cooper Union (an extra $60,000, bringing its total to $750,000), Pittsburgh University ($200,000), the Hampton Institute ($300,000), and the Stevens Institute ($100,000). Other institutions given money by Carnegie, to help young people gain knowledge and skills, were Berea College ($237,000), the Franklin Union ($408,396), and the Tuskegee Institute ($620,000). Many such institutions received Carnegie money through the Carnegie Corporation.

SOME OTHER GIFTS

Three interesting donations by Carnegie were to the Academy of Paris ($50,000) for scholarships in connection with the work of Madame Curie on radium, to the Koch Institute in Berlin ($120,000) to help Robert Koch in his research on tuberculosis, and to the Iron and Steel Institute in London ($89,000), of which Carnegie was the first non-British president. Carnegie also gave $200,000 to the St Andrew's Society, $100,000 to the American Library Association, $500,000 to the King Edward's Hospital Fund; he gave substantial sums to the New York Zoological Society, the New York Association for the Blind, the Foreign Students Friendly Relations Committee, Scots Charitable Society of Boston, Massachusetts—with innumerable other gifts, some from his own pocket, many through the Carnegie Corporation.

CARNEGIE HALL, NEW YORK

Opened: 1891   *Investment:* $2,000,000

It was on Carnegie's honeymoon trans-Atlantic voyage to Scotland, in 1887, that he met Walter Damrosch, conductor of New York's Oratorio Society, founded by his father, Leopold. Damrosch seized his chance to plead the cause of a new concert hall for the Society, which had hitherto been forced to hold rehearsals in the Knabe Piano warehouse, for lack of suitable space. Carnegie was soon convinced.

He organized a music hall company, not as a philanthropic enterprise but as a business undertaking in which he was the chief stockholder. William Tuthill, architect and music lover, studied hundreds of concert halls around the world before designing the luxurious and acoustically successful interior. The five-day opening, in May 1891, attracted the cream of New York society to performances by the Oratorio Society and companion Symphony Society under the direction of Damrosch and Tchaikovsky, invited specially for the occasion. Tuthill himself missed the performance; having watched the crowds entering the balcony for the first time, he rushed home to recalculate his estimates of stress that a full house would place on the support columns. Tchaikovsky, however, wrote glowingly of the Hall and of the abilities of the orchestra and soloist. The *New York Herald* noted that, 'All was quiet, dignified, soft, slow and noiseless, as became the dedication of a great temple.'

The name 'Music Hall' was changed by Carnegie to 'Carnegie Hall' because, as he explained, a music hall denoted a vaudeville palace rather than a serious concert hall—and he had been persuaded that it would be an advantage to use his own name for the building. After his death, the Hall became part of his residuary estate and, as such, was owned for a period of about thirty days by the Carnegie Corporation of New York, which sold it to a private enterprise. In late 1959, the owners prepared to sell the Hall to commercial interests which planned to demolish it and erect another large building on

Exterior and Interior
of Carnegie Hall, New York

the site. Outraged citizens stopped the destruction of the Hall. In July 1960, special state legislation allowed New York City to purchase it and charter a new non-profit organization, the Carnegie Hall Corporation, to manage and rent the Hall and also to sponsor events at the Hall. In 1964, it was designated a National Historical Landmark.

There have been many modifications to the Hall over the years but one aspect has not changed—the variety and standard of the performers. The world's finest orchestras, conductors, singers and soloists, from classical music to jazz, folk and pop, have welcomed chances to take advantage of the superb acoustics and the reputation of Carnegie's musical 'flagship.' Jazz had its debut in 1912, with a concert by the Clef Club, followed by every important jazz performer in the decades since. In 1932, John Jacob Niles was the first folk singer to perform at the Hall. In 1964, the Beatles made their U.S. debut there. On 5th May 1981, the New York Philharmonic recreated the opening night programme which Tchaikovsky had conducted ninety years earlier. Recognized throughout the world as a focus for musical talent, Carnegie Hall can call on some equally outstanding artists when it comes to the centenary in a few years' time.

Meanwhile business leaders have continuously been supporting Carnegie Hall ever since Andrew Carnegie built the famous 'Music Hall on 57th Street' in 1891. Today more than 400 local, national and international corporations and numerous individuals annually contribute to its corporate fund because they value the association with excellence.

CARNEGIE MANSION: THE COOPER-HEWITT MUSEUM

In December 1898, Carnegie announced his intention to build 'the most modest, plainest, and roomiest house in New York.' The site on Fifth Avenue, between 90th and 91st Streets, was then in a pocket of semi-rural land, beyond the normal limit of the houses of the very rich. It was three years before Carnegie and his wife and daughter moved in. The mansion cost $1,500,000 to build and contained sixty-four rooms on six levels, complete with organ, library, public and private living rooms, servants' quarters and large utility areas, including massive boilers, in the basement, and an extensive garden. This continued to be Carnegie's New York home for the rest of his life. He slept there on the same simple brass bed that he had used as a child in Pittsburgh.

The Cooper-Hewitt Museum did not move into the Mansion until 1976 but it was fitting that, in his will, Carnegie included a bequest to the Cooper Union for $60,000, 'making my total gift to it, $750,000.' Peter Cooper had opened the Cooper Union for the Advancement of Science and Art in 1859; it consisted of a free school, a library and a lecture forum, and was open to the respectable needy without regard for race, creed, colour or sex. It provided education for thousands of men and women, many of them immigrants, who might otherwise have been bound to employment with little future.

In 1897, Cooper's grand-daughters—Sarah, Eleanor and Amy Hewitt—having travelled much in Europe, added a Museum for the Arts and Decoration, believing that

Exhibition installation photograph, for the exhibition 'Palladio in America,' June 7 to October 5, 1977. The scale model of a Palladian building in Italy is shown on a platform in the drawing room of the Mansion. The panels and lights and wall decorations are the originals.

OPPOSITE

TOP The Carnegie Mansion, from the South, or Garden side. The wisteria climbing the wall was planted in about 1902; it continues to bloom every season. Because this building was designated a National Historic and New York Landmark, the exterior may never be altered.

BELOW LEFT The front door of the Cooper-Hewitt Museum, with the original wrought iron and glass installed when the building was erected as the Carnegie Mansion. From the 'Great Hall' looking out.

BELOW RIGHT The main staircase leading from the Great Hall to the family quarters on the second floor. The furnishings are those that were in place when the Carnegie family lived in the house.

Installation photograph, for the exhibition 'Now I lay me down to eat, A Salute to the Unknown Art of Living.' This installation is in the former billiard room of the Mansion; the windows and shutters are intact; the woodwork on the stairwell is the original.

such a museum would be useful in raising the standards of design in America. The acquisition of a number of important private collections, including European textiles, Italian architectural and decorative drawings, samples of eighteenth-century French decoration in drawings, woodwork, hardware, prints and books quite soon made the museum one of the foremost repositories of decorative arts and design in the world.

By 1968, however, the Trustees of the Cooper Union were being forced by financial pressure to consider closing down the museum. The collections were eventually entrusted to the Smithsonian Institution and, at that time, the museum's name was changed to Cooper-Hewitt, to honour the founders. In 1972, the Carnegie Corporation deeded the Carnegie property to the Smithsonian as a new home for the Cooper-Hewitt. The museum reopened in the fall of 1976, after the restoration and renovation of the Mansion at a cost of $3,000,000, met entirely by private funds.

The Mansion's principal public rooms have been restored to what they were like in Carnegie's lifetime, providing an interesting contrast between the old building, the temporary exhibitions and the permanent collections; the latter are used for reference and study and occasional display; they are categorized by medium and technique rather than by culture, period or historical chronology.

Recent exhibitions have included holiday ephemera, a collection of 2,000 buttons from the eighteenth to the twentieth centuries, architectural cast-iron penny banks from 1870 to the 1900s, theatre designs, and a display of Fabergé's work, including some of his famous jewelled eggs from the collection of Her Majesty Queen Elizabeth II. The permanent collections encompass objects from all parts of the world and from every historical period over a span of 3,000 years: there are drawings, prints, wallpapers, textiles, ceramics, glass, furniture, woodwork, metalwork, jewelry, and there are categories including architecture, urban and industrial design, advertising, fashion, interiors and home furnishings. Miscellanea include a collection of theatre designs and pre-cinema toys, with peep shows, sand toys and shadow puppets; sand, tinsel and feather pictures; bird cages; pressed flowers; straw-work boxes; valentines; candy Christmas tree ornaments; and examples of packaging and paper folding.

The Library contains the most complete assemblage of books on the textile arts in America, including architecture books of the seventeenth and eighteenth centuries, early natural history books with hand-coloured plates, books of festival decorations, catalogues of the world's fairs, and a collection of auction sales catalogues spanning more than 150 years. The museum's combined library and picture archive has become one of the outstanding design reference centres in America. In terms of education, both for students and for public pleasure, the museum fits well into Carnegie's scheme of things and into the Carnegie Mansion.

Carnegie Mansion: The Cooper-Hewitt Museum

The Smithsonian Institution's National Museum of Design, housed in the Carnegie Mansion, New York.

Cooper-Union Museum founded:	1897
Carnegie Mansion constructed:	1902
Cooper-Hewitt Museum reopened in Carnegie Mansion:	1976

Finance:

Original cost of Carnegie Mansion:	$1,500,000
Cost of remodelling the Mansion:	$3,000,000
Additional spent on renovation:	$1,000,000
Annual income/expenditure, in excess of:	$3,000,000
Value of property, estimated at:	$12,000,000

Visitors, collections and exhibits:

Annual number of visitors:	(approx) 250,000
Total number of visitors since reopening:	1,500,000
Annual number of exhibitions:	12-16
Total number of exhibitions since reopening:	120
Total items in permanent collection	300,000

Administration:
Director: Lisa Taylor
Staff: 65 full-time; 35 part-time; 30 full- and part-time security staff
Address: 2 East 91st Street, New York, NY 10028

SKIBO CASTLE

At one time the estate and manor of the Roman Catholic Bishops of Caithness, Skibo was purchased by Carnegie in 1897 for £85,000, together with 32,000 acres, to be the Scottish home for himself, his wife and daughter. He rebuilt the castle with walls of mediaeval design which hid structural steel rolled in Pittsburgh and all the modern conveniences of the time. The total cost of Skibo, including the building of its extensions, was about $1,170,000 (£234,000), paid for, according to Professor Wall, almost to the dollar by a rival's lost deposit in a business deal, that Carnegie kept.

Carved in the mantel of the oak fireplace, Carnegie had his favourite motto inscribed—the same one that he had at his mansion in New York.

> He that cannot reason is a fool;
> He that will not is a bigot;
> He that dare not is a slave.

He commissioned the collection of a library of all the best literature in the world but was furious when he discovered that instead of having everyday, workmanlike editions, he had been provided with the finest leather bindings; he threatened to return the books

Skibo Castle, South face

Stairway and Organ   Groundfloor hall

Library

Mr Carnegie at his castle

but kept them and hardly ever looked at them. He was woken each morning by the bagpipes of his personal Scottish piper—and so were his guests. Overhead, the flag that flew from the mast showed on one side the Stars and Stripes and on the other side the Union Jack. Royalty, politicians, intellectuals all visited Carnegie at Skibo. From 1898 until 1914, he spent his summers there and revelled in all the characteristic activities of a Scottish laird.

The castle and estate remained in the possession of his wife, after his death, and then of his daughter, Mrs Margaret Carnegie-Miller, who recently added the Castle to the list of Carnegie's gifts by offering it, in 1981, for educational use to the Carnegie UK Trust. Unable to use it economically, or to support it realistically, the UK Trust had to decline the offer, so Mrs Miller included the castle and its policies within the sale of the larger estate of nearly 19,000 acres. In 1982, the estate was purchased by Inverness-born Derek Holt, of Holt Leisure Parks, with an offer thought to be about £2,500,000. A sum of around £600,000 is due to be added to the endowment of the UK Trust, seventy years after Carnegie had provided his original endowment. Holt, meanwhile, assured the public that, in his eyes, Skibo 'will always be Andrew Carnegie's home.'

Conclusion

I was asked at the outset by the Carnegie United Kingdom Trust to give some account of the origins of the main Carnegie Trusts and to explore the range of activities in which they have been and still are involved. The intent was to produce a book, to coincide with the 150th anniversary of Carnegie's birth, that would enable a wider public to understand what the Trusts do. The UK Trust gave me a free hand to select whatever material and themes I liked and introduced me to the other Carnegie Trusts on both sides of the Atlantic. They, too, have allowed me freedom of selection, while at the same time drawing my attention to those activities that each considered to be the most interesting. I was able to visit almost all the Trusts and to see for myself.

Knowing almost nothing about Carnegie himself or the Trusts when I started, I felt that I was on a level with the reader of average curiosity for whom the book was intended. I was delighted to discover, as I began my research, that one Trust or another was closely connected with a great many activities of which I already knew but to which I had no idea the name of a Carnegie Trust was attached. At the same time, I began rapidly to learn, through the Trusts, about a wide range of educational and other activities of which I had no previous knowledge at all; I had not known that such a piece of research or such an organization even existed. Indeed, it was only after I had completed the first draft of the book that I suddenly learned of the continued existence, in another guise, of one of the Trusts about which all the other Trusts had 'forgotten' to tell me.

In like manner, I have received invaluable information on major areas of Trust work right up until the book has gone to print; I have no doubt that I shall learn a great deal more in subsequent months as old projects are brought to my notice and as new projects develop. For example, I have only just received information on the Carnegie Medal for children's literature, which will have its 50th anniversary in 1987. This award by the Library Association in the United Kingdom is not connected with any of the Trusts but was first announced to celebrate the centenary of Carnegie's birth in honour of his work in establishing the free public library system. The award is widely recognized among parents, publishers, teachers and writers, as well as librarians, as a hallmark of quality. Another 50th anniversary, in 1985, is that of the Haskins

◄ Sea Breeze 1910. Photo of Andrew Carnegie with his close companions, Sir John Ross and Sir William Robertson, which he entitled 'Words of wisdom—no charge.' Both men influenced Carnegie on his endowments in the United Kingdom.

Laboratories in the United States, which have a link with the Trusts through their founder, Caryl P. Haskins, for long associated with the Carnegie Institution of Washington. The laboratories have achieved remarkable work in helping the blind to 'see' through sound. An example of developing work that came to my notice only as I was preparing this chapter was the Carnegie Interpret Britain Awards, sponsored by the UK Trust, and announced at the very end of 1984. The awards by the Society for the Interpretation of Britain's Heritage are for outstanding displays and trails linked to conservation. These are three examples of what will undoubtedly prove to be hundreds of omissions of worthwhile subjects.

Not unreasonably, some of the Trusts regarded my ignorance with suspicion but most of them subsequently became most generous in providing me with assistance. Almost everything I learned was gleaned from the records of the Trusts themselves, from my visits to the Trusts and from conversations with officers of the Trusts. I have simply selected what I thought to be interesting or what seemed to reflect the range of incidental as well as fundamental work of each Trust; I have also sought to draw out some of the basic themes that underlie the work of all the Trusts—for example, their interest in education, their relative independence, their emphasis on initiative and adaptability—as I have described in the Introduction.

In deciding what to include, I have had to be highly selective. Each Trust had an opportunity to see the draft of what I had written on that Trust and some felt that I had not always chosen the best examples of their work. They considered, for example, that I had included too many incidental activities for the purpose of catching the interest of the reader at the expense of some of their steady background work. The Carnegie Corporation of New York believes that its major contribution throughout its history has been in the field of higher education, whereas I have chosen to allot much of the available space to a range of other activities to show the spread of the Corporation's interests. The Carnegie Endowment for International Peace considered that I passed too glibly over its work in the 1950s and 1960s, whereas I preferred to concentrate on its philosophy in the 1980s.

As I assembled this material, I encountered many critical questions about the Trusts and about Carnegie himself. For example, he failed dismally with the Simplified Spelling Board, and his hopes for the Carnegie Endowment for International Peace and the Church Peace Union were too high for either to live up to. Both Trusts have had to work with an element of 'unreality' imposed by Carnegie's expectations for them and I found their pragmatic approach in the 1980s both interesting and constructive. Even so, I met many who felt that the Endowment for International Peace might in the past have considered adopting a higher radical profile, bearing in mind Carnegie's Chartist background. Carnegie's official biographer was among those who wondered whether Carnegie might not have expected a little more action in the streets to protest future wars.

There were many important questions about the activities of all the Trusts. How much should the Carnegie Corporation concern itself with a peace policy when already two Trusts are devoted to this area, or is the Corporation simply recognizing the fundamental connection between education and peace? How much can the Trust for the Universities of Scotland achieve now that the help it can offer is reduced to such an insignificant proportion of the money available for research from other sources? Is Carnegie-Mellon University becoming too select? Should it open itself out to provide opportunities for those with social or physical handicaps, for example? Does the Dunfermline Trust cater for the interests of the average Dunfermline townsfolk? Does it act to hold the community together? Does the Carnegie Institute have the right balance between research and education? Could it do still more to bring together the community and the museums—perhaps by bringing the craft demonstrations of the Three Arts Festival into the building itself to show practical, creative, arts activities alongside museum exhibits? Is the Carnegie Foundation for the Advancement of Teaching moving fast enough toward embracing the whole curriculum, from infants through to university, and making education relevant to what follows? Are the Hero Funds in danger of providing simply a token acknowledgement of self-sacrifice or could they do more to lobby for much deeper social support for the personal side of their work? With its increasingly expensive research programmes to support, can the Institution continue to avoid the pressures for quick results demanded by outside finance? Does the UK Trust's policy of sustained support sometimes work against the Trust? Its support for the Drama Board dragged on for thirty years, draining meagre resources that might have been better used elsewhere. The UK Trust acknowledges that it would be much easier to provide one-off grants, as do many of the other Trusts, but nonetheless it sees merit in sustained support for the right projects and is prepared to take the risks.

One of the biggest questions is whether Carnegie put his money in the right place at all? Would his aims have been better served had he continued in business and perhaps established truly revolutionary working practices within them, in the style of Robert Owen and his 'Villages of Cooperation'? Might he have done better to have left some areas entirely alone, such as Peace? Should he have put all his money in a single Trust, even bigger than the Corporation, and directed it to one purpose to maximise its effect? Would that have been more likely to achieve his purpose, to provide for 'the improvement of mankind'? It seems an attractive notion but doubtful of success. In Carnegie's day, the sums devoted to each Trust appeared vast; it did indeed seem as if Carnegie was concentrating almost unlimited resources on each area of activity. But today, even the sum total is relatively insignificant now that government is involved in so many areas in which the Carnegie Trusts pioneered. Because of this, it is now not so much the *amount* of money that is spent by the Trusts each year but the ways in which that money is spent that is important. Had it all been concentrated into one pot, it is not certain that it would have solved more quickly any one of the problems to which the Trusts have addressed themselves. Certainly, there would have been left unexplored a great many worthwhile lines of activity.

It is the diversity of those activities that I have found the most interesting aspect of the

Trusts' work and have thought worth displaying in this book. The range is astonishing and yet all the activities come within three interlinked themes: education, research and peace, at formal and informal levels, with individuals and with communities. It has been easy to see all of us being touched in some way by the activities deriving from these themes and it has been tempting to see most of us benefitting unwittingly from Carnegie money. We are 'beneficiaries under the skin.' Of course, the Trusts have their individual character and are completely independent from each other. Carnegie did not create them as a 'whole'; he created them as his interests and opportunity arose. And yet there is a 'wholeness' about them and an unrehearsed kinship of priorities about those who find themselves associated with the work of the Trusts either at first or second hand.

Inevitably, that wholeness comes from the character of Carnegie himself. It is difficult to consider the Trusts without considering the man, and impossible not to have one's judgement of the Trusts coloured by one's opinion of the man. What he achieved in creating his wealth and in disposing of it was quite remarkable. He was a true philanthropist in that he gave away his money in the days before tax incentives became a fine inducement to philanthropy. His evident energy, positiveness, individuality, his belief in 'self-help,' even his relish for fame and his naïvety, all these are attractive in him. But there are aspects of his character and occasions in his life that are less attractive. He appears almost embarrassingly gauche in his self-appointed task as European peace-maker and ambassador-extraordinary to the Kaiser. His competitive urge had its destructive edge. His rôle in the Homestead strike seems equivocal at best. Despite having overcome the limitations of his own background, or *because* he had done so, he expected everyone to be able to do the same. He seems ignorant of true handicap.

Underlying the firm resolve of his public statements about the acquisition and distribution of wealth, his position is awkward, his philosophy seems tainted. The *Gospel of Wealth*, to return to society what he had taken from it, may be little more than 'a refuge from self-questioning'; Professor Wall, his biographer, said that he was convinced that with his endowments for enlightenment and international peace Carnegie had also endowed himself with an enlightened inner peace. 'The *Gospel of Wealth*,' said Wall, 'was absolutely essential for him to justify his own life.'

Whatever his good intentions, Carnegie's 'Gospel' does sound patronizing. He was convinced that he knew better than the people themselves what was good for them. The happy chance, or stroke of genius, was that Carnegie did in fact hit on ways of using his money to advance many of the causes dear to liberal hearts. Above all, it is possible to forgive his conceit because he made provision for others, not himself, to determine how his money should be spent after his death.

It is this that is the chief key to the success and survival of the Trusts. Carnegie admitted that he might not know what was best for society for all time and by so doing he saved the Trusts from being dismissed by succeeding generations as irrelevant. His stipulation that the trustees might adapt the purpose and function of the Trusts 'as the needs and expectations of society changed' provided a remarkable flexibility that has

Andrew Carnegie, the philanthropist

allowed them to flourish and not either be stifled by the past or be forced to spend precious resources in the courts to change the terms of their endowments.

The characters of the men and women who have translated Carnegie's intentions in subsequent decades have been as important to the work of the Trusts as the character of the founder himself. The celebrations of the 150th anniversary of Carnegie's birth being held in 1985 should not merely be in memory of Carnegie but of all those who have developed his philanthropy. Despite his sociable life on both sides of the Atlantic, Carnegie does not appear to have been a very happy man in his last decade. He recognized that he could not bring about peace at a stroke nor educate the masses overnight; he accepted that mankind might only be elevated by degrees. The skill of those responsible for his Trusts has been to pinpoint those degrees that might prove most worthwhile, the small seeds that might with encouragement bear fruit. At the same time they have endeavoured to preserve their funds to enable succeeding generations to have a similar freedom to pick out what they too see as opportunities. 'We have learned or are learning in the distribution of funds,' wrote Carnegie, 'money is never the main consideration, convenient though its presence may be. The essential factor is the human element.' His faith in this tenet has been well founded.

In August 1985, during the first week of the Edinburgh Festival, representatives of all the Carnegie Trusts and Foundations, together with members of Carnegie's immediate family, gather in Dunfermline to exchange information and to discuss 'The Importance of Philanthropy in a Changing World.' A number of joint activities have been planned by the four British Trusts. These include the sponsorship of an educational pack on Carnegie's life and achievements, the issue of a special anniversary illustrated calendar, a visit by the Pittsburgh Symphony Orchestra and an exhibition of water colours from the Carnegie Institute's Museum of Art.

At this gathering, the individuals currently responsible for determining the ways in which Carnegie's money is being spent will exchange views on the matter, quite possibly controversial, maybe self-critical. They will be aware of an opinion that they hold an increasingly privileged position in a world where such independence as their money and current legislation provides is a rare luxury. They will affirm that their work is *not* a luxury but an urgent necessity, and that by their ability to stand back from the immediate political, social and economic pressures that tend to shoulder aside all but primary considerations they are able to give thought to long-term issues and politically unattractive byways, and to support innovation without fear of reprisals for failure. Their self-imposed brief is not simply to pick up the pieces but to anticipate and to forestall the first signs of cracking.

In adopting such a rôle, the trustees assume a social and scientific wisdom that can only be justified by the widest possible consultation with all sectors of society. Since the survival of the Trusts and the continuation of their work depends, apart from money, on public and political faith in what they are doing and how they are going about it, then it seems important that the Trusts should open themselves to public scrutiny. The simple act of discussing their work freely and widely can be seen to provide an adequate check on their activities and need not prejudice their independence. In a way, this book is already working to that purpose; the achievements of the Trusts are quite obvious.

I have already suggested that, in Carnegie's day, neither he nor the spirit of the age properly recognized any limitations to achievement or to opportunity. Carnegie himself believed passionately in equality of opportunity but he was torn between two aspects of that principle. On the one hand, in a fiercely competitive world, full of promise, he believed in the opportunity for the fittest to fulfil themselves to the utmost. On the other hand, there was the principle of service, of helping others to fulfil themselves, of creating opportunities for everyone, at many levels, regardless of how fit or unfit they might be. Perhaps it was only a symptom of the age, that Carnegie seems to have had little time for the weak; he lacked tolerance. In terms of ambitions and the kind of money that only a rare individual like Carnegie could bring to bear in society, the world that Carnegie envisaged was one that lived *above* its means. His ideals are admirable but, despite the dedication of more than one of his Trusts to the welfare of the common people, he appears out of touch with reality.

Those who have come after him to execute his Trust Deeds have done much to redress the balance. They, too, seek peace and justice. But instead of telling us what to do and trying to elevate us toward a future ideal, they are concerned with making the best of the resources and limitations of individuals, communities and our planet. Carnegie exploited resources to the full and did not acknowledge limitations. Today's trustees recognize that our resources impose restraints on society just as much as they create opportunities. This approach is fundamental to living *within* our means. It reflects as much, for example, on our approach to wealth or poverty or the social consequences of the micro-computer age as on our attitude to those with disabilities or to the potential of the work force. Everything we plan must spring from and carry with itself all these pluses and minuses; they represent an integral part of our society—of ourselves. The Carnegie Trusts and other independent Trusts serve their greatest purpose in reminding us of these twin poles of our existence.

In his speech at the laying down of the cornerstone of Carnegie Hall, Andrew Carnegie said, 'It is built to stand for ages and during those ages it is probable that this hall will intertwine itself with the history of our country.' It was true of the Hall; it has also been true of the Trusts themselves, on a worldwide front. For that achievement, we should applaud Carnegie for some remarkable foundation work; we should also be grateful that he left the superstructure for others to design. Let them continue to be imaginative, bold, perceptive and secure.

Summary of Dates

Here are some of the main dates in Carnegie's life and in the history of the Trusts:

1835 25 November, Andrew Carnegie born in Dunfermline
1848 Carnegie family emigrate to America
1849 Andrew Carnegie becomes a telegraph messenger boy
1853 Starts work for Thomas L. Scott, Superintendent of the Pittsburgh Division of the Pennsylvania Railroad
1855 Death of Carnegie's father
1856 Buys his first shares, in Adams Express Company
1859 Becomes Superintendent of the Pittsburgh Division of the Pennsylvania Railroad; invests in Woodruff Sleeping Car Company
1861 Outbreak of Civil War; Carnegie goes to Washington D.C., as assistant in charge of military railroads and telegraphs
1862 First return visit to Scotland, with his mother
1863 Beginning of Keystone Bridge Company
1864 Forms Cyclops Iron Company
1865 End of Civil War; Carnegie leaves Pennsylvania Railroad
1867 Moves to New York City
1868 St Nicholas Hotel Memorandum; personal assessment
1870 Construction of Lucy Blast Furnace
1872 Visits Bessemer works in Britain
1873 Edgar Thomson Steel Mill founded
      Gives $25,000 for swimming baths in Dunfermline (opened 1877)
      Gives first grant for church organ, in Swedenborgian Church
1877 Receives the Freedom of Dunfermline, his first such honour
1878 Journey round the world (book published 1881)
1881 Foundation of Carnegie Brothers, with $5m capital
      Foundation stone laid in Dunfermline for the first Carnegie free public library
      Coaching trip in Britain (book published 1883, as *An American Four-in-Hand in Britain*)
1882 Buys half stock in Frick Coke Company
1883 Gains control of the Homestead Steel Works
1886 Carnegie's mother and brother died of typhoid
      First publication of *Triumphant Democracy*
1887 Married Louise Whitfield
1889 *Gospel of Wealth* published
1890 Offered $1m for construction of a Pittsburgh Library
1891 Carnegie Hall, New York, opened
1892 Foundation of the Carnegie Steel Company
      Homestead strike
1893 Armor Plate scandal
1895 Carnegie Institute founded
1897 Birth of daughter Margaret and purchase of Skibo Castle, Scotland
1900 Carnegie Technical School founded

1901	Sale of Carnegie Company for $480m; Carnegie retires from business and devotes himself to philanthropy
	Carnegie Trust for the Universities of Scotland founded
	Carnegie Relief Fund created
1902	Carnegie Institution of Washington founded
	Pittencrieff Park purchased
	Moved into Carnegie Mansion, New York
1903	Carnegie Dunfermline Trust founded
	Finance offered for construction of Peace Palace, The Hague (opened 1913)
1904	Carnegie Hero Fund Commission in America founded
	Engineering Societies Building in New York founded
1905	Carnegie Foundation for the Advancement of Teaching founded
1906	Simplified Spelling Board founded
1907	Pan American Union Building proposed (dedicated 1910)
	Art Gallery and Museum of Natural History added to Carnegie Institute of Pittsburgh
1908	Carnegie Hero Fund Trust for Great Britain founded
	Central American Court of Justice proposed (opened 1910)
1909	Fondation Carnegie, France
1910	Carnegie Endowment for International Peace founded
	Carnegie-Stiftung fur Lebensretter, Germany
1911	Carnegie Corporation of New York founded
	Carnegie Belonningsfud for Heltemod, Denmark
	Carnegie Heltefond for Norge, Norway
	Carnegie Heldenfonds, Netherlands
	Carnegie Stiftelsens, Sweden
	Fondation Carnegie, Belgium
	Fondazione Carnegie, Italy
1912	Carnegie Institute of Technology in Pittsburgh founded (now Carnegie-Mellon University)
	Fondation Carnegie pour les Sauveteurs, Switzerland
1913	Carnegie United Kingdom Trust founded
1914	Church Peace Union founded (became the Council on Religion and International Affairs, in 1961)
	Carnegie finished *Autobiography* at Skibo and left for America for the last time
	Outbreak of First World War
1917	United States officially enters the war
1918	End of the First World War;
	Teachers Insurance and Annuity Association founded
1919	11 August, Andrew Carnegie died at Lenox, Massachusetts
1926	Carnegie Birthplace Memorial Fund and Museum founded in Dunfermline
1938	TIAA became independent of Carnegie Corporation
1946	Andrew Carnegie's wife, Louise, died
1952	College Retirement Equities Fund (CREF) added to TIAA
1959	Carnegie Institute of Technology became independent of the Carnegie Institute
1961	The Council on Religion and International Affairs replaces the Church Peace Union (founded 1914)
1967	Carnegie-Mellon University founded, incorporating the Carnegie Institute of Technology and the Mellon Institute
1976	Cooper-Hewitt Museum reopened in the Carnegie Mansion
1983	Sale of Skibo Castle. Donation from proceeds to the Carnegie UK Trust

Summary of Books

Anyone wishing to find out more about the Carnegie Trusts should look first in their respective Year Books, Annual Reports and other periodicals and booklets. Here are some further titles by and about Carnegie and the Trusts that might prove interesting, informative or idiosyncratic for the general reader:

Andrew Carnegie, The Trusts and Their Work, printed by Pillans & Wilson, Edinburgh, 1935

Anderson, Florence, *Carnegie Corporation Library Program 1911-1961*, Carnegie Corporation of New York, 1963

Ash, Marinell, *The Star-Spangled Scotsman*, Educational Pack, Carnegie UK Trust, Dunfermline, 1985

Boyer, Ernest L., *High School, A Report on Secondary Education in America*, Harper & Row, New York, 1983

Carnegie, Andrew, *An American Four-in-Hand in Britain*, Charles Scribner's Sons, New York, 1883

Carnegie, Andrew, *Autobiography*, Houghton Mifflin Co., New York, 1920

Carnegie, Andrew, *The Gospel of Wealth, And Other Timely Essays*, The Century Co., New York, 1900

Carnegie, Andrew, *My Own Story*, reprinted for the Carnegie Dunfermline Trust, 1920 and 1984

Carnegie, Andrew, *Problems of Today: Wealth—Labour—Socialism*, Doubleday, Page & Co., New York, 1908

Carnegie, Andrew, *Round the World*, Charles Scribner's Sons, New York, 1884

Carnegie Andrew, *Triumphant Democracy, Sixty Years' March of the Republic*, Charles Scribner's Sons, New York, 1893

Carnegie Endowment for International Peace, *A Manual of the Public Benefactions of Andrew Carnegie*, Washington, 1919

Carnegie Corporation of New York, *Andrew Carnegie Centenary, 1835-1935*, New York, 1935

Haskins, Caryl P., ed., *The Search for Understanding*, Carnegie Institution of Washington, 1967

Hendrick, Burton J., *The Life of Andrew Carnegie*, William Heinemann, London, 1933

Hubbard, Elbert, *Andrew Carnegie*, Roycrofters, New York, 1909

Lagemann, Ellen C., *Private Power for the Public Good, A History of the Carnegie Foundation for the Advancement of Teaching*, Wesleyan University Press, Connecticut, 1983

Lester, Robert M., *Forty Years of Carnegie Giving, 1901-1941*, Charles Scribner's Sons, New York, 1941

Mackie, J. B., *Andrew Carnegie, His Dunfermline Ties and Benefactions*, Dunfermline Journal Printing Works, 1916

Markowitz, Jack, *A Walk on the Crust of Hell*, Stephen Green Press, Vermont, 1973

Peddie, J. R., *The Carnegie Trust for the Universities of Scotland—the First Fifty Years*, Pillans & Wilson, Edinburgh, 1951

Robertson, William, *Welfare in Trust, a History of the Carnegie United Kingdom Trust, 1913-1963*, CUKT, Dunfermline, 1964

Wall, Joseph, *Andrew Carnegie*, Oxford University Press, New York, 1970

Wall, Joseph, *Skibo*, Oxford University Press, New York, 1984

Wilson, Margaret B., *A Carnegie Anthology*, privately printed, New York, 1915

Winkler, John K., *Incredible Carnegie*, Vanguard Press, New York, 1931

Index

*Page references in **bold** type denote a major text entry*